Cambridge Lower Secondary
Mathematics

WORKBOOK 7

Lynn Byrd, Greg Byrd & Chris Pearce

Shaftesbury Road, Cambridge CB2 8EA, United Kingdom

One Liberty Plaza, 20th Floor, New York, NY 10006, USA

477 Williamstown Road, Port Melbourne, VIC 3207, Australia

314–321, 3rd Floor, Plot 3, Splendor Forum, Jasola District Centre, New Delhi – 110025, India

103 Penang Road, #05-06/07, Visioncrest Commercial, Singapore 238467

Cambridge University Press & Assessment is a department of the University of Cambridge.

We share the University's mission to contribute to society through the pursuit of education, learning and research at the highest international levels of excellence.

www.cambridge.org
Information on this title: www.cambridge.org/9781108746366

© Cambridge University Press & Assessment 2021

This publication is in copyright. Subject to statutory exception and to the provisions of relevant collective licensing agreements, no reproduction of any part may take place without the written permission of Cambridge University Press & Assessment.

First published 2014
Second edition 2021

20 19 18 17 16

Printed in Italy by L.E.G.O. S.p.A.

A catalogue record for this publication is available from the British Library

ISBN 978-1-108-74636-6 Paperback + Digital Access (1 year)

Cambridge University Press & Assessment has no responsibility for the persistence or accuracy of URLs for external or third-party internet websites referred to in this publication, and does not guarantee that any content on such websites is, or will remain, accurate or appropriate. Information regarding prices, travel timetables, and other factual information given in this work is correct at the time of first printing but Cambridge University Press & Assessment does not guarantee the accuracy of such information thereafter.

....

NOTICE TO TEACHERS
It is illegal to reproduce any part of this work in material form (including photocopying and electronic storage) except under the following circumstances:
(i) where you are abiding by a licence granted to your school or institution by the Copyright Licensing Agency;
(ii) where no such licence exists, or where you wish to exceed the terms of a licence, and you have gained the written permission of Cambridge University Press;
(iii) where you are allowed to reproduce without permission under the provisions of Chapter 3 of the Copyright, Designs and Patents Act 1988, which covers, for example, the reproduction of short passages within certain types of educational anthology and reproduction for the purposes of setting examination questions.

....

NOTICE TO TEACHERS
The photocopy masters in this publication may be photocopied or distributed [electronically] free of charge for classroom use within the school or institution that purchased the publication. Worksheets and copies of them remain in the copyright of Cambridge University Press, and such copies may not be distributed or used in any way outside the purchasing institution.

> Contents

How to use this book 5
Acknowledgements 6

1 Integers

1.1 Adding and subtracting integers 7
1.2 Multiplying and dividing integers 9
1.3 Lowest common multiples 12
1.4 Highest common factors 14
1.5 Tests for divisibility 16
1.6 Square roots and cube roots 17

2 Expressions, formulae and equations

2.1 Constructing expressions 20
2.2 Using expressions and formulae 24
2.3 Collecting like terms 28
2.4 Expanding brackets 32
2.5 Constructing and solving equations 35
2.6 Inequalities 39

3 Place value and rounding

3.1 Multiplying and dividing by powers of 10 43
3.2 Rounding 47

4 Decimals

4.1 Ordering decimals 51
4.2 Adding and subtracting decimals 54
4.3 Multiplying decimals 57
4.4 Dividing decimals 59
4.5 Making decimal calculations easier 62

5 Angles and constructions

5.1 A sum of 360° 66
5.2 Intersecting lines 68
5.3 Drawing lines and quadrilaterals 70

6 Collecting data

6.1 Conducting an investigation 73
6.2 Taking a sample 76

7 Fractions

7.1 Ordering fractions 80
7.2 Adding mixed numbers 83
7.3 Multiplying fractions 88
7.4 Dividing fractions 93
7.5 Making fraction calculations easier 97

8 Shapes and symmetry

8.1 Identifying the symmetry of 2D shapes 102
8.2 Circles and polygons 107
8.3 Recognising congruent shapes 111
8.4 3D shapes 115

9 Sequences and functions

9.1 Generating sequences 1 121
9.2 Generating sequences 2 124
9.3 Using the nth term 129
9.4 Representing simple functions 134

10 Percentages

10.1 Fractions, decimals and percentages 137
10.2 Percentages large and small 139

Contents

11 Graphs
11.1	Functions	141
11.2	Graphs of functions	144
11.3	Lines parallel to the axes	146
11.4	Interpreting graphs	148

12 Ratio and proportion
12.1	Simplifying ratios	153
12.2	Sharing in a ratio	157
12.3	Using direct proportion	161

13 Probability
13.1	The probability scale	164
13.2	Mutually exclusive outcomes	166
13.3	Experimental probabilities	168

14 Position and transformation
14.1	Maps and plans	172
14.2	Distance between two points	176
14.3	Translating 2D shapes	179
14.4	Reflecting shapes	185
14.5	Rotating shapes	189
14.6	Enlarging shapes	193

15 Shapes, area and volume
15.1	Converting between units for area	199
15.2	Using hectares	202
15.3	The area of a triangle	204
15.4	Calculating the volume of cubes and cuboids	209
15.5	Calculating the surface area of cubes and cuboids	214

16 Interpreting and discussing results
16.1	Two-way tables	220
16.2	Dual and compound bar charts	227
16.3	Pie charts and waffle diagrams	234
16.4	Infographics	239
16.5	Representing data	245
16.6	Using statistics	247

How to use this book

This workbook provides questions for you to practise what you have learned in class. There is a unit to match each unit in your Learner's Book. Each exercise is divided into three parts:

- **Focus:** these questions help you to master the basics
- **Practice:** these questions help you to become more confident in using what you have learned
- **Challenge:** these questions will make you think very hard.

You will also find these features:

Words you need to know. ⎯⎯⎯⎯⎯⎯⎯⎯

> **Key words**
> integers
> inverse
> number line
> positive integers
> negative integers

Step-by-step examples showing how to solve a problem. ⎯⎯⎯⎯⎯⎯⎯⎯

> **Worked example 1.1**
>
> Work out:
>
> a $-5+9$ b $2--5$
>
> **Answer**
>
> a Draw a **number line** if you need to.
>   Start at -5. Move 9 places to the right.
>   You finish at 4. $-5+9=4$
>
> b To subtract -5, add the **inverse**, 5.
> $2--5=2+5=7$

Questions marked with this symbol help you to practise thinking and working mathematically. ⎯⎯⎯⎯⎯⎯⎯⎯

> 13 a This diagram is similar to the diagrams in Question **10**.
>   Copy and complete the diagram. All the numbers are integers.
>   b Is there more than one solution? Have you found all of the solutions?
>
>
>
> 14 a Use the integers 3, 4 and -5 to complete this calculation.
>   ($\square$+$\square$)×$\square$=-8
>   b What is the largest answer you can get when you put the integers 2, -4 and 7 in this calculation?
>   ($\square$+$\square$)×$\square$
>   Give evidence to explain your answer.

> Acknowledgements

Thanks to the following for permission to reproduce images:

Cover image: ori-artiste/Getty Images

Inside: GettyImages/GI; Yoshiyoshi Hirokawa/GI; Lew Robertson/GI; Fajrul Islam/GI; Norberto Leal/GI; Dave Greenwood/GI; Roman Milert/GI.

Key: GI= Getty Images.

1 Integers

> 1.1 Adding and subtracting integers

> **Worked example 1.1**
>
> Work out:
>
> a $-5+9$
> b $2--5$
>
> **Answer**
>
> a Draw a **number line** if you need to.
>   Start at -5. Move 9 places to the <u>right</u>.
>   You finish at 4. $-5+9=4$
>
> b To subtract -5, add the **inverse**, 5.
> $2--5=2+5=7$

Key words

integers
inverse
number line
positive integers
negative integers

Exercise 1.1

Focus

1 Add these **positive** and **negative integers**.

  a $-3+-4$ b $6+-5$ c $-7+2$ d $-5+10$

2 Subtract these positive and negative integers.

  a $4-6$ b $-6-3$ c $1--8$ d $-5--6$

3 Copy and complete this addition table.

+	4	−5
2		
−6		

4 Work out:

  a $20+-5$ b $-10+-15$ c $-2+-13$ d $-3+20$

1 Integers

5 Work out:
   a 20 − −5   b −10 − −15   c −2 − −13   d −3 − 20

Practice

6 Fill in the missing numbers.
   a 8 + ☐ = 1   b −3 + ☐ = 3
   c −10 + ☐ = −6   d 5 + ☐ = −5

7 Fill in the missing numbers.
   a ☐ − 3 = 6   b ☐ − 3 = 2
   c ☐ − 3 = −1   d ☐ − 3 = −6

8 Estimate the answers to these questions by rounding the numbers to the nearest integer.
   a −6.15 + 9.93   b 7.88 − −9.13
   c −11.3 + −8.81   d 12.19 − 5.62

9 Estimate the answers to these questions by rounding the numbers.
   a −28 − 53   b 514 + −321
   c −888 − −111   d −61.1 + −29.3

10 Two **integers** add up to 2. One of the integers is 8. What is the other integer?

11 When you subtract one integer from another integer, the answer is 3.
    One integer is 1. Find the other integer.

12 Here are six integers: −5, −3, −2, 3, 4, 5.
    Use each integer once to complete these additions.
    a ☐ + ☐ = 1   b ☐ + ☐ = −2   c ☐ + ☐ = 3

Challenge

13 Copy and complete this addition table.

+	3	
	5	−2
	1	−6

14 This subtraction table shows that 3 − 6 = −3. Copy and complete the table.

−	−4	6	
3		−3	1
−3			

15 Copy and complete these addition pyramids.

a 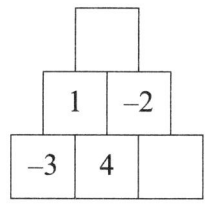   b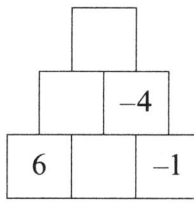

16 This addition pyramid is more difficult than the pyramids in Question **13**.

Copy and complete the pyramid. Explain how you worked out the missing numbers.

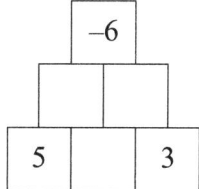

> 1.2 Multiplying and dividing integers

> **Worked example 1.2**
>
> Work out:
> a 4×-8 b $20 \div (-3 + -2)$
>
> **Answer**
> a $4 \times 8 = 32$, so $4 \times -8 = -32$.
> b First, do the addition in the bracket.
> $-3 + -2 = -5$
>   So, $20 \div (-3 + -2) = 20 \div -5 = -4$.

Key word

product

Exercise 1.2

Focus

1 Work out:
   a 10×-3 b 4×-9 c 5×-11 d 7×-7

2 Work out:
   a $-24 \div 2$ b $24 \div -6$ c $-50 \div 10$ d $63 \div -9$

1 Integers

3 Copy and complete this multiplication table.

×	4	7
−2		
−6		

4 Work out:
 a $(-5 + 2) \times 4$
 b $(-6 + -4) \times 3$
 c $(1 - -3) \times -7$
 d $(-2 - -5) \times -10$

5 Work out:
 a $(-5 + -7) \div 4$
 b $(10 - -4) \div -2$
 c $(-6 + 14) \div -4$
 d $(-5 - 13) \div 3$

Practice

6 Work out the missing numbers.
 a $3 \times \square = -24$
 b $6 \times \square = -18$
 c $-2 \times \square = -26$
 d $-12 \times \square = -60$

7 Work out the missing numbers.
 a $-27 \div \square = -3$
 b $36 \div \square = -9$
 c $\square \div 6 = -6$
 d $\square \div -4 = -8$

8 Estimate the answers to these questions by rounding the numbers.
 a -4.1×2.8
 b -7.1×-3.2
 c -1.1×-7.9
 d $-9.1 \div 3.2$

9 Estimate the answers to these questions by rounding the numbers.
 a 423×-2.9
 b 32×-28
 c -6.1×219
 d $-612 \div 2.92$

 10 The **product** of 2 and −9 is −18.
 a Find three more pairs of integers with a product of −18.
 b Are there more pairs of integers with a product of −18? How can you be sure?

1.2 Multiplying and dividing integers

11 Copy and complete this multiplication grid.

×	6	4
	−30	
		−32

Challenge

12 In these diagrams, the integer in a square is the product of the integers in the circles next to it.

a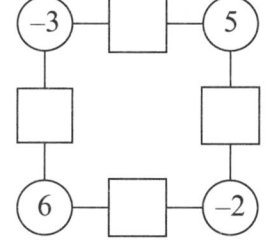

b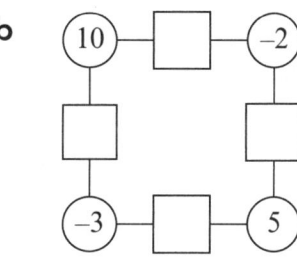

   i Copy each diagram and fill in the squares.
   ii Add the numbers in the squares in each diagram.

13 a This diagram is similar to the diagrams in Question 10. Copy and complete the diagram. All the numbers are integers.

   b Is there more than one solution? Have you found all of the solutions?

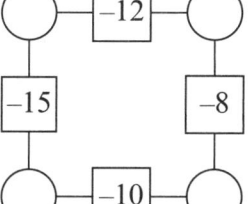

14 a Use the integers 3, 4 and −5 to complete this calculation.

   (☐ + ☐) × ☐ = −8

   b What is the largest answer you can get when you put the integers 2, −4 and 7 in this calculation?

   (☐ + ☐) × ☐

   Give evidence to explain your answer.

15 a The product of two integers is −20. Find the largest possible value of the sum of the two integers.

   b The product of two integers is −30. Find the largest possible sum of the two integers.

   c Can you generalise the result of part **a** and part **b**?

1 Integers

> 1.3 Lowest common multiples

> **Worked example 1.3**
>
> Find the **lowest common multiple** (LCM) of 6 and 9.
>
> **Answer**
>
> The **multiples** of 6 are 6, 12, <u>18</u>, 24, 30, <u>36</u>, 42, 48, <u>54</u>, …
>
> The multiples of 9 are 9, <u>18</u>, 27, <u>36</u>, 45, <u>54</u>, …
>
> The **common multiples** are 18, 36, 54, …
>
> The lowest common multiple is 18.

You may not need to list so many multiples each time.

Key words

common multiple
lowest common multiple (LCM)
multiple

Exercise 1.3

Focus

1 Write down the first four multiples of:
   a 4   b 7   c 12   d 30

2 How many multiples of 10 are less than 100?

3 a Work out the multiples of 8 that are less than 50.
   b Work out the multiples of 5 that are less than 50.
   c Write down the lowest common multiple of 8 and 5.

4 a Find the first five common multiples of 2 and 3.
   b Copy and complete this sentence:
      The common multiples of 2 and 3 are multiples of ▢
   c Find the lowest common multiple of 2 and 3.

5 a Write down the first three common multiples of 6 and 4.
   b Copy and complete this sentence:
      The common multiples of 6 and 4 are multiples of ▢
   c Write down the lowest common multiple of 6 and 4.

6 Find the lowest common multiple of:
   a 3 and 10   b 4 and 10   c 5 and 10

1.3 Lowest common multiples

Practice

7 Show that the multiples of 3 and 5 are multiples of 15.

8 Find the lowest common multiple of 6 and 14.

9 **a** Find the lowest common multiple of:
    i 7 and 2   **ii** 7 and 4   **iii** 7 and 6
  b Is there an easy method to find the lowest common multiple of 7 and a number less than 7?
  c Does the method in part **b** work for 7 and a number more than 7?

10 Look at these numbers: 90 92 94 96 98 100
  a **i** Which number is a multiple of 9 and 10?
     ii Is this number the lowest common multiple?
  b **i** Which number is a multiple of 2 and 7?
     ii Is this number the lowest common multiple?
  c **i** Which number is a multiple of 12 and 8?
     ii Is this number the lowest common multiple?

11 Work out the lowest common multiple (LCM) of 2, 5 and 6.

Challenge

12 Find the LCM of 3, 8 and 9.

13 $24 \times 4 = 96$
  a Explain why 96 is a common multiple of 4 and 24.
  b Is 96 the lowest common multiple of 4 and 24? Give evidence to justify your answer.

14 Two numbers have a LCM of 45. The two numbers add up to 14. Find the two numbers.

15 The LCM of two numbers is 63. Work out the two numbers.

1 Integers

> 1.4 Highest common factors

> **Worked example 1.4**
>
> a Find the **factors** of 24.
>
> b Find the **highest common factor** (HCF) of 24 and 80.
>
> **Answer**
>
> a $24 = 1 \times 24, 2 \times 12, 3 \times 8, 4 \times 6$
>
>   The factors of 24 are 1, 2, 3, 4, 6, 8, 12 and 24.
>
> b You must find the highest factor of 24 that is also a factor of 80.
>
>   8 is a factor of 80 because $80 \div 8 = 10$.
>
>   12 is not a factor of 80 because $80 \div 12 = 6$ remainder 4.
>
>   24 is not a factor of 80.
>
>   The highest common factor of 24 and 80 is 8.

Key words

common factor
conjecture
consecutive
factor
highest common factor (HCF)

Exercise 1.4

Focus

1 Find the factors of:
   a 21   b 32   c 50   d 72   e 43

2 Find the factors of:
   a 51   b 52   c 53   d 54   e 55

3 a Find the **common factors** of 16 and 28.
   b Find the highest common factor of 16 and 28.

4 a Find the common factors of 30 and 45.
   b Find the highest common factor of 30 and 45.

Practice

5 Find the highest common factor of:
 a 18 and 21   b 18 and 27   c 18 and 36

6 Find the highest common factor of:
 a 27 and 45   b 50 and 75   c 40 and 72   d 24 and 35

7 Find the highest common factor of:
 a 70 and 77   b 70 and 85   c 70 and 84

8 a Find the highest common factor of 32 and 40.
 b Use your answer to part **a** to simplify the fraction $\frac{32}{40}$.

9 a Find the highest common factor of 52 and 91.
 b There are 91 rooms in a hotel. 52 rooms are reserved. What fraction of the rooms are reserved?

Challenge

10 Two numbers have a highest common factor of 5. The two numbers add up to 35. Show that there are three possible pairs of values for the two numbers.

11 The HCF of two numbers is 4. Both numbers are more than 4 and less than 30.
 a Show that the numbers could be 8 and 12.
 b Show that the numbers are not 8 and 16.
 c Find all the other possible values of the two numbers.

12 The HCF of two numbers is 3. One of the numbers is 9. What are the possible values of the other number?

13 a Find the highest common factor of:
  i 9 and 10   ii 20 and 21   iii 32 and 33
 b 9 and 10 are **consecutive** numbers. 20 and 21 are consecutive numbers.
  Use part **a** to make a **conjecture** about the highest common factor of two consecutive numbers.
 c What is the lowest common multiple of two consecutive numbers?

1 Integers

> 1.5 Tests for divisibility

> **Worked example 1.5**
>
> Use **tests for divisibility** to show that 3948 is **divisible** by 3 and 6 but not by 9.
>
> **Answer**
>
> The sum of the digits is $3+9+4+8=24$.
>
> 24 is divisible by 3, so 3948 is also divisible by 3.
>
> 3948 is even and divisible by 3, so 3948 is also divisible by 6.
>
> 24 is not divisible by 9, so 3948 is also not divisible by 9.

Key words

divisible

tests for divisibility

Exercise 1.5

Focus

1   Use tests for divisibility to show that 5328 is divisible by 4 and by 9.

2   a   Show that 2739 is divisible by 11.
    b   When the digits are reversed, the number is 9372.
        Is 9372 divisible by 11? Give a reason for your answer.

3   a   Show that 67 108 is divisible by 4.
    b   Is 67 108 divisible by 8? Give a reason for your answer.

4   The number 3812* is divisible by 3. The final digit is missing. What can you say about the missing digit?

Practice

5   What integers less than 12 are factors of 7777?

6   a   Use the digits 5, 4, 2 and 1 to make a number that is divisible by:
        i   5   ii   3
    b   Can you arrange the digits 5, 4, 2 and 1 to make a number that is divisible by:
        i   9?   ii   11?

7   322 is divisible by 7. Use this fact to find a number that is divisible by 7, 2 and 3.

8   Find the smallest positive integer that is <u>not</u> a factor of 2520. Give reasons for your answer.

9 Here are some numbers where all the digits are 9:
   9   99   999   9999   99999   ...
   In numbers where all the digits are 9, which are multiples of 11?

Challenge

10 A number is divisible by 15 if it is divisible by 3 and 5.
    a   Show that 7905 is divisible by 15.
    b   The number 208** is divisible by 15. Find the possible values of the two missing digits.

11 Find three numbers less than 20 that are factors of 3729.
    Give reasons for your answers.

12 Show that 8897 is divisible by only one number between 1 and 12.

13 The numbers 4, 5, 6, … are consecutive numbers; for example, 4567 is a number with four consecutive digits.
    Find all the numbers with four consecutive digits that are divisible by:
    a   2   b   3   c   5   d   11

> 1.6 Square roots and cube roots

Worked example 1.6

Work out $\sqrt[3]{125} - \sqrt{49}$.

Answer

$5^3 = 5 \times 5 \times 5 = 125$, so $\sqrt[3]{125} = 5$.

$7^2 = 7 \times 7 = 49$, so $\sqrt{49} = 7$.

$\sqrt[3]{125} - \sqrt{49} = 5 - 7 = -2$

Key words

consecutive
cube number
cube root
square number
square root

Exercise 1.6

Focus

1 Work out:
   a $3^2 + 4^2$ b $6^2 + 7^2$ c $9^2 + 10^2$

1 Integers

2 Work out:
a $\sqrt{64}$
b $\sqrt{100}$
c $\sqrt{225}$
d $\sqrt{169}$

3 Work out:
a $1^3 + 2^3$
b $3^3 + 5^3$
c $4^3 - 2^3$

4 Work out:
a $\sqrt{64} - \sqrt[3]{64}$
b $\sqrt{25} - \sqrt[3]{125}$
c $\sqrt[3]{27} - \sqrt{16}$

5 Work out:
a $\sqrt[3]{216}$
b $\sqrt[3]{512}$
c $\sqrt[3]{1000}$
d $\sqrt[3]{1728}$

Practice

6 Copy and complete:
a $\sqrt{\Box} = 20$
b $\sqrt{\Box} = 25$
c $\sqrt{\Box} = 30$
d $\sqrt{\Box} = 35$

7 Copy and complete:
a $\sqrt[3]{\Box} = 6$
b $\sqrt[3]{\Box} = 10$
c $\sqrt[3]{\Box} = 11$
d $\sqrt[3]{\Box} = 15$

8 Find the integer that is closest to:
a $\sqrt{38}$
b $\sqrt{220}$
c $\sqrt[3]{70}$

9 $\sqrt{45}$ is between 6 and 7.

Write down a similar statement for:
a $\sqrt{90}$
b $\sqrt{135}$

 10 Mustafa thinks of a number. The number is between 100 and 200. The **square root** of the number is a multiple of 3.
What is Mustafa's number?

11 a Find all the numbers between 100 and 200 that have an integer square root.
b Find all the numbers between 100 and 200 that have an integer **cube root**.

Challenge

12 Find the highest common factor of $1^2 + 2^2 + 3^2$ and $4^2 + 5^2 + 6^2$.

13 Jiale thinks of a number. She works out the square root of the number. Then she works out the cube root of the square root of the number. The answer is 2.
a Find Jiale's number.
b Show that Jiale gets the same answer if she finds the cube root first and then the square root.

14 289 and 324 are two **consecutive square numbers**. Find the next square number after 324.

15 1331 and 1728 are two consecutive **cube numbers**. Find the next cube number after 1728.

16 a Show that 64 is a square number and a cube number.

b There is one number between 100 and 1000 that is a square number and a cube number. What is this number?

c What method did you use to answer part **b**? Could you use the same method to look for another number that is both a square number and a cube number?

2 Expressions, formulae and equations

> 2.1 Constructing expressions

Here are three bags, each with a different number of balls inside.

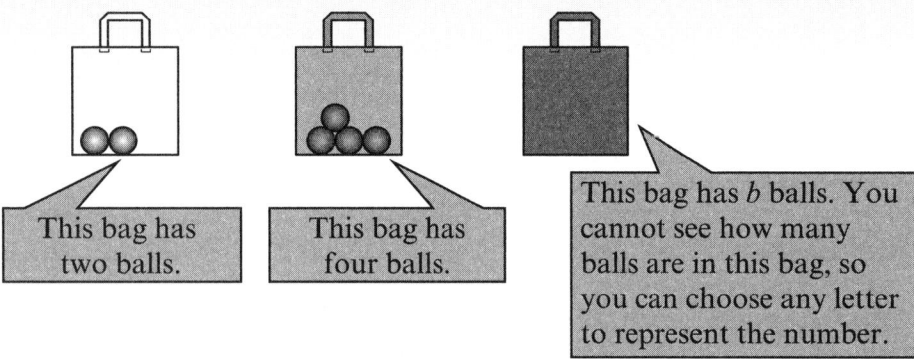

This bag has two balls.

This bag has four balls.

This bag has b balls. You cannot see how many balls are in this bag, so you can choose any letter to represent the number.

> **Key word**
>
> expression

> **Tip**
>
> Remember that the correct order of operations is used in algebra as well as in number calculations. Divisions and multiplications come before additions and subtractions.

Exercise 2.1

Focus

1   Write down the missing number for each of the following.

    If you do not know the number, choose your own letter to represent it.

    a   This box has ☐ counter.

    b   This box has ☐ counters.

    c   This box has ☐ counters.

> **Tip**
>
> In part **c** you do not know how many counters are in this box, so choose your own letter.

20

2.1 Constructing expressions

d This bag has ☐ apples.

e This bag has ☐ apples.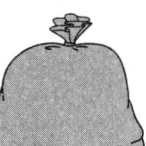

2 Two balls are added to each of these bags. Write down the missing numbers.

a There is one ball in the bag.

Add two balls, so there are now 1 + 2 = ☐ balls in the bag.

b There are ☐ balls in the bag.

Add two balls, so there are now ☐ + 2 = ☐ balls in the bag.

c There are ☐ balls in the bag.

Add two balls, so there are now ☐ + 2 balls in the bag.

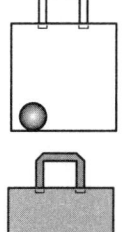

Tip

In part **c** choose your own letter for the number of balls; for example, *b*. You cannot work out *b* + 2, so just leave the **expression** as it is.

3 A bag has *n* counters in it.

Match the statement in each rectangle to its correct expression in the ovals. The first one has been done for you: **A** and **iv**.

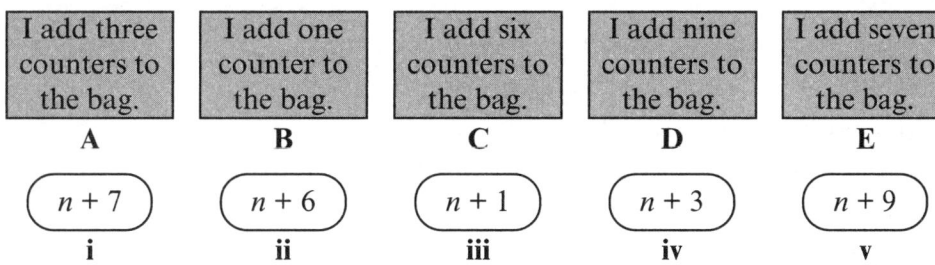

Tip

An expression is a statement that contains letters and sometimes numbers; for example, $n + 7$.

4 Sofia has a box that contains *t* toys. Write an expression for the total number of toys she has in the box when:

a she puts in four more toys
b she takes out two toys
c she adds five toys
d she takes out half of the toys.

Tip

In each part of the question Sofia starts with *t* toys.

2 Expressions, formulae and equations

5 Cheng has s strawberries. Write an expression for someone who has:
  a two more strawberries than Cheng
  b three times as many strawberries as Cheng
  c six fewer strawberries than Cheng
  d half as many strawberries as Cheng.

Practice

6 Write down an expression for the answer to each of these questions.
  a Ali has x paintings. He buys two more paintings.
     How many paintings does he now have?
  b Hamza has t free text messages on his phone each month.
     So far this month he has used 15 text messages.
     How many free text messages does he have left?
  c Ibrahim is i years old and Tareq is t years old. What is the total of their ages?
  d Aya can store v video clips on one memory card. How many video clips can he store on two memory cards?

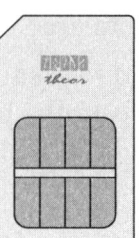

7 Nesreen thinks of a number, n. Write an expression for the number Nesreen gets each time.
  a She multiplies the number by 6.
  b She divides the number by 5.
  c She multiplies the number by 5, then adds 1.
  d She multiplies the number by 7, then subtracts 2.
  e She divides the number by 10, then adds 3.
  f She multiplies the number by 3, then subtracts the result from 25.

8 The cost of an adult meal in a fast-food restaurant is $\$a$. The cost of a child's meal in the same restaurant is $\$c$.

Write an expression for the total cost of the meals for these groups.
  a one adult and one child
  b one adult and three children
  c four adults and one child
  d four adults and five children

2.1 Constructing expressions

9 Match each description (**a** to **f**) to the correct expression (**i** to **vii**).

	Description		Expression
a	Multiply x by 5 and add 4.	i	$4x + 5$
b	Multiply x by 4 and add 5.	ii	$4x - 5$
c	Multiply x by 5 and subtract 4.	iii	$4 - 5x$
d	Multiply x by 5 and subtract from 4.	iv	$5 - 4x$
e	Multiply x by 4 and subtract 5.	v	$5x - 4$
f	Multiply x by 4 and subtract from 5.	vi	$5 - 5x$
		vii	$5x + 4$

Marcus writes this description for the expression that did not have a match:

Multiply x by 5 then subtract 5.

Is Marcus correct? Explain your answer.

10 Write an expression for each of these situations.
You can choose your own letters, but make sure you write what your letters represent.
  a The total cost of seven drinks and six bags of potato chips.
  b The total value of three rings is doubled.

Challenge

11 Write an expression for each of these descriptions.
  a k more than g
  b h less than t
  c y more than eight times x
  d three times a multiplied by b

12 Write a description for each of these expressions.
  a $v + 7u$
  b $8w - d$
  c $5x + 3y$
  d $7pq$

> **Tip**
> Remember the correct order of operations. Multiplication comes before addition and subtraction.

2 Expressions, formulae and equations

13 Kai has two pieces of wood. The lengths of the pieces of wood are shown in the diagram.

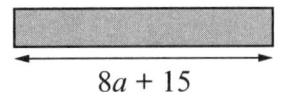
$8a + 15$

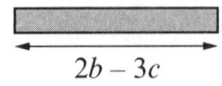
$2b - 3c$

Write an expression for:
a the total length of the pieces of wood
b the difference in the lengths of the pieces of wood.

 14 p and q are whole numbers, such that $p + q = -2$ and $pq = -8$. Also $p > q$.
a Sadie thinks that $p = -12$ and $q = 10$. Explain why Sadie is wrong.
b Work out the values of p and q.

> 2.2 Using expressions and formulae

An expression is a statement that contains letters and sometimes numbers but has no = sign.

For example: p $x + 2$ $n - 3$ $4m$

You can **substitute** numbers into an expression to work out the value of the expression.

For example, the value of $x + 2$ when $x = 5$ is $5 + 2 = 7$.

A **formula** is a statement that contains letters and sometimes numbers and has an = sign.

For example: $A = 2p$ $y = x - 2$ $v = 5n - 3$ $R = m + k$

Key words

formula
substitute

Tip

Substitute the x for the number 5 and then work out $5 + 2$.

Exercise 2.2

Focus

1 For each of these statements, write the letter E if it is an expression or write the letter F if it is a formula. The first two have been done for you.
a $8h$ E
b $v = 9u$ F
c $9u + 3$
d $m = 4 + n$
e $G = 2x + y$
f $b - c$

2 Work out the value of $x + 6$ when:
a $x = 1$
b $x = 2$
c $x = 3$
d $x = 4$

Tip

In part **a**, $x + 6 = 1 + 6 = \boxed{}$

2.2 Using expressions and formulae

3 Work out the value of $n-1$ when:

    a $n=5$ **b** $n=6$ **c** $n=7$ **d** $n=8$

> **Tip**
>
> In part **a**, $n-1=5-1=\boxed{}$

4 Work out the value of the expression in each rectangle and match it to its correct answer in the oval. The first one has been done for you: **A** and **iii**.

A	B	C	D	E
$y+2$ when $y=3$	$y-2$ when $y=10$	$4+y$ when $y=2$	$10-y$ when $y=1$	$y+3$ when $y=0$

i	ii	iii	iv	v
8	6	5	3	9

5 Write down 'True' or 'False' for each of these statements.
If a statement is false, work out the correct value of the expression.
The first one has been done for you.

  a The value of $2m$ when $m=5$ is 7.   False; when $m=5$, $2m=10$.

  b The value of $3m$ when $m=8$ is 24.

  c The value of $9p$ when $p=2$ is 11.

  d The value of $\frac{w}{2}$ when $w=6$ is 3.

  e The value of $\frac{x}{3}$ when $x=12$ is 6.

> **Tips**
>
> $2m$ means $2 \times m$, so $2 \times 5 = 10$.
>
> $\frac{w}{2}$ means $w \div 2$.

Practice

6 Work out the value of each expression.

  a $a+10$ when $a=6$ **b** $b-3$ when $b=120$

  c $c+z$ when $c=3$ and $z=17$ **d** $d-y$ when $d=40$ and $y=15$

  e $3e$ when $e=20$ **f** $\frac{f}{5}$ when $f=35$

  g $g+2x$ when $g=1$ and $x=6$ **h** $h-4w$ when $h=17$ and $w=2$

  i $2i+3v$ when $i=3$ and $v=2$ **j** $\frac{j}{2}+u$ when $j=30$ and $u=3$

  k $\frac{24}{k}-3$ when $k=8$ **l** $\frac{p+q}{3}$ when $p=11$ and $q=22$

2 Expressions, formulae and equations

7 Jana uses this formula to work out how much money her friends will collect from their sponsored walk.

> Money collected = distance walked (km) × sponsored rate ($ per km)

How much money do the following friends collect?
- **a** Miriam walks 5 kilometres at a sponsored rate of $16 per kilometre.
- **b** Yara walks 8 kilometres at a sponsored rate of $18 per kilometre.

8
- **a** Write a formula for the number of hours in any number of days, using:
  - **i** words
  - **ii** letters
- **b** Use your formula in part **a ii** to work out the number of hours in four days.

9
- **a** Use the formula $A = bh$ to work out A when:
  - **i** $b = 4$ and $h = 5$
  - **ii** $b = 3$ and $h = 12$
- **b** Work out the value of b when $A = 52$ and $h = 4$.

> **Tip**
> bh means $b \times h$.

10
- **a** Write a formula for the number of hours for any number of minutes, in:
  - **i** words
  - **ii** letters
- **b** Use your formula in part **a ii** to work out the number of hours in 360 minutes.

11 Hiroto uses this formula to work out the times it should take him to travel from his house to any of his friends' houses.

$T = \dfrac{D}{S}$, where: T is the time, in hours
D is the distance, in kilometres
S is the average speed, in kilometres per hour.

> **Tip**
> $\dfrac{D}{S}$ means $D \div S$.

How long does it take Hiroto to travel from his house to:
- **a** Souta's house, which is 60 kilometres away, at an average speed of 20 kilometres per hour?
- **b** Hina's house, which is 140 kilometres away, at an average speed of 40 kilometres per hour?

Challenge

12 The weight of an object is calculated using the formula $W = mg$, where:

  W is the weight, in newtons (N)

  m is the mass, in kg

  g is the acceleration due to gravity, in m/s^2

On Earth $g = 10$ m/s^2, and on the Moon $g = 2$ m/s^2.

The mass of a man is 75 kg and the mass of a lunar landing module is 10 344 kg.

  a Work out the weight of the:
  - **i** man on Earth
  - **ii** lunar landing module on Earth.

  b Work out the weight of the:
  - **i** man on the Moon
  - **ii** lunar landing module on the Moon.

13 What value of x can you substitute into each of these expressions to give you the <u>same</u> answer?

$x + 12$ $4x$ $6x - 8$

14 Kwame uses the formula $F = ma$, where:

  F is the force, in newtons (N)

  m is the mass, in kg

  a is the acceleration, in m/s^2

He works out that $F = 75$ N when $m = 25$ kg.

What value of a did he use? Explain how you worked out your answer.

 **15** This is part of Kali's homework. She has spilt tea on some of her work.

> <u>Question:</u>
> Use the formula M = ▓
> to work out the value of M when:
>   i   P = 51 and h = 17
>   ii P = 65 and h = 13
> <u>Solution:</u>
>   i   M = ▓ = 3
>   ii M = ▓ = 5

  a What is the formula that Kali uses?

  b Work out the value of M when $P = 56$ and $h = 4$.

2 Expressions, formulae and equations

16 A cookery book shows how long it takes to cook a piece of meat.

Electric oven	$T = 70W$
Microwave oven	$T = 28W$

Where:
T is the time, in minutes
W is the weight of the piece of meat, in kg.

a How much longer will it take to cook a 2 kg piece of meat in an electric oven than in a microwave oven?

b A piece of meat takes 1 hour and 52 minutes to cook in a microwave oven. How long would this same piece of meat take to cook in an electric oven?

> 2.3 Collecting like terms

Like terms are **terms** that contain the same letter.

The letter in an expression represents an unknown number but, if you find it easier, you can think of the letter as an object.

You **simplify** an expression by **collecting like terms**.

Example: $a + a = 2a$
$2b + 3b = 5b$

Key words

collecting like terms
like terms
simplify
term

Tip

2a and 3a are like terms. 2a and 3b are not like terms. Think of a as an apple, so

Think of b as a banana, so

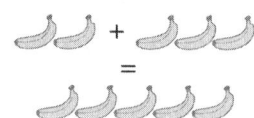

Exercise 2.3

Focus

1 Match the expression in each rectangle to its correct simplified expression given in the oval.

The first one has been done for you: **A** and **iii**.

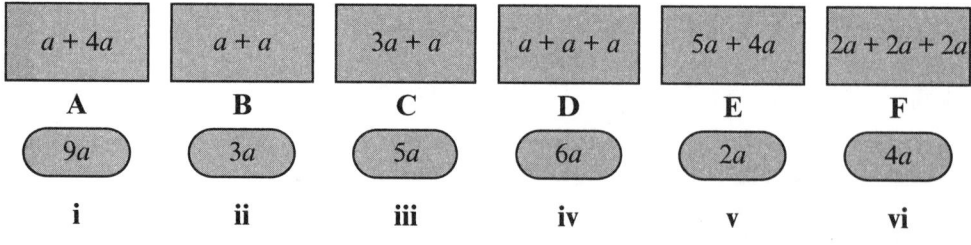

Tip

Remember that a means 1a.

2.3 Collecting like terms

2 Look at these statements. Three of the statements are true and three of the statements are false.

Write 'true' or 'false' for each statement. If the statement is false, write the correct statement.

   a $b + 2b = 3b$ **b** $4d + 2d = 5d$

   c $6f + 4f = 11f$ **d** $c + c + c = 3c$

   e $h + 3h + 5h = 8h$ **f** $7v + 2v + v = 10v$

3 Each of these expressions simplifies to $3s$ or $5s$.

For each rectangle **A** to **E**, write down whether it simplifies to:
i $3s$ or **ii** $5s$.

The first one has been done for you: **A** and **ii**.

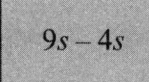 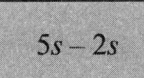 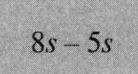 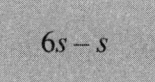 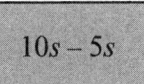
    A   **B**   **C**   **D**   **E**

> **Tip**
> Think of s as a strawberry. For example, for **A**, you start with nine, you eat four, so you have five strawberries left.

4 Look at these statements. Three of the statements are true and three of the statements are false.

Write 'true' or 'false' for each statement. If the statement is false, write the correct statement.

   a $7b - 2b = 3b$ **b** $4d - 2d = 2d$

   c $6f - f = 6$ **d** $8c - 2c - 3c = 3c$

   e $9h - h - h = 7h$ **f** $10v - 6v - v = 4v$

5 Look at these expressions. Some of the expressions can be simplified and some cannot be simplified. Copy the expressions.

If the expression can be simplified, write a tick and work out the simplified answer.

If the expression cannot be simplified, write a cross.

For example: $4m + 2m$ ✓ $6m$

                  $2a + 3b$ ✗

   a $5p + p$ **b** $6p + 2$ **c** $5n - 2w$ **d** $8u - u$

> **Tip**
> You can simplify only when the letters are the same.

Practice

6 Pedro has striped, checked and spotted bricks.

The length of a striped brick is x.
The length of a checked brick is y.
The length of a spotted brick is z.

 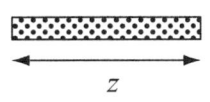
        x y z

Work out the total length of each arrangement of bricks. Give each answer in its simplest form.

a
b
c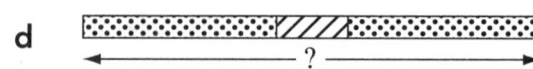
d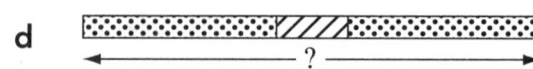
e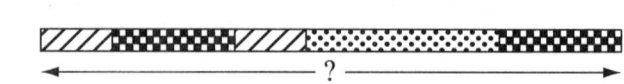
f

7 Simplify each expression.
   a $a+a+a+a$
   b $4b+3b$
   c $4c+7c$
   d $2d+3d+4d$
   e $6e+6e+e$
   f $10f+f+4f$
   g $9g-3g$
   h $4h^2-3h^2$
   i $9i-i$
   j $8j+2j-4j$
   k $k+6k-3k$
   l $12y^3-4y^3-7y^3$

8 In an algebraic pyramid, you find the expression in each block by <u>adding</u> the expressions in the two blocks below it.
   Copy and complete these pyramids.

   a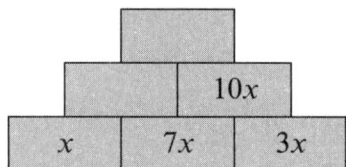
   b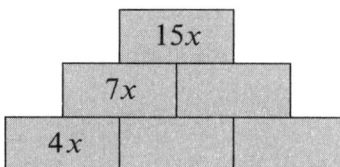

9 Simplify these expressions by collecting like terms.
   a $3x+4x+5y$
   b $5z+5z+5a+a$
   c $3a+4b+4a+5b$
   d $4x+5+3x+2$
   e $d+1+d+1$
   f $5f-3f+12g-3g$
   g $45-15+12w-w$
   h $7x+5y-3x+y$
   i $8a+6b-4a-5b$
   j $4w+3x+7y-2w-3x+13y$
   k $200a+20g+100-15g-70$

10 Write each expression in its simplest form.
   a $4ab+2ab+3xy+5xy$
   b $3rd+3rd+5th+6th$
   c $5tv+6tv+9jk-5kj$
   d $8ej+7yh-3je-4hy$
   e $5v+15rv-2v+vr$
   f $7un-4nu+11ef-11fe$

2.3 Collecting like terms

Challenge

11 This is part of Maddi's homework.

> *Question*
> *Write these expressions in their simplest form.*
> a $2x + 8 + 7x - 4$ b $5rg + 4t - t + 2gr$
>
> *Solution*
> a $2x + 8 = 10x$, $7x - 4 = 3x$, $10x + 3x = 13x$
> b $5rg + 4t - t + 2gr = 5rg + 4 + 2gr$

Maddi has made several mistakes. Explain the mistakes Maddi has made.

12 Copy and complete this algebraic pyramid.

Remember, you find the expression in each block by <u>adding</u> the expressions in the two blocks below it.

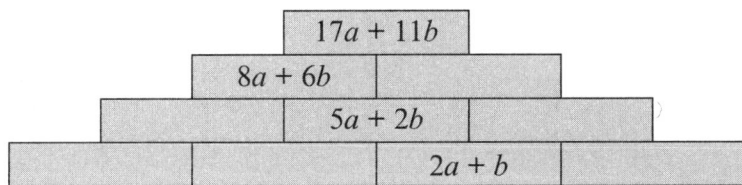

13 Simplify these expressions. Write your answers in their simplest form.

a $\dfrac{3a}{4} - \dfrac{a}{2}$ b $\dfrac{b}{5} + \dfrac{3b}{10}$ c $3c + \dfrac{c}{7}$

14 In this diagram, the expressions in each rectangle simplify to the expression in the circle.

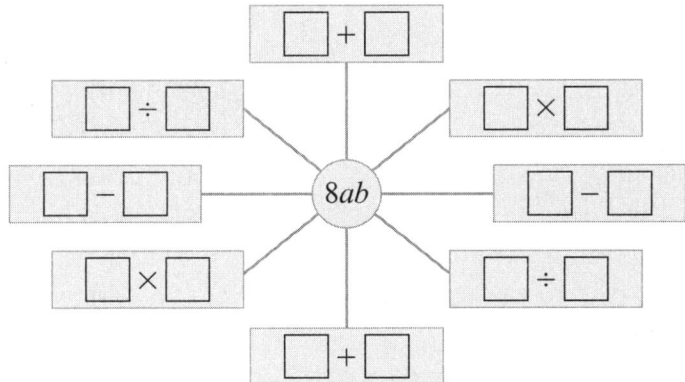

Tip

Remember:
$x \times y = xy$, so
$2x \times y = 2xy$ and
$4x \times 3y = 12xy$.

a Copy and complete the diagram in two different ways.
b Is it possible to say how many ways there are to complete the diagram? Explain your answer.

2 Expressions, formulae and equations

15 In a magic square, the rows, columns and diagonals all add up to the same number. Copy the magic squares in parts **a** and **b**.

   a Write the numbers 1 to 9 in this magic square, so that all the rows, columns and diagonals add up to 15.
   You can use each number only once.
   Three numbers have been written in the magic square for you.

8		
	5	
	9	

   b Write the algebraic expressions from the cloud in the magic square, so that all the rows, columns and diagonals add up to $3b$.

   Cloud: $b-c$, $b-a-c$, $a+b-c$, $b+c$, $b-a$, $b+c-a$, $a+b$

	$a+b$	
	b	
	$a+b+c$	

   (The magic square shows: top-middle $a+b$, middle-middle b, bottom-middle $a+b+c$)

> 2.4 Expanding brackets

Key words
brackets
expand

You can use a box method to multiply numbers together, like this:

$4 \times 16 = 4 \times (10+6)$

×	10	6
4	40	24

$4 \times 16 = 40 + 24 = 64$

Tips

You can write $4 \times (10+6)$ as $4(10+6)$.

You use the table to **expand** the **brackets** $4(10+6)$ to get $(4 \times 10) + (4 \times 6)$.

2.4 Expanding brackets

Exercise 2.4

Focus

1 Copy and complete the boxes to work out the answers.

a 5×13

×	10	3
5		

$5 \times 13 = \square + \square = \square$

b 2×38

×	30	8
2		

$2 \times 38 = \square + \square = \square$

c 7×21

×	20	1
7		

$7 \times 21 = \square + \square = \square$

d 4×17

×	10	7
4		

$4 \times 17 = \square + \square = \square$

2 Simplify these expressions.

   a $3 \times x$ **b** $4 \times p$ **c** $9 \times f$ **d** $5 \times m$

> **Tip**
>
> $3 \times x$ can be written simply as $3x$.

3 Copy and complete the boxes to simplify these expressions. The first one has been done for you.

a $2(x+3)$

×	x	3
2	$2x$	6

$2(x+3) = 2x + 6$

b $3(x+4)$

×	x	4
3		

$3(x+4) = \square + \square$

c $5(m+1)$

×	m	1
5		

$5(m+1) = \square + \square$

d $4(n+2)$

×	n	2
4		

$4(n+2) = \square + \square$

4 Copy and complete the boxes to simplify these expressions. The first one has been done for you.

a $3(x-2)$

×	x	-2
3	$3x$	-6

$3(x-2) = 3x - 6$

b $5(x-6)$

×	x	-6
5		

$5(x-6) = \square - \square$

2 Expressions, formulae and equations

c $2(y-4)$

×	y	-4
2		

$2(y-4) = \square - \square$

d $6(k-3)$

×	k	-3
6		

$6(k-3) = \square - \square$

Practice

5 Expand the brackets.

a $3(a+2)$ b $5(b+3)$ c $3(c+2)$ d $5(d-1)$
e $4(e-9)$ f $3(f-8)$ g $4(2+f)$ h $8(7+z)$
i $9(3+y)$ j $4(4-x)$ k $7(1-w)$ l $7(2-v)$

6 Multiply out the brackets.

a $5(2p+1)$ b $7(3q+2)$ c $9(2r+3)$
d $11(3s-4a+7)$ e $2(2t-5)$ f $4(5u-1)$
g $6(1+2v)$ h $8(6+4w-3g)$ i $10(6+7x)$
j $5(3-5x)$ k $5(4-3x)$ l $5(5k-8x-6h)$

7 This is part of Paul's homework. Paul has made a mistake in every solution.

Question
Multiply out the brackets.
a $5(a+3)$ b $3(4b-5)$ c $4(3-c)$

Solution
a $5(a+3) = 5a+3$
b $3(4b-5) = 12b-8$
c $4(3-c) = 12-4c = 8c$

Explain the mistakes Paul has made.

8 Which one of these expressions is the odd one out?
Explain your answer.

$2(9x+12)$ $2(10x+8)$ $6(4+3x)$ $3(8+6x)$ $1(18x+24)$

Tip
The 'odd one out' means the expression that is different from all of the others.

Challenge

9 The diagram shows a rectangle.
The width of the rectangle is $2x - 3y$ cm.
The length of the rectangle is 12 cm.

Write an expression, in its simplest form, for the:
- **a** area of the rectangle
- **b** perimeter of the rectangle.

10 Expand and simplify these expressions.
- **a** $3(x+2) + 4x$
- **b** $4(9+x) - 24$
- **c** $5(2x-2) + x + 17$
- **d** $6(3x-4) - 8x + 4$
- **e** $4(x+4) + 7(x+1)$
- **f** $8(5+2x) + 3(x-6)$

11 Show that $4(2x+7) + 3(6x-5) \equiv 13(2x+1)$.

12 Work out the missing numbers in these expansions.
- **a** $9(3x+2) = 3(\square x + \square)$
- **b** $5(8-6z) = 10(\square - \square z)$

Tip
$\equiv$ means 'is equivalent to' or 'is the same as'.

13 Work out the missing numbers in these expansions.
All the numbers are in the cloud. Only use each number once.
- **a** $\square(2x + \square) = 8x + \square$
- **b** $5(\square x - \square) = \square x - 35$
- **c** $\square(6y - 10) = \square y - 80$
- **d** $7(\square y + \square) = \square y + 42$

Cloud: 2, 3, 4, 6, 7, 8, 9, 14, 15, 36, 48

> 2.5 Constructing and solving equations

When you **solve** an equation, you find the value of the unknown letter.
You can use a flow chart like this to solve an equation using **inverse operations**.

Solve: $x + 5 = 12$ $x \rightarrow +5 \rightarrow 12$
So $x = 7$ $7 \leftarrow -5 \leftarrow 12$

Key words
inverse operation
solve

Tip
Reverse the flow chart to work out the value of x.

Exercise 2.5

Focus

1 Write down the missing numbers.
- **a** $\square + 4 = 6$
- **b** $\square + 1 = 6$
- **c** $\square + 2 = 10$
- **d** $8 - \square = 5$
- **e** $9 - \square = 2$
- **f** $17 - \square = 10$

2 Expressions, formulae and equations

2 Copy and complete these flow charts to work out the value of x.

a) $x + 3 = 7$ $x \to [+3] \to 7$
   $x = \square \quad \square \leftarrow [-3] \leftarrow 7$

b) $x + 1 = 9$ $x \to [+1] \to 9$
   $x = \square \quad \square \leftarrow [-1] \leftarrow 9$

c) $x + 6 = 11$ $x \to [+6] \to 11$
   $x = \square \quad \square \leftarrow [-\square] \leftarrow 11$

d) $x + 2 = 13$ $x \to [+2] \to 13$
   $x = \square \quad \square \leftarrow [\square] \leftarrow 13$

e) $x + 4 = 12$ $x \to [+4] \to 12$
   $x = \square \quad \square \leftarrow [\square] \leftarrow \square$

f) $x + 9 = 15$ $x \to [\square] \to \square$
   $x = \square \quad \square \leftarrow [\square] \leftarrow \square$

3 Copy and complete these flow charts to work out the value of x.

a) $x - 1 = 5$ $x \to [-1] \to 5$
   $x = \square \quad \square \leftarrow [+1] \leftarrow 5$

b) $x - 3 = 8$ $x \to [-3] \to 8$
   $x = \square \quad \square \leftarrow [+3] \leftarrow 8$

c) $x - 2 = 9$ $x \to [-2] \to 9$
   $x = \square \quad \square \leftarrow [+\square] \leftarrow 9$

d) $x - 5 = 12$ $x \to [-5] \to 12$
   $x = \square \quad \square \leftarrow [\square] \leftarrow 12$

e) $x - 10 = 8$ $x \to [-10] \to 8$
   $x = \square \quad \square \leftarrow [\square] \leftarrow \square$

f) $x - 4 = 5$ $x \to [\square] \to \square$
   $x = \square \quad \square \leftarrow [\square] \leftarrow 12$

4 Copy and complete these flow charts to work out the value of y.

a) $2y = 6$ $y \to [\times 2] \to 6$
   $y = \square \quad \square \leftarrow [\div 2] \leftarrow 6$

b) $4y = 8$ $y \to [\times 4] \to 8$
   $y = \square \quad \square \leftarrow [\div 4] \leftarrow 8$

Practice

5 Solve each of these equations. Check your answers by substituting your answer back into the original equation.

a) $x + 2 = 6$
b) $x + 6 = 9$
c) $4 + x = 11$
d) $15 + x = 21$
e) $x - 5 = 10$
f) $x - 4 = 6$
g) $x - 15 = 12$
h) $5x = 20$
i) $3x = 30$
j) $4x = 28$

6 Solve each of these equations. Check your answers by substituting your answer back into the original equation.

a) $14 = x + 3$
b) $9 = x + 5$
c) $12 = x - 6$
d) $20 = x - 5$
e) $14 = 2x$
f) $50 = 10x$

2.5 Constructing and solving equations

7 Write an equation for each of these statements. Solve each equation to find the value of the unknown number.

a I think of a number and then add 5. My answer is 21. What is the number I first thought of?

b I think of a number and then subtract 5. My answer is 21. What is the number I first thought of?

8 Write an equation for each of these statements. Solve each equation to find the value of the unknown number.
   a I think of a number and add 14. The answer is 20.
   b I think of a number and subtract 17. The answer is 20.
   c I think of a number and multiply it by 5. The answer is 20.

9 Solve each of these equations. Check your answers by substituting your answer back into the original equation.
   a $2a + 4 = 18$
   b $5a - 2 = 18$
   c $30 = 7b + 9$
   d $18 = 6b - 12$

Challenge

10 This is part of Sofia's homework.

> Question:
> The diagram shows a right angle divided into two smaller angles, 3x and 2x.
> Work out the size of the angles in this diagram.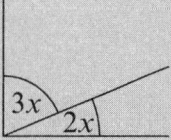
>
> Solution:
> Equation $3x + 2x = 90°$
> Simplify $5x = 90°$
> Solve $x = \dfrac{90}{5} = 18°$
> Answers   3x angle is $3 \times 18 = 54°$.
>   2x angle is $2 \times 18 = 36°$.
> Check $54 + 36 = 90°$ ✓

For each of these diagrams:
  i   Write an equation involving the angles.
  ii Simplify your equation by collecting like terms.
  iii Solve your equation to find the value of x.
  iv Work out the sizes of the angles in the diagram.
  v   Check that your answers are correct by substituting your answer back into the original equation.

Tip

What do the angles on a straight line and in a triangle add up to?

a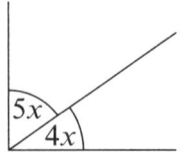
b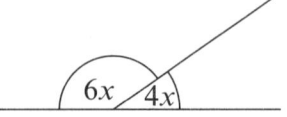
c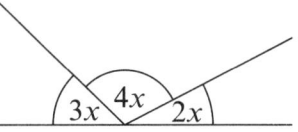
d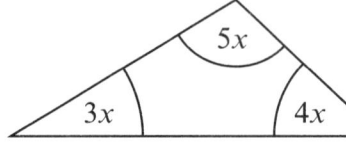

11 Solve each of these equations and check your answers.
  a $x + 12 = -6$
  b $y - 9 = -4$
  c $3z + 6 = -30$
  d $4w - 3 = -27$

 12 Zara solves these equations:

| $2a - 11 = -7$ | $4 = b + 16$ |
| $6c + 7 = 25$ | $-12 = 3d + 9$ |

Is Zara correct? Show all your working and explain your answer.

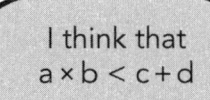
I think that a × b < c + d

13 Use the formula $w = 2x + y - 3z$ to work out:
  a w when $x = 8$, $y = -3$ and $z = 7$
  b x when $w = 15$, $y = 9$ and $z = -4$
  c y when $w = -10$, $x = 6$ and $z = 2$
  d z when $w = 20$, $x = 15$ and $y = 8$

> 2.6 Inequalities

Remember: < means 'is less than'
 > means 'is greater than'.

Key words
inequality
integer

Exercise 2.6

Focus

1 Write 'true' or 'false' for each of these statements. The first one has been done for you.
 a $x < 9$ means 'x is less than 9'. True
 b $x > 3$ means 'x is less than 3'.
 c $x < 2$ means 'x is greater than 2'.
 d $x > 7$ means 'x is greater than 7'.

2 Match each **inequality** (**A** to **D**) with its correct meaning (**i** to **iv**).
 The first one has been done for you: **A** and **ii**.

 A $x > 4$ i x is less than 12.
 B $x < 4$ ii x is greater than 4.
 C $x > 12$ iii x is less than 4.
 D $x < 12$ iv x is greater than 12.

3 Write these statements as inequalities. The first one has been done for you.
 a x is greater than 2. $x > 2$ b y is greater than 5.
 c m is less than 15.   d b is less than 7.

4 Match each inequality (**A** to **D**) with its correct number line (**i** to **iv**). The first one has been done for you: **A** and **iv**.

 A $x > -5$ i
 B $x < 5$ ii
 C $x < -5$ iii
 D $x > 5$ iv

Tip
Remember: You use an open circle (o) for the < and > inequalities.

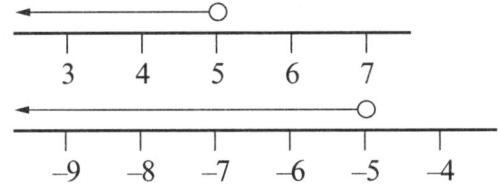
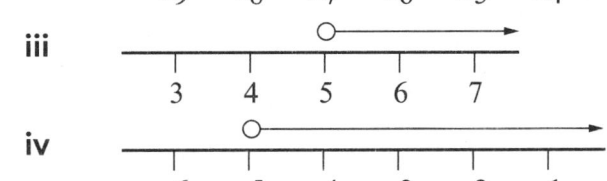

2 Expressions, formulae and equations

5 a Copy this number line. 12 13 14 15 16 17

Show the inequality $y < 15$ on the number line.

b Copy this number line. 12 13 14 15 16 17

Show the inequality $y > 15$ on the number line.

c Write down the inequality shown on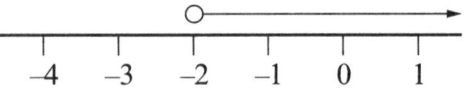

this number line. Use the letter x.

d Write down the inequality shown on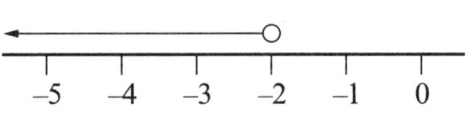

this number line. Use the letter x.

Practice

6 Copy each number line and show each inequality on the number line.

  a $x > 8$ 7 8 9 10 11   **b** $x < 6$ 3 4 5 6 7

  c $x < -3$ −5 −4 −3 −2 −1   **d** $x > 0$ −1 0 1 2 3

7 Write down the inequality shown on these number lines. Use the letter x.

  a 12 13 14 15 16   **b** 30 31 32 33 34

  c −9 −8 −7 −6 −5   **d** 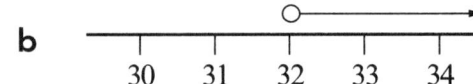 −4 −3 −2 −1 0

8 Write down if **A**, **B** or **C** is the correct answer to each of the following.

  a For the inequality $h > 5$, the smallest **integer** that h could be is:
  A 4   B 5   C 6

  b For the inequality $j > -7$, the smallest integer that j could be is:
  A −8   B −7   C −6

  c For the inequality $k < 12$, the largest integer that k could be is:
  A 11   B 12   C 13

  d For the inequality $m < -1$, the largest integer that m could be is:
  A −3   B −2   C −1

9 Zara looks at the inequality $z < -5$.

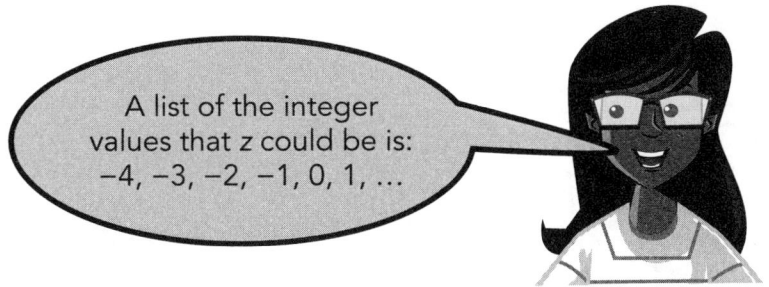

A list of the integer values that z could be is: −4, −3, −2, −1, 0, 1, ...

Is Zara correct? Explain your answer.

10 For each of these inequalities, write down:
  i the smallest integer that p could be
  ii a list of the integer values that p could be.
  a $p > 8$ **b** $p > -3$ **c** $p > 4.7$

11 For each of these inequalities, write down:
  i the largest integer that q could be
  ii a list of the integer values that q could be.
  a $q < -1$ **b** $q < 16$ **c** $q < 3.9$

Challenge

12 Copy each number line and show each inequality on the number line.

  a $x > 1.5$ **b** $x < 3.75$

  c $y > 4.6$ **d** $y < 8.25$

13 Write down the inequality shown on these number lines. Use the letter y.

  a 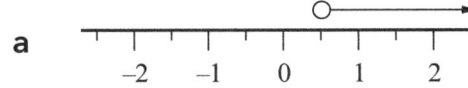 **b**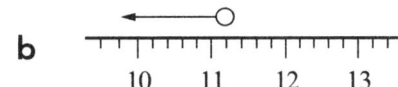

  c 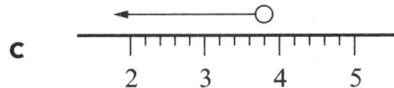 **d**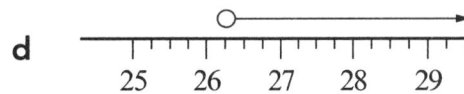

2 Expressions, formulae and equations

14 Arun looks at this number line: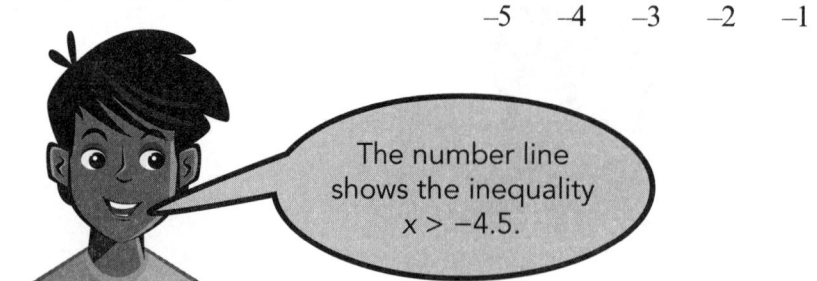

> The number line shows the inequality $x > -4.5$.

Explain the mistake that Arun has made.

15 Write down the inequality shown on these number lines. Use the letter w.

a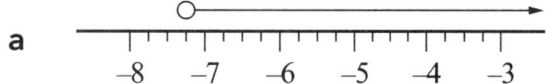

b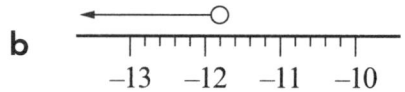

16 Copy each number line and show each inequality on the number line.

a $y < -1.5$

b $y > -4.4$

3 Place value and rounding

> 3.1 Multiplying and dividing by powers of 10

Exercise 3.1

> **Key words**
> power
> powers of 10

Focus

1 Each oval card has the same value as a square card.

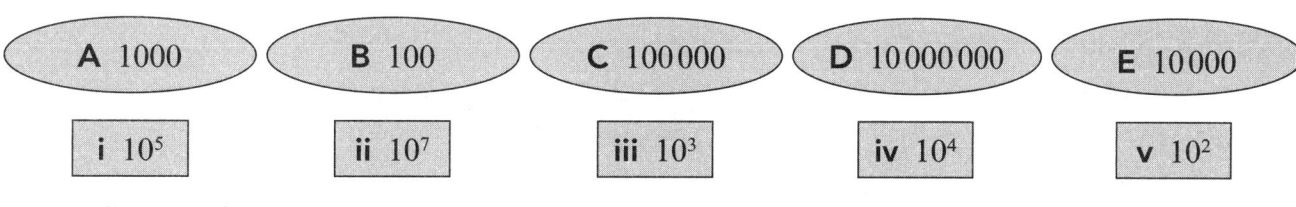

Copy and complete the list of pairs of cards with the same value.
The first one has been done for you.

A and **iii** because $1000 = 10^3$.
B and ☐ because $100 =$ ☐
C and ☐ because $100\,000 =$ ☐
D and ☐ because $10\,000\,000 =$ ☐
E and ☐ because $10\,000 =$ ☐

> **Tip**
> The number of zeros after the 1 is the same as the **power of the 10**.
> 3 zeros after the 1 = **power** of 3

2 Copy and complete the following.
a $6 \times 10^4 = 6 \times 10\,000 = 60\,000$
b $9 \times 10^4 = 9 \times$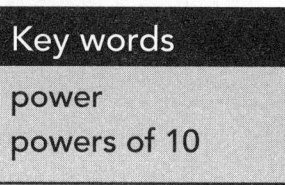
c $3 \times 10^4 = 3 \times$ ☐ = ☐

> **Tip**
> Remember:
> $10^4 = 10\,000$

43

3 Place value and rounding

3 Copy and complete the following.
   a. $2 \times 10^5 = 2 \times 100\,000 = 200\,000$
   b. $7 \times 10^5 = 7 \times \boxed{} = \boxed{}$
   c. $5 \times 10^5 = 5 \times \boxed{} = \boxed{}$

> **Tip**
> Remember:
> $10^5 = 100\,000$

4 Write whether **A**, **B** or **C** is the correct answer for each of these.
   a. $8 \times 10^3 =$ **A** 800   **B** 8000   **C** 80 000
   b. $4 \times 10^6 =$ **A** 4 000 000   **B** 400 000   **C** 40 000 000
   c. $3 \times 10^8 =$ **A** 3 000 000   **B** 30 000 000   **C** 300 000 000

5 Rafa uses this method to work out $6\,000\,000 \div 10^5$.

> 10^5 has 5 zeros, so I will cross 5 zeros off the number 6 000 000.
>
> 60 ØØ ØØØ, which gives me an answer of 60.

Use Rafa's method to work out:
   a. $800\,000 \div 10^5$ b. $2\,000\,000 \div 10^5$ c. $400\,000 \div 10^4$
   d. $90\,000 \div 10^4$ e. $3\,000\,000 \div 10^6$ f. $500\,000\,000 \div 10^6$

6 Write whether **A**, **B** or **C** is the correct answer.
   a. $50\,000 \div 10^3 =$ **A** 50   **B** 5   **C** 500
   b. $710\,000 \div 10^4 =$ **A** 7100   **B** 710   **C** 71
   c. $89\,000\,000 \div 10^6 =$ **A** 890   **B** 89   **C** 8900
   d. $470\,000\,000 \div 10^5 =$ **A** 47   **B** 470   **C** 4700

Practice

7 Work out:
   a. 56×10^2 b. 877×10^4 c. 13×10^6
   d. 6.5×10^4 e. 33.2×10^3 f. 0.65×10^6

8 Copy and complete these calculations.
   a. $3.7 \times 10^4 = \boxed{}$
   b. $34.6 \times \boxed{} = 34\,600$
   c. $\boxed{} \times 10^6 = 8\,900\,000$
   d. $78.34 \times 10^{\boxed{}} = 783\,400\,000$

9 Work out:
   a. $9000 \div 10^3$ b. $520\,000 \div 10^4$ c. $8\,000\,000 \div 10^5$

10 Copy and complete this table.

	÷ 10^2	÷ 10^3	÷ 10^4	÷ 10^5	÷ 10^6
400 000	4000				
56 000			5.6		
3000				0.03	
720		0.72			

11 Write down whether **A**, **B** or **C** is the correct answer.
   a $240\,000 ÷ 10^5$ A   24   B   2.4   C   0.24
   b $7020 ÷ 10^6$ A   0.00702   B   0.0702   C   0.702
   c $8\,700\,000 ÷ 10^8$ A   87   B   0.87   C   0.087

 12 Arun thinks of a starting number. He multiplies his number by 10^3, then divides the answer by 10^5. He multiplies this answer by 10^6 and finally divides this answer by 10^2.

Arun thinks that a quicker method would be to just multiply his starting number by 10.

Is Arun correct?

Show your working and explain your answer.

Tip

Try different starting numbers and work out the answers.

Challenge

13 These formulae show how to convert between different metric units of mass.

> Number of milligrams = number of grams × 10^3

> Number of milligrams = number of kilograms × 10^6

> Number of milligrams = number of tonnes × 10^9

Tip

The units are:
milligram (mg)
gram (g)
kilogram (kg)
tonne (t)

Use the formulae to work out the missing numbers in these conversions.
   a   ☐ mg = 28 g   b   ☐ mg = 0.75 g
   c   ☐ mg = 2 kg   d   ☐ mg = 0.083 kg
   e   ☐ mg = 53 t   f   ☐ mg = 0.0025 t

3 Place value and rounding

14 a Use the formulae in Question **13** to complete the following formulae.

> Number of grams = number of milligrams ÷ 10^3

> Number of kilograms = number of milligrams ÷ $10^{...}$

> Number of tonnes = number of milligrams ÷ $10^{...}$

b Use your formulae in part **a** to work out the missing numbers in these conversions.

i ☐ g = 45 000 mg

ii ☐ kg = 7 600 000 mg

iii ☐ t = 65 700 000 mg

15 The table shows the distances from Earth to different objects in space. The distances are shown as a decimal number multiplied by a power of 10.

Object	Distance from Earth (km)
Moon	3.844×10^5
space station	4.08×10^2
Venus	4.14×10^7
Neptune	4.35×10^9
weather satellite	3.6×10^4
Jupiter	6.287×10^8

Aki wants to write the objects in order, from the closest to Earth to the farthest from Earth.

a Without doing any calculations, write down what you think Aki's list will be. Explain how you made your decisions.

b Work out the multiplications and then compare the distances. Was your list in part **a** correct? If it was incorrect, write down the correct list.

16 In this diagram, the calculations in each rectangle simplify to the answer given in the circle.

Copy and complete the diagram with a different calculation in each box. Two have been done for you.

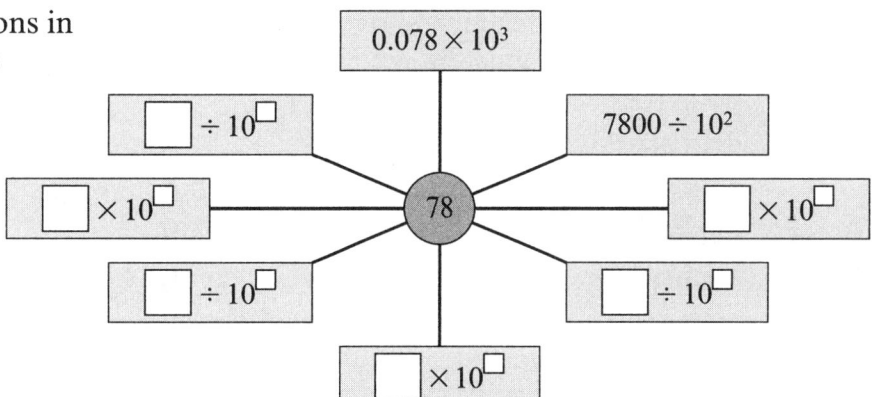

17 Work out the following.

a $(3.6 \times 10^4) + \dfrac{15\,000}{3}$ b $4 \times (2\,310\,000 \div 10^6)$

c $(0.005 \times 10^3)^2$ d $(256\,000\,000 \div 10^7) - (0.000049 \times 10^5)$

Tip

Remember to use the correct order of operations.

> ## 3.2 Rounding

Exercise 3.2

Key words

degree of accuracy

round

Focus

1 **Round** each of these numbers to one decimal place. The first two have been done for you.

   a $4.53 = 4.5$ (1 d.p.)   b $3.69 = 3.7$ (1 d.p.)   c 8.82

   d 7.24   e 2.37   f 4.09

2 Round each of these numbers to one decimal place. Write whether **A** or **B** is the correct answer.

   a 4.671 =   **A** 4.6   **B** 4.7

   b 9.055 =   **A** 9.0   **B** 9.1

   c 3.733 =   **A** 3.7   **B** 3.8

   d 6.915 =   **A** 6.9   **B** 7.0

   e 0.858 =   **A** 0.8   **B** 0.9

3 Round each of these numbers to two decimal places. The first two have been done for you.

   a $2.473 = 2.47$ (2 d.p.)   b $8.659 = 8.66$ (2 d.p.)   c 3.314

   d 8.065   e 1.938   f 2.422

3 Place value and rounding

4 Round each of these numbers to two decimal places. Write whether **A** or **B** is the correct answer.

a	0.6651 =	A	0.66	B	0.67
b	2.3015 =	A	2.30	B	2.31
c	8.5544 =	A	8.55	B	8.56
d	0.0593 =	A	0.05	B	0.06
e	5.6058 =	A	5.60	B	5.61

Practice

5 Round each of these numbers to two decimal places (2 d.p.). The first one has been done for you.

- a 4.983 = 4.98 (2 d.p.)
- b 9.037
- c 24.332
- d 128.641
- e 0.66582
- f 0.03174

6 Round each of these numbers to three decimal places (3 d.p.). The first one has been done for you.

- a 7.2845 = 7.285 (3 d.p.)
- b 65.8823
- c 134.9028
- d 0.67893
- e 300.00442
- f 0.0085411

7 Round each of these numbers to four decimal places (4 d.p.). The first one has been done for you.

- a 3.882615 = 3.8826 (4 d.p.)
- b 61.89022
- c 143.56228
- d 200.006789
- e 300.000555
- f 18.25252525

8 Write whether **A** or **B** is the correct answer to each of the following.

a	34.9892 to 1 d.p. =	A	35	B	35.0
b	7.4955 to 2 d.p. =	A	7.50	B	7.5
c	0.009666 to 3 d.p. =	A	0.010	B	0.01

9 A red blood cell has a length of 0.0065982 millimetres. Write down the length, correct to five decimal places.

10 Use a calculator to work out the answers to the following. Round each of your answers to the given **degree of accuracy**.

- a $19 \div 11$ (2 d.p.)
- b $12 - \dfrac{11}{13}$ (4 d.p.)
- c $\sqrt{89} + 26$ (3 d.p.)

Challenge

11 Write the number 476.8925636952, correct to:

a the nearest 10
b the nearest whole number
c one decimal place
d two decimal places
e three decimal places
f four decimal places
g five decimal places
h six decimal places
i seven decimal places
j eight decimal places

12 a Copy and complete the division below to work out $7 \div 11$. Work out the answer as far as five decimal places.

$$11 \overline{\smash{\big)}\, 7\,.\,^{7}0\,^{4}0\,0\,0\,0}^{0\,.\,6}$$

Write your answer correct to four decimal places.

b Work out $11 \div 7$ as far as four decimal places.
Write your answer correct to three decimal places.

c Work out $13 \div 9$ as far as three decimal places.
Write your answer correct to two decimal places.

d Marcus and Arun both work out $58 \div 7$, correct to three decimal places.
Here are the methods they use:

I am going to work out $58 \div 7$ as far as three decimal places. Then I will have the correct answer.

I am going to work out $58 \div 7$ as far as four decimal places and then round to three decimal places. Then I will have the correct answer.

3 Place value and rounding

  - i Work out 58 ÷ 7 using Marcus's method and Razi's method.
  - ii Do you get the same answer?
  - iii Whose method gives the correct answer? Explain why.

13 Alan rounds a number to three decimal places and his answer is 45.638.

Write down 10 different numbers that round to 45.638, correct to three decimal places.

14 a Work out 28.67284 − 3.42649. Write your answer correct to three decimal places.

  b Work out 28.67284 − 3.42649 again, but this time round each number correct to three decimal places <u>before</u> you do the subtraction.

  c Are your answers to parts **a** and **b** the same? Explain your answer.

  d In general, why is it a good idea to round only the final answer of a calculation and <u>not</u> to round any numbers or answers you get before the final answer?

4 Decimals

> 4.1 Ordering decimals

Exercise 4.1

Key words
- compare
- decimal number
- decimal part
- order
- third
- whole-number part

Focus

1   Write these numbers in **order** of size, starting with the smallest. The first one has been done for you.

| 176 | 204 | 23 | 498 | 45 | 12 |

12 ☐ ☐ ☐ ☐ ☐

2   For each of these lists of numbers:
    i   Write down the number that is in the incorrect place.
    ii Write the list in the correct order of size, starting with the smallest.

    a   34   59   70   215   152   251
    b   67   88   39   95   101   321
    c   6   8.2   14.5 67   10.9 100.7

Tip
Start by comparing the numbers in the tens, then the numbers in the hundreds.

3   a   Copy the diagram. Write these measurements in the spaces under the ruler. One has been done for you.

    18.6 cm   18.9 cm   18.1 cm   18.5 cm   18.3 cm

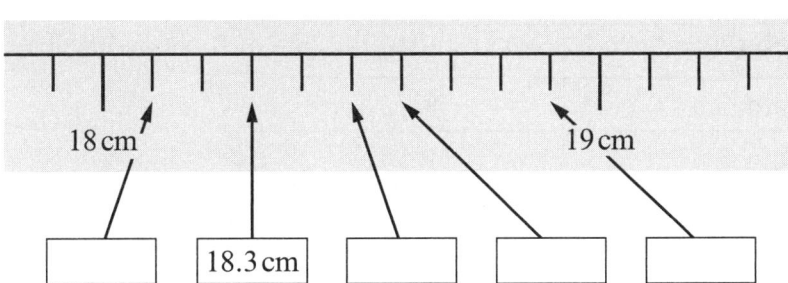

    b   Use your answer in part **a** to write these numbers in order of size, starting with the smallest.
        18.6   18.9   18.1   18.5   18.3
    c   Write these numbers in order of size, starting with the smallest.
        9.5   9.3   9.8   9.2   9.7

51

4 Decimals

d Write these numbers in order of size, starting with the smallest. The first one has been done for you.

3.32   3.21   3.56   3.42

3.21   ☐   ☐   ☐

Tip

The whole-number parts are the same, so compare the numbers after the decimal point: 32, 21, 56, 42.

4 Complete the workings to write these numbers in order of size, starting with the smallest.

6.5   6.08   6.21   6.1

Start by writing each number to
two decimal places: 6.50, 6.08, 6.21, 6.10
Now write the **decimal parts** only: 50, 08, 21, 10
Now write in order the decimal parts only: 08, 10, ☐, ☐
Now write the complete numbers in order: 6.08, ☐, ☐, ☐

5 Write these numbers in order of size, starting with the smallest.

a   4.67   4.21   4.5   4.02
b   12.9   12.41   12.08   12.3

Tip

Use the same method as you did in Question **4**.

Practice

6 Write down the smallest **decimal number** from each pair.

a 3.5, 9.1	**b** 214.92, 311.67	**c** 34.56, 43.652	**d** 638.06, 336.9
e 0.22, 0.3	**f** 5.6, 5.41	**g** 25.67, 25.76	**h** 0.02, 0.013
i 0.009, 0.01	**j** 0.05, 0.049		

7 The table shows six of the fastest times run by men in a 100 metre race.

Name	Country	Time (seconds)
Donovan Bailey	Canada	9.84
Nesta Carter	Jamaica	9.78
Tyson Gay	USA	9.69
Asafa Powell	Jamaica	9.72
Usain Bolt	Jamaica	9.58
Maurice Greene	USA	9.79

a Write the times in order of size, starting with the smallest.
b Which man has the **third** fastest time?

4.1 Ordering decimals

8   Write the correct inequality, < or >, between each pair of numbers.
    a   2.05 ☐ 2.24   b   8.55 ☐ 8.41   c   0.48 ☐ 0.51
    d   18.05 ☐ 18.02   e   8.2 ☐ 8.01   f   2.18 ☐ 2.205
    g   0.072 ☐ 0.02   h   28.882 ☐ 28.88

9   Write the correct sign, = or ≠, between each pair of numbers.
    a   8.3 ☐ 8.30   b   2.92 ☐ 2.29
    c   5.505 ☐ 5.055   d   4.660 ☐ 4.66
    e   87.0 ☐ 87   f   0.0076 ☐ 0.076

Tip

The symbol ≠ means 'is <u>not</u> equal to'.

10 For each list, write the decimal numbers in order of size, starting with the smallest.
    a   4.46, 2.66, 4.41, 4.49   b   0.71, 0.52, 0.77, 0.59
    c   6.09, 6.92, 6.9, 6.97   d   5.212, 5.2, 5.219, 5.199
    e   42.449, 42.42, 42.441, 42.4   f   9.09, 9.7, 9.901, 9.04, 9.99

Challenge

11 Write these measurements in order of size, starting with the smallest.
    a   83 mm, 8.15 cm, 0.081 m
    b   0.00672 t, 6750 g, 6.7 kg
    c   0.00347 km, 3455 mm, 3.48 m, 346 cm

12 Zack has put these decimal number cards in order of size, starting with the smallest.

    6.46   6.▓   6.471

    There is a mark covering part of the number on the middle card.
    a   Write down three possible numbers that could be on the middle card.
    b   How many different numbers with three decimal places do you think could be on the middle card?
    c   Show how you can check if your answer to part **b** is correct.

13 Put the following in order of size, starting with the smallest.

    2110 ÷ 100   0.0208 × 100   1.9 × 10   2320 ÷ 1000   2000 ÷ 1000   0.23 × 10

4 Decimals

> 4.2 Adding and subtracting decimals

Exercise 4.2

Key words

digits
mentally/using a mental method
written method

Focus

1   Work out the answers to these whole-number additions.

   a   75
       + 22
       ___

   b   36
       + 45
       ___

   c   79
       + 53
       ___

   d   125
       + 314
       ___

   e   562
       + 36
       ___

   f   286
       + 77
       ___

Tip

Remember to start from the right column. Add the units first, then the tens, then the hundreds.

2   Work out the answers to these decimal additions.

   a   3.4
       + 2.1
       ___
       .

   b   5.2
       + 3.9
       ___
       .

   c   6.8
       + 8.4
       ___
       .

   d   42.5
       + 33.7
       ___
       .

   e   73.7
       + 9.1
       ___
       .

   f   8.49
       + 0.84
       ___
       .

Tip

Use the same method as you did in Question **1**. Do not let the decimal point distract you!

3   Work out the answers to these decimal additions.
    Use a grid like the one shown on the right to help you.

   Remember to line up the decimal points in each question so that they are underneath each other. The first one has been started for you.

   a   6.1 + 5.7
   b   8.3 + 4.8
   c   12.9 + 5.3
   d   3.21 + 0.58

a		6	.	1
	+	5	.	7

4.2 Adding and subtracting decimals

4 Work out the answers to these subtractions.

a) 78 − 42

b) 49 − 21

c) 843 − 28

d) 6.7 − 1.4

e) 8.2 − 4.6

f) 2.63 − 0.45

> **Tip**
> Start from the right column. Remember to 'borrow' if you need to.

5 Work out the answers to these decimal subtractions. Use a grid like the one in Question **3** to help you.

Remember to line up the decimal points in each question so that they are underneath each other.

a) 3.9 − 2.5
b) 7.4 − 3.8
c) 12.92 − 5.3

Practice

6 Use a **mental method** to work out the following.
a) 5.5 + 2.3
b) 12.3 + 5.5
c) 8.7 + 6.5
d) 8.8 − 3.4
e) 18.6 − 7.4
f) 12.3 − 5.3

7 Write whether **A** or **B** is the correct answer to each of these.
a) 1 − 0.65 =   A 0.45   B 0.35
b) 1 − 0.324 =   A 0.676   B 0.786

8 Work out the following by rounding one of the numbers to a whole number.
a) 5.9 + 3.3
b) 8.7 + 8.9
c) 5.8 + 6.3
d) 7.3 − 2.9
e) 9.7 − 4.6
f) 13.5 − 8.8

9 Use a **written method** to work out the following.
a) 7.67 + 0.15
b) 7.77 + 5.55
c) 23.4 + 6.78
d) 45.67 + 76.5
e) 8.64 − 6.42
f) 9.75 − 7.95
g) 23.4 − 4.32
h) 77.7 − 38.66
i) 5.23 − − 15.5

10 Amira records the mass of her dog at the start and end of every month. Here are her records for April and May.

Date	Mass (kg)	Date	Mass (kg)
Start of April	6.43	End of April	7.22
Start of May	7.22	End of May	8.05

4 Decimals

   a   During which month, April or May, does the mass of the dog increase the most?
   b   During June the mass of the dog increases by 0.93 kg. What is the mass of the dog at the end of June?

11 Work out:
   a $10 - 3.74$
   b $20 - 13.56$
   c $30 - 2.183$
   d $40 - 25.661$

Challenge

12 At the cinema, Bijoux spends $1.50 on a ticket, $1.75 on food and $0.85 on a drink.
   a   How much does she spend in total?
   b   Bijoux pays with a $5 note. How much change does she receive?

13 Dewain makes curtains. He has four pieces of fabric that are 0.6 m, 1.35 m, 1.6 m and 3 m long.
   a   What is the total length of the four pieces of fabric?
   b   Dewain needs 8 m of fabric in total. How much more fabric does he need to buy?

14 Work out:
   a $2.45 - 6.69$
   b $9.38 - 12.9$
   c $-14.2 + 6.54$
   d $2.457 - (3.7 + 4.584)$
   e $-6.92 - 5.37$
   f $-1.43 - -13.7$

 15 Work out the missing **digits** in these calculations.

a
```
    ☐ 7 . ☐ 2
  + 2 ☐ . 5 ☐
  ─────────────
    6 6 . 1 5
```

b
```
    ☐ 4 . 5 6
  - 2 ☐ . 5 ☐
  ─────────────
    5 5 . ☐ 7
```

> 4.3 Multiplying decimals

Exercise 4.3

Focus

Key word

fill in

1 **Fill in** the missing numbers in these number patterns.

a	$200 \times 4 = 800$	b	$300 \times 2 = 600$	c	$500 \times 3 = 1500$
	$20 \times 4 = 80$		$30 \times 2 = \square$		$50 \times 3 = \square$
	$2 \times 4 = \square$		$3 \times 2 = 6$		$5 \times 3 = \square$
	$0.2 \times 4 = 0.8$		$0.3 \times 2 = \square$		$0.5 \times 3 = 1.5$
d	$700 \times 5 = 3500$	e	$900 \times 2 = \square$	f	$600 \times 7 = \square$
	$70 \times 5 = \square$		$90 \times 2 = \square$		$60 \times 7 = \square$
	$7 \times 5 = \square$		$9 \times 2 = \square$		$6 \times 7 = \square$
	$0.7 \times 5 = \square$		$0.9 \times 2 = \square$		$0.6 \times 7 = \square$

Tip

Look at how the numbers at the end of each pattern become smaller.

2 Write down two of your own number patterns. Make the patterns similar to those in Question **1**, but choose your own numbers.

Tip

You could start with 400 × 6 or 800 × 3. You decide.

3 Copy and complete these workings. The first one has been done for you.

a 0.3×6 First work out $3 \times 6 = 18$,   so $0.3 \times 6 = 1.8$.
b 0.2×8 First work out $2 \times 8 = \square$,   so $0.2 \times 8 = \square$
c 0.4×4 First work out $4 \times 4 = \square$,   so $0.4 \times 4 = \square$
d 0.7×9 First work out $\square \times \square = \square$,   so $0.7 \times 9 = \square$
e 0.5×5 First work out $\square \times \square = \square$,   so $0.5 \times 5 = \square$

4 Copy and complete this number pattern.

$0.1 \times 5 = 0.5$ $0.6 \times 5 = \square$
$0.2 \times 5 = 1$ $0.7 \times 5 = \square$
$0.3 \times 5 = 1.5$ $0.8 \times 5 = \square$
$0.4 \times 5 = 2$ $0.9 \times 5 = \square$
$0.5 \times 5 = \square$ $1 \times 5 = \square$

Tip

To work out 0.2×5, do $2 \times 5 = 10$, so $0.2 \times 5 = 1.0$, which is the same as 1.

4 Decimals

5 Use a grid to help you work out the answers to these questions. The first one has been done for you.

		3	2	
	×		7	
	2	2	4	
		1		

Tip

First work out
32 × 7 = 224, so
3.2 × 7 = 22.4.

a 3.2 × 7 = 22.4   b 4.5 × 2 = ☐   c 2.4 × 3 = ☐
d 4.6 × 4 = ☐   e 8.9 × 5 = ☐   f 9.2 × 2 = ☐

Practice

6 Use a mental method to work out the following.
- a 0.3 × 2
- b 0.2 × 4
- c 0.4 × 6
- d 5 × 0.6
- e 7 × 0.7
- f 0.8 × 6

7 Use a mental method to work out the following.
All the answers are given in the cloud.
- a 6 × 0.03
- b 9 × 0.2
- c 3 × 0.006
- d 180 × 0.1

Cloud: 0.018   18   0.18   1.8

8 Use the numbers given in the box to complete these calculations.
You can use each number only once. You should have no numbers left by the end.
- a 0.2 × 3 = ☐
- b 0.6 × ☐ = 2.4
- c ☐ × 9 = 4.5
- d 6.3 × ☐ = 37.8
- e 7.6 × 0.5 = ☐
- f ☐ × 5 = ☐

Box: 0.4   0.5   0.6   2   4   6   3.8

9 In 1 g of pink gold there is 0.05 g of silver.
How many grams of silver are there in 30 g of pink gold?

10
- a Work out 118 × 56.
- b Use your answer to part **a** to write down the answers to the following.
  - i 118 × 5.6
  - ii 118 × 0.56
  - iii 118 × 0.056
  - iv 11.8 × 56
  - v 1.18 × 56
  - vi 0.118 × 56

11 Work out these multiplications. Show how to check your answers using rounding.
- a 4.8 × 34
- b 2.1 × 476
- c 0.32 × 71
- d 0.57 × 635

Challenge

12 In 1 g of rose gold there is 0.0275 g of silver.
How many grams of silver are there in 28 g of rose gold?

13 The mean mass of the players in a rugby team is 94.35 kg.
There are 15 players in the team.

What is the total mass of the players in the team?

Tip

Mean mass = $\dfrac{\text{total mass}}{\text{number of players}}$

14 Asha manages an activity centre. The table shows the cost of some items she buys for the centre.

Asha buys:
- 120 T-shirts
- 50 baseball caps
- 32 safety hats
- 200 water bottles.

What is the total cost of these items?

Item	Cost (each)
T-shirts	$5.65
baseball caps	$3.49
safety hats	$12.38
water bottles	$1.17

15 Use the fact that $0.43 \times 28 = 12.04$, to work out:

    a 4.3×28 **b** 43×2.8 **c** 0.43×280 **d** 0.043×28

> 4.4 Dividing decimals

Exercise 4.4

Key words

conjecture
estimation
inverse calculation

Focus

1 Copy and complete these divisions.

    a $4\overline{)8\;4}$ quotient 2   **b** $4\overline{)8.4}$ quotient 2.   **c** $4\overline{)0.84}$ quotient 0.

    d $6\overline{)8\;{}^24}$ quotient 1   **e** $6\overline{)8.4}$ quotient 1.   **f** $6\overline{)0.84}$ quotient 0.

2 Work out the following. Use the same method as in part **b** of Question **1**.

    a $6.3 \div 3$ **b** $4.6 \div 2$ **c** $9.1 \div 7$ **d** $8.4 \div 3$ **e** $4.9 \div 7$

3 Copy and complete these divisions.

    a $3\overline{)6\;9\;3}$ quotient 2   **b** $3\overline{)6\;9.3}$ quotient 2.   **c** $3\overline{)6.9\;3}$ quotient 2.

    d $2\overline{)7\;{}^10\;4}$ quotient 3   **e** $2\overline{)7\;0.4}$ quotient 3.   **f** $2\overline{)7.0\;4}$ quotient 3.

4 Decimals

4 Work out:
- **a** 8.26 ÷ 2
- **b** 9.33 ÷ 3
- **c** 4.84 ÷ 4
- **d** 18.66 ÷ 6
- **e** 45.05 ÷ 5

5 Copy and complete these divisions.

- **a** 4)4.9 ¹2 8 → 1.2
- **b** 3)9.5 ²1 6 → 3.1
- **c** 7)7.8 ¹5 4 → 1.1

Practice

6 Copy and complete these divisions.

- **a** 3)3.5 ²2 8 → 1.1
- **b** 5)6.¹3 ³9 5 → 1.2
- **c** 8)8.9 ¹3 6 → 1.1
- **d** 4)7.³1 5 2 → 1.
- **e** 7)9.²5 8 3 → 1.
- **f** 6)1.¹5 3 6 → 0.

7 Work out:
- **a** 4.628 ÷ 2
- **b** 7.926 ÷ 6
- **c** 27.845 ÷ 5
- **d** 0.976 ÷ 8

8 Kai pays $7.45 for five bags of cement. How much does one bag of cement cost?

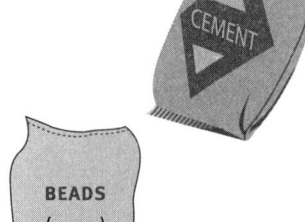

9 Rosi pays $7.56 for six bags of beads. How much does one bag of beads cost?

10 Copy and complete these divisions.

- **a** 12)3 8.²7 1 2 → 3.
- **b** 11)8 1.⁴9 6 1 → 7.

11 a Copy and complete the table below, which shows the 18 times table.

1	2	3	4	5	6	7	8	9
18	36	54						

b Use the table to help you work out 242.208 ÷ 18.

c Use **estimation** and an **inverse calculation** to show how to check that your answer to part **b** is correct.

> **Tip**
> Your answer to part **b** × 18 should equal 242.208.

4.4 Dividing decimals

12 a Copy and complete the table below, which shows the 25 times table.

1	2	3	4	5	6	7	8	9
25	50	75						

b A hockey club pays $808 a year to hire a hockey pitch. The 25 members of the club share the price equally between them. How much do they each pay?

c Use estimation and a reverse calculation to show how to check that your answer to part **b** is correct.

Challenge

13 Shaun and four friends eat a meal at a restaurant. The total cost of the meal is $68.60.

Shaun eats chicken korma $9.45, pilau rice $2.20 and a plain naan $1.95.

Is it better for Shaun to pay for his own food or to pay for an equal share of the bill?

14 Jiachi times how long it takes two racing cars to travel a distance of 400 m. The tables show her results.

Car A (five attempts)				
Time (seconds)				
7.882	7.663	7.910	7.562	8.008

Car B (four attempts)			
Time (seconds)			
8.015	7.972	7.735	7.582

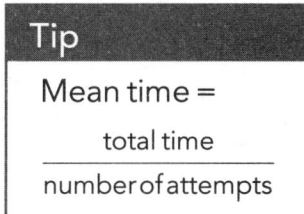

a Make a **conjecture**. Which car do you think has the fastest mean time?

b Work out the mean time for each car.

c Is your answer to part **a** correct?

15 Mick works out that $148 \times 68 = 10064$. Use this information to work out:
    a $10064 \div 68$ **b** $1006.4 \div 68$ **c** $100.64 \div 68$ **d** $10.064 \div 68$

16 Use the fact that $47.7 \div 5.3 = 9$ to work out:
    a $477 \div 5.3$ **b** $47.7 \div 0.53$ **c** $4.77 \div 0.53$ **d** $4770 \div 5.3$

17 Work out the following. Round each of your answers to the given degree of accuracy.
    a $9.94 \div 8$ (1 d.p.)   **b** $11.4 \div 7$ (2 d.p.)   **c** $5.8 \div 14$ (3 d.p.)

18 Copy and complete this division.

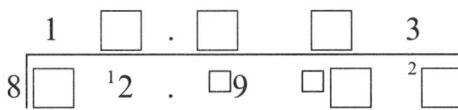

4 Decimals

> 4.5 Making decimal calculations easier

Exercise 4.5

Key words
equivalent fraction
partitioning
place value

Focus

1. Match each of these decimals to their **equivalent fraction**. The first one has been done for you: **A** and **v**.

   | A 0.1 | B 0.05 | C 0.4 | D 0.7 | E 0.06 | F 0.8 | G 0.02 | H 0.3 | I 0.04 |

   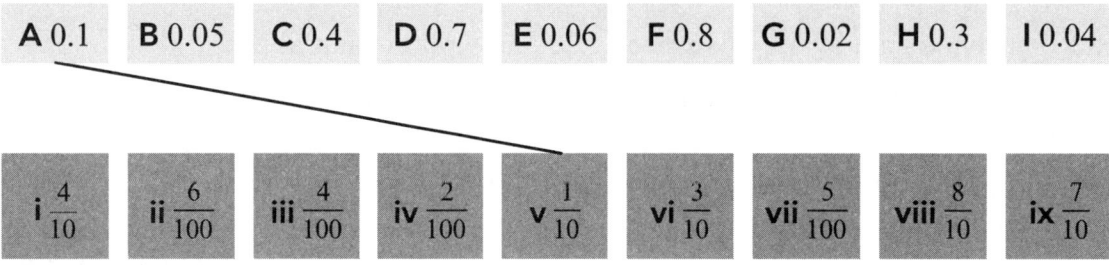

   i $\frac{4}{10}$ ii $\frac{6}{100}$ iii $\frac{4}{100}$ iv $\frac{2}{100}$ v $\frac{1}{10}$ vi $\frac{3}{10}$ vii $\frac{5}{100}$ viii $\frac{8}{10}$ ix $\frac{7}{10}$

2. Complete the working to make these calculations easier.

   a 150×0.2

   $0.2 = \frac{2}{10} = 2 \div 10$ $150 \times 2 \div 10 = 150 \div 10 \times \square$
   $= 15 \times \square$
   $= \square$

   b 70×0.3

   $0.3 = \frac{3}{10} = 3 \div 10$ $270 \times \ldots \div 10 = 70 \div \square \times \square$
   $= \square \times \square$
   $= \square$

   c 120×0.6

   $0.6 = \frac{6}{10} = \square \div \square$ $120 \times \square \div \square = 120 \div \square \times \square$
   $= \square \times \square$
   $= \square$

4.5 Making decimal calculations easier

3 For each of the following, complete the working to make the calculation easier.

a 1200×0.03

$0.03 = \dfrac{3}{100} = 3 \div 100$ $\qquad 1200 \times 3 \div 100 = 1200 \div 100 \times \square$
$\qquad\qquad\qquad\qquad\qquad\qquad\qquad\qquad = 12 \times \square$
$\qquad\qquad\qquad\qquad\qquad\qquad\qquad\qquad = \square$

b 900×0.05

$0.05 = \dfrac{5}{100} = 5 \div 100$ $\qquad 900 \times \ldots \div 100 = 900 \div \square \times \square$
$\qquad\qquad\qquad\qquad\qquad\qquad\qquad\qquad = \square \times \square$
$\qquad\qquad\qquad\qquad\qquad\qquad\qquad\qquad = \square$

c 700×0.04

$0.04 = \dfrac{4}{100} = \square \div \square$ $\qquad 700 \times \ldots \div \ldots = 700 \div \square \times \square$
$\qquad\qquad\qquad\qquad\qquad\qquad\qquad\qquad = \square \times \square$
$\qquad\qquad\qquad\qquad\qquad\qquad\qquad\qquad = \square$

4 Zara uses this method to multiply a number by the decimal 0.5.

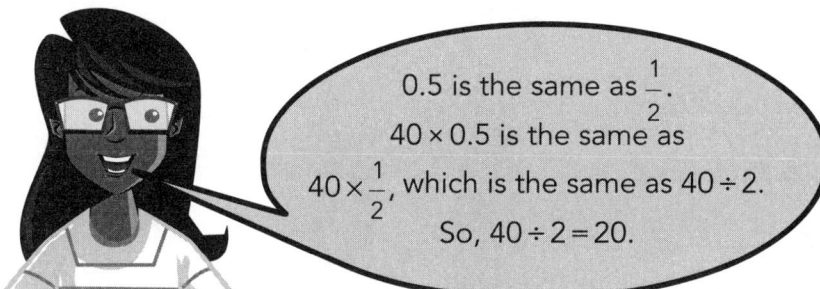

0.5 is the same as $\dfrac{1}{2}$.
40×0.5 is the same as
$40 \times \dfrac{1}{2}$, which is the same as $40 \div 2$.
So, $40 \div 2 = 20$.

> **Tip**
>
> The easiest way to work out $0.5 \times$ a number is to work out the number $\div 2$.

Use Zara's method to work out the following.

a $20 \times 0.5 = 20 \div 2 = \square$ **b** 50×0.5 **c** 16×0.5

d 48×0.5 **e** 52×0.5 **f** 23×0.5

5 Complete the workings to make these calculations easier.

a 2.3×9
$= 2.3 \times (10 - 1)$
$= 2.3 \times 10 - 2.3 \times 1$
$= \square - \square$
$= \square$

b 5.7×9
$= 5.7 \times (10 - 1)$
$= 5.7 \times 10 - 5.7 \times 1$
$= \square - \square$
$= \square$

4 Decimals

Practice

6 Complete the workings to make these calculations easier. Use the **place value** method.

a 0.3×270
$= \frac{3}{10} \times 270$
$= 3 \div 10 \times 270$
$= 3 \times 270 \div 10$
$= 3 \times \square$
$= 3 \times \square + 3 \times \square$
$= \square + \square$
$= \square$

b 0.07×4300
$= \frac{7}{100} \times 4300$
$= 7 \div 100 \times 4300$
$= 7 \times 4300 \div 100$
$= 7 \times \square$
$= 7 \times \square + 7 \times \square$
$= \square + \square$
$= \square$

Tip

Remember to use **partitioning** to help with the multiplications; e.g. $3 \times 27 = (3 \times 20) + (3 \times 7)$.

7 Use the same method as shown in Question **6** to work out:

a 0.4×630 b 0.8×250 c 0.07×5100 d 0.05×4200

8 Ana has $650 to share between her two children. The table shows the amount she will give to each child.

Item	Amount
Ayida	$0.4 \times \$650 = \$\square$
Dayana	$0.6 \times \$650 = \$\square$

a Copy and complete the table.
b Show how you can check that your answers are correct.

9 Work out:

a 6.8×9 b 4.7×9 c 12.6×9

10 Work out:

a 4.2×6 b 7.8×5 c 6.3×8

Tips

Use the same method as that shown in Question **5**.

Use partitioning to help.

a $4.2 \times 6 = 4 \times 6 + 0.2 \times 6$

11 Copy and complete the workings to make these divisions easier. Then work out the answer.

a $16.47 \div 30 = \frac{16.47}{30}$
$= \frac{16.47 \div 10}{30 \div 10}$
$= \frac{1.647}{\square}$

b $89.25 \div 70 = \frac{89.25}{70}$
$= \frac{89.25 \div \square}{70 \div \square}$
$= \frac{\square}{\square}$

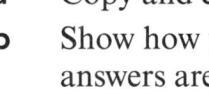

64

Challenge

12 An equilateral triangle has a side length of 4.7 m.

The formula to work out the perimeter of an equilateral triangle is:

$P = 3l$, where: P is the perimeter

l is the side length.

Use the formula to work out the perimeter of the equilateral triangle.

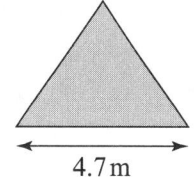

13 Copy and complete the workings to make these divisions easier. Then work out the answer.

a $38.16 \div 600 = \dfrac{38.16}{600}$

$= \dfrac{38.16 \div 100}{600 \div 100}$

$= \dfrac{0.3816}{\square}$

b $676.5 \div 500 = \dfrac{676.5}{500}$

$= \dfrac{676.5 \div \square}{500 \div \square}$

$= \dfrac{\square}{\square}$

14 Forty members of a club go to a restaurant for a meal. The total cost of the meal is $742.84. They share the total cost of the meal equally between them.

  a How much do they each pay? Round your answer to the nearest:

    i cent ii dollar

  b Is your answer from part **a i** or from part **a ii** the most suitable amount for each member to pay? Explain your answer.

15 The total mass of the 20 members of a gymnastics team is 1219.64 kg. Work out the mean mass of the members. Round your answer correct to one decimal place.

Tip

Mean mass = $\dfrac{\text{total mass}}{\text{number of gymnasts}}$

5 Angles and constructions

> 5.1 A sum of 360°

> **Worked example 5.1**
>
> Three of the angles of a **quadrilateral** are 55°, 108° and 123°. Calculate the fourth angle.
>
> **Answer**
>
> The **sum** of the four angles is 360°.
>
> 55° + 108° + 123° = 286°, so the fourth angle is 360° − 286° = 74°.

Key words

sum
quadrilateral

Exercise 5.1

Focus

1 *AB* and *CD* are straight lines. Calculate the size of the angles that have a letter.

a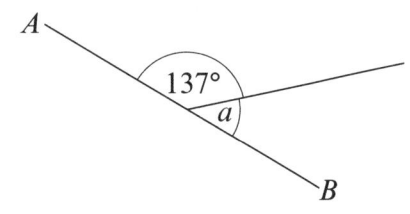

b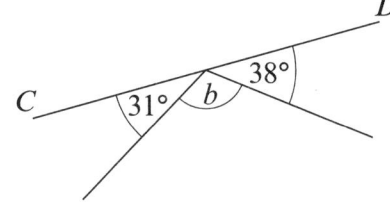

2 Work out the size of the angles that have a letter.

a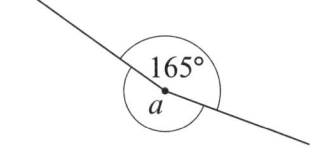

b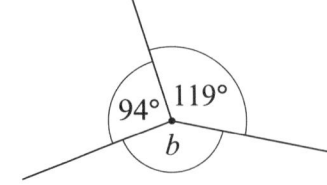

c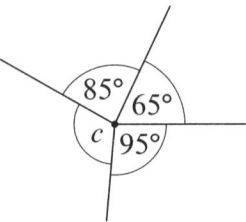

66

5.1 A sum of 360°

3   Calculate the value of each angle that has a letter.

a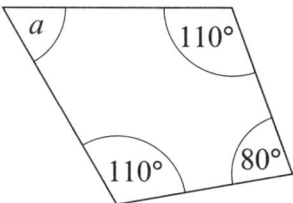

b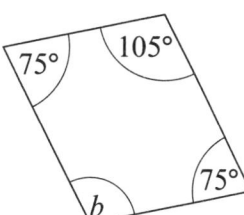

Practice

4   Give a reason why diagram **c** is the odd one out.

a 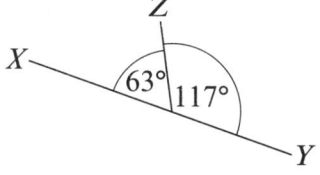   b 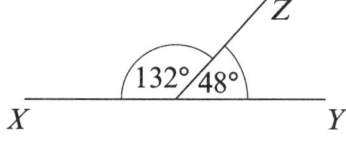   c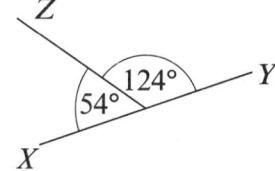

5   One angle of a quadrilateral is 135°. All the other angles are the same size. Work out the size of the other angles.

6   Calculate the values of a and b.

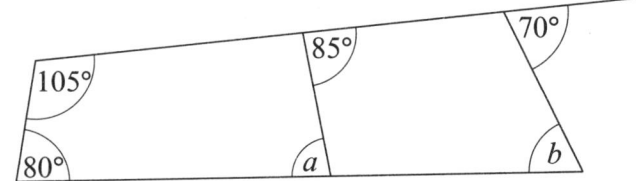

7   One angle of a parallelogram is 62°. Work out the size of the other three angles.

Challenge

8   Calculate the value of x.

9   This diagram is made from a square and two equilateral triangles. Calculate the value of y.

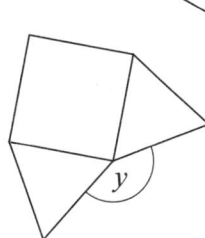

10 Two quadrilaterals have eight angles in total.
    a   Show that the angles could not be 50°, 60°, 70°, 80°, 90°, 100°, 110° and 120°.
    b   Show that the angles could be 20°, 40°, 60°, 80°, 100°, 120°, 140° and 160°.

5 Angles and constructions

 11 A kite is a quadrilateral with a line of symmetry.
One angle of a kite is 120°. Another angle is 90°.
What could the other angles be?

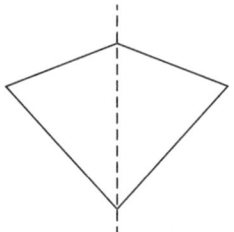

> 5.2 Intersecting lines

Key word

parallel

Exercise 5.2

Focus

1   *AB*, *CD* and *EF* are straight lines.

   Write the correct word to complete each sentence.
   a   *AB* and *CD* are .... lines.
   b   *CD* and *EF* are .... lines.
   c   *AB* and *EF* are .... lines.

2   This diagram shows two straight lines.
    Work out the values of *x*, *y* and *z*.

3   Work out the size of the angles that have letters.

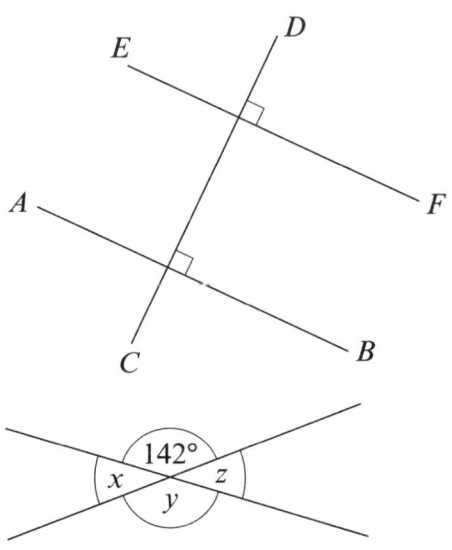

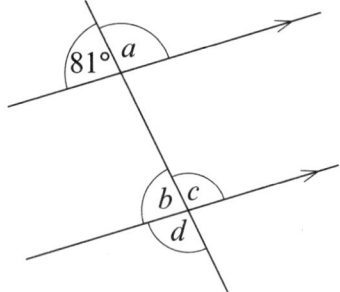

Practice

 4   Work out the values of *a*, *b* and *c*.

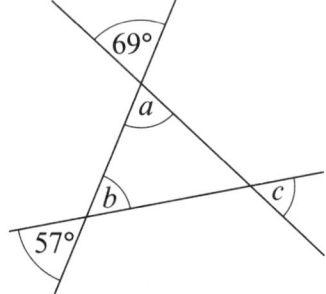

68

5.2 Intersecting lines

5 Calculate the size of the angles that have letters.

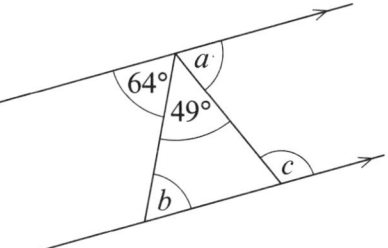

6 Calculate the size of the angles that have letters.

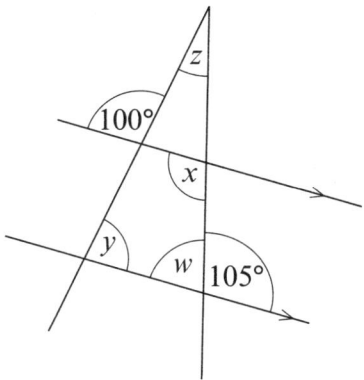

7 Calculate the value of x.

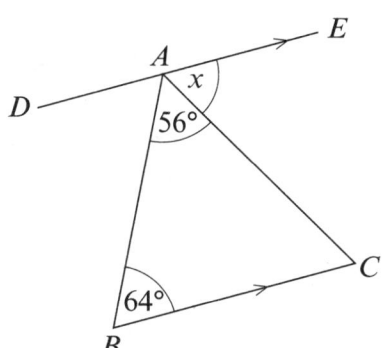

Challenge

8 Here are three statements. Which statement, **A**, **B** or **C**, is correct?

- **A** Lines AB and CD are **parallel**.
- **B** Lines AB and CD are not parallel.
- **C** You need more information to decide if the lines AB and CD are parallel.

Give a reason for your choice.

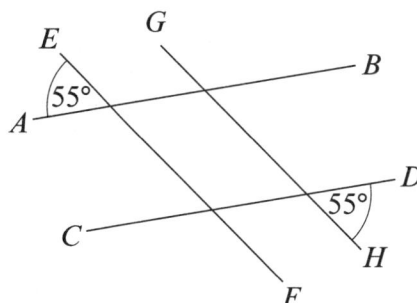

5 Angles and constructions

9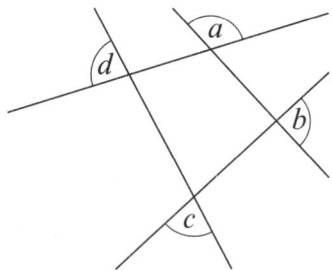

Explain why the sum of the four angles that have letters is 360°.

10 *AB*, *CD* and *EF* are three straight lines.

Explain why two of the lines are parallel but the third line is not parallel.

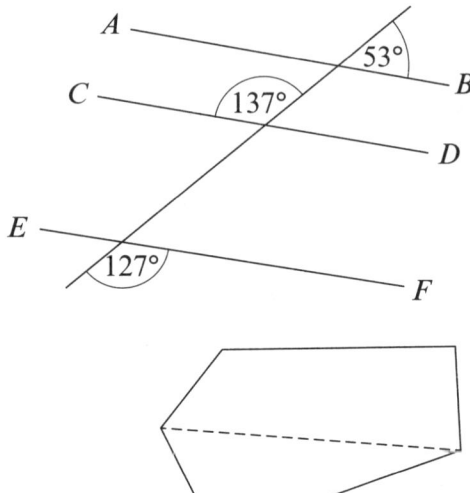

11 This five-sided shape is divided into a quadrilateral and a triangle.

a Explain why the sum of the angles of the five-sided shape must be 540°.

b In general, is the sum of the angles of any five-sided shape equal to 540°? Give a reason for your answer.

> 5.3 Drawing lines and quadrilaterals

Exercise 5.3

Key words

parallel
perpendicular
quadrilateral

Focus

1   a   Draw the line *ABC*.
    b   Draw the line through *B* **perpendicular** to *AB*.
    c   Mark the point *D*.
    d   Draw the line *CD* and measure the length.

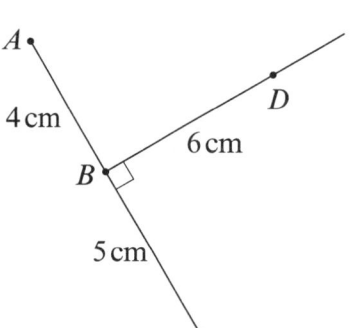

2   a   Draw the line *AB*.
    b   *AB* is one side of a square *ABCD*. Draw the square.
    c   Measure the length of the diagonal *AC*.

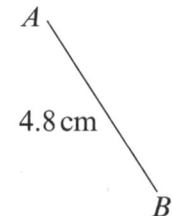

70

3 a Draw this parallelogram.
   b Measure the diagonal *BD*.

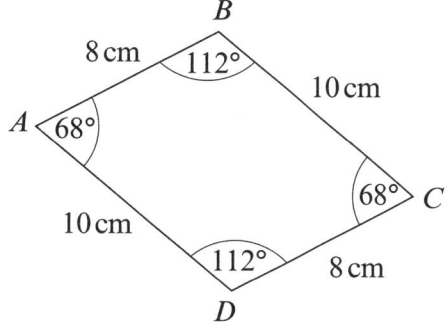

Practice

4 a Draw this diagram.
   b Draw a perpendicular line from *C* to *AB*.
   c The perpendicular line meets *AB* at *D*. Measure the length of *AD*.

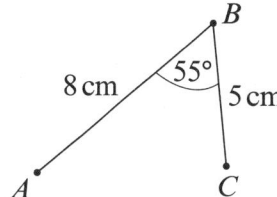

5 a Draw the triangle *PQR*.
   b Draw a line through *Q* **parallel** to *PR*.
   c Draw a line through *P* parallel to *RQ*.

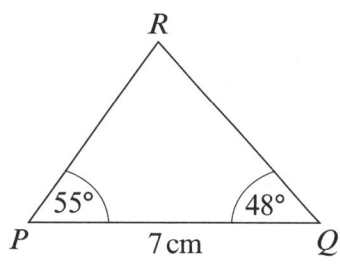

 6 a Draw the **quadrilateral** *ABCD*.
   b Measure angle *D*. How can you check that your answer is correct?
   c Measure the length of the side *CD*.

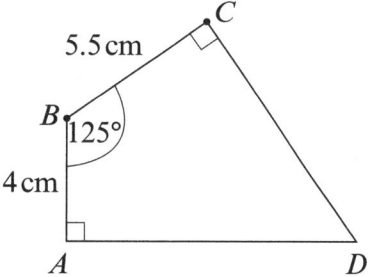

Challenge

 7 a Draw the quadrilateral *ABCD*.
   b Measure the length of *AD*.
   c Measure the angles of the quadrilateral. How can you check the accuracy of your measurements?

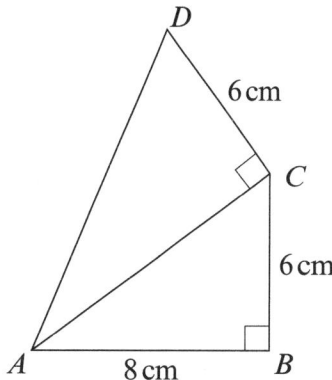

5 Angles and constructions

8
  a Draw the quadrilateral ABCD.
  b Measure the fourth angle of the quadrilateral at C.
  c Do a calculation to check the accuracy of your answer to part **b**.
  d Draw the line AC and measure the length.

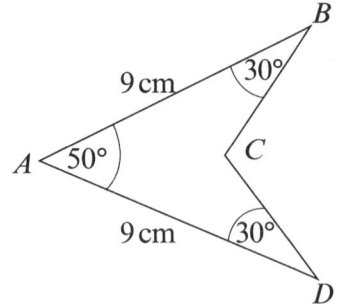

9 This shape is made from two parallelograms and a triangle.
  a Draw the shape.
  b Measure the length of AB.

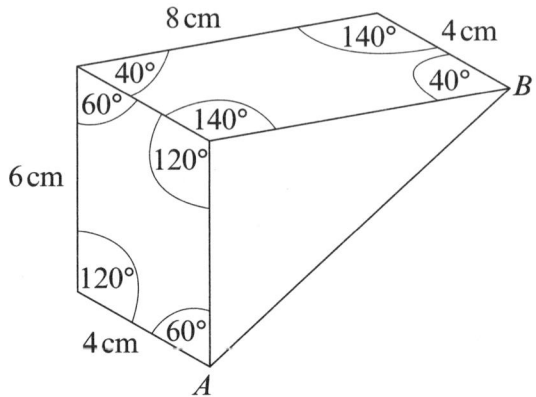

72

6 Collecting data

> 6.1 Conducting an investigation

> **Worked example 6.1**
>
> A nurse is collecting **data** about babies. Write down the type of data in each case.
>
> a length   b date of birth   c mass
>
> d age of mother   e colour of eyes
>
> **Answer**
>
> **a** and **c** are **continuous data**; length and mass are both measured.
>
> **d** is **discrete data**; age is a whole number.
>
> **b** and **d** are **categorical data**; date of birth and colour of eyes are not numerical.

Key words

categorical data
continuous data
data
discrete data
prediction

Exercise 6.1

Focus

1. categorical   discrete   continuous

   Choose the correct word from the box to describe the following recipe ingredients.

   a the number of eggs   b the mass of rice   c the type of vegetables

2. Marcus is collecting data about a room. Give two examples of each of the following types of data.

   a categorical data   b discrete data   c continuous data

3. The manager of a gym wants to investigate how people use the gym.

   Here are two questions from a questionnaire. The questionnaire is given to members as they leave the gym.

   Question 1: Did you enjoy your visit to the gym today? ....

   Question 2: Which equipment did you use? ....

6 Collecting data

a Write an improved version of Question 1.

b How could you improve Question 2?

Practice

 4 This is a question from a questionnaire. The questionnaire is given to people who use a website to find information.

How easily did you find the information you wanted?
Choose one number.

Not easy at all 1 2 3 4 5 Very easy

a What does it mean if you choose '4'?

This table shows the total scores at the end of one day.

Score	1	2	3	4	5
Frequency	12	25	17	14	5

b How many people answered the question?

c Draw a suitable chart to show the data.

d Write down the modal score.

e A **prediction** is that most people find the website easy to use. Is the prediction correct? Give reasons for your answer.

5 A teacher gives 40 learners a spelling test. The test has a total of 10 marks.

The teacher predicts that, on average, learners will get at least 8 marks. Here are the marks.

a Put the marks in a frequency table.

b Find the modal mark.

c Find the median mark.

d The total of all the marks is 276. Work out the mean mark.

e Is the teacher's prediction correct? Give a reason for your answer.

9	7	4	8	9
5	5	6	8	6
7	6	5	4	8
8	8	9	4	9
8	5	10	5	5
6	10	6	4	7
5	8	8	8	8
8	9	5	10	6

6 A medical clinic records the pulse rate of 125 patients.

The lowest rate collected is 48 beats per minute (bpm) and the highest rate collected is 83 bpm.

a You have been asked to show these results in a bar chart. Why is it a good idea to group the data first?

> **Tip**
>
> Pulse rate is the number of times the heart beats in 1 minute.

b   Shown here is part of a grouped frequency table. Add more columns to the table.

Pulse rate (bpm)	45–49	50–54	55–59	
Frequency				

c   The table is used to draw a bar chart. How many bars will the bar chart have?

d   How would you find the modal group from your bar chart?

e   A prediction is that very few people have a low pulse rate. How will the bar chart show that this prediction is true?

f   What calculation can you do to test whether the prediction is true?

Challenge

7   A shop is doing a survey of its customers. Here are some questions from the survey. Critique the questions by giving a reason why each question is not good. Suggest a way to improve each question.

a   How much did you enjoy shopping here today?

b   How often do you shop here?

c   How old are you?

8   A college uses a survey to investigate student satisfaction with a lecturer.

Students must say how much they agree with a number of statements. Here is an example:

The lecturer gives clear explanations.

1	2	3	4	5
Strongly disagree	*Disagree*	*Neither agree nor disagree*	*Agree*	*Strongly agree*

a   Give some advantages of writing a question in this way.

b   Write two more statements for the same type of question.

c   Are there any disadvantages when using this format?

6 Collecting data

9 Here is part of an advertisement for a brand of coffee.

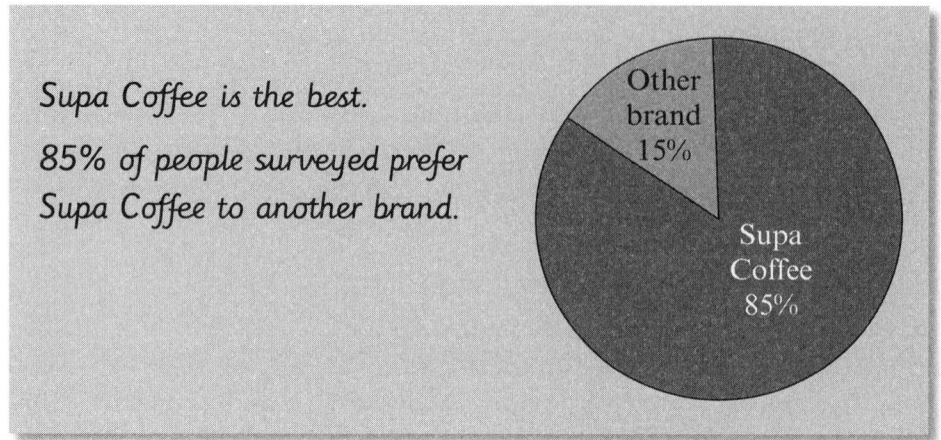

Supa Coffee is the best.

85% of people surveyed prefer Supa Coffee to another brand.

Other brand 15%

Supa Coffee 85%

  a Does the survey show that Supa Coffee is the best brand?
  b The advertisement does not give any information about the survey. What information should be included?

> 6.2 Taking a sample

Exercise 6.2

Key words

sample
sample size

Focus

1 Kimsant is investigating the heights of 13-year-old boys. He finds the heights of a **sample** of five boys.
   a What average could Kimsant work out from these five boys? Explain how he would calculate this average.
   b Explain why five is not a good **sample size**.
   c Would 1000 boys be a good sample size? Give a reason for your answer.

2 A questionnaire is given to people who have stayed at a hotel. Here is one question:
   Was the hotel good value for money? Circle one number.
   Very bad value   1   2   3   4   5   6   7   8   9   10   *Excellent value*

a Why is the question asked in this way?

Here is a summary of the results.

Score	1	2	3	4	5	6	7	8	9	10
Frequency	4	18	25	15	10	18	8	0	2	0

b What is the sample size?
c Draw a suitable chart to show the data.
d Find a suitable average value.
e Is there evidence that the hotel is good value for money?
Give reasons for your answer.

3 A website sells shoes. After customers receive their shoes, the company asks them to fill in an online questionnaire.
  a Give one advantage of sending a questionnaire in this way.
  b Write down two predictions the questionnaire could test.
  c Is this a good way to choose a sample?

Practice

4 Students at a large college are aged between 17 and 22 years.
Zara predicts:

Older students are likely to study more subjects.

She collects data from a sample of students to test this prediction.
  a Show how Zara could set up a table to display the data she collects.
  b There are 10 students in the sample who are 18 years old and who study four subjects. Show this information in your table.
  c Explain why a sample size of 20 is not large enough.

6 Collecting data

5 Rosario is investigating adults who use a library. He predicts that older adults use the library more often than younger adults.

    a Write down two ways that Rosario can choose a sample to test his prediction.

Rosario collects some data and presents it in this table.

		Age (years)		
		21–35	36–50	More than 50
Number of visits in a 3-month period	1–5	5	2	2
	6–10	3	2	3
	More than 10	1	4	6

    b What is the sample size?
    c Is there evidence that Rosario's prediction is correct?
    d Do you think the sample is large enough?

6 A large company has over 2000 employees. There is a staff restaurant for the employees. The manager wants to investigate what employees think about the food provided so that the company can make improvements. The manager wants to question a sample of employees.

    a What is a suitable sample size?
    b How can the manager choose the sample?
    c How can the manager collect the data?

Challenge

7 A company employs 265 people. Here are the ages (in years) of a sample of 30 employees.

29	53	27	30	32	69	50	32	54	43
25	46	33	62	37	54	37	38	44	31
44	41	36	57	63	37	29	53	33	40

    a Show the data in a suitable chart.
    b What can you say about the ages of the employees in the company?

8 There are 150 learners of your age at your school. You want to investigate what they think about mathematics and the quality of the teaching at your school. You decide to choose a sample of 30 learners and to give them a questionnaire.

  a Why would it <u>not</u> be a good idea just to choose 30 of your friends?

  b How would you choose your sample to make it representative of the whole school?

  c Write one question that you could ask.

  d Explain how you would analyse the answers you get to the question in part **c**.

9 A spinner has five sections numbered 1 to 5. This table shows the results of 40 spins.

4	4	1	1	5	1	3	4	2	5
1	3	5	5	3	3	5	1	1	3
5	2	1	4	5	4	4	3	4	5
4	4	1	2	5	2	3	3	5	2

  a Use the columns as 10 samples of size 4. Find the mean of each sample. For example, the first sample is 4, 1, 5, 4 and the mean is $(4 + 1 + 5 + 4) \div 4 = 3.5$.

  b Use the rows as four samples of size 10. Find the mean of each sample. For example, the mean of the first sample is $(4 + 4 + 1 + 1 + 5 + 1 + 3 + 4 + 2 + 5) \div 10$.

  c Sofia wants to investigate the mean score of the spinner for a large number of spins. She says:

A large sample is better than a small sample.

Use your answers to parts **a** and **b** to decide if Sofia's statement is true.

7 Fractions

> 7.1 Ordering fractions

Exercise 7.1

Key words
- common denominator
- equivalent fractions
- improper fractions
- mixed number
- order of size

Focus

1 Write the correct symbol, = or ≠, between each pair of numbers. The first one has been done for you.

   a 27 ≠ 29
   b 36 ☐ 36
   c 0.60 ☐ 0.6
   d 5.50 ☐ 5.55

2 Copy and complete these **equivalent fractions**.

   a $\dfrac{2}{3} = \dfrac{2 \times 3}{3 \times 3} = \dfrac{\Box}{9}$
   b $\dfrac{3}{5} = \dfrac{3 \times 2}{5 \times 2} = \dfrac{\Box}{10}$
   c $\dfrac{1}{2} = \dfrac{1 \times 7}{2 \times 7} = \dfrac{\Box}{14}$

3 Write the correct symbol, = or ≠, between each pair of fractions. Use your answers to Question **2** to help you.

   a $\dfrac{2}{3} \Box \dfrac{7}{9}$
   b $\dfrac{3}{5} \Box \dfrac{6}{10}$
   c $\dfrac{1}{2} \Box \dfrac{8}{14}$

4 Write each of these **improper fractions** as a **mixed number**. The first one has been done for you.

   a $\dfrac{7}{3}$ → 7 ÷ 3 = 2 remainder 1 → $\dfrac{7}{3} = 2\dfrac{1}{3}$

   b $\dfrac{15}{4}$ → 15 ÷ 4 = ☐ remainder ☐ → $\dfrac{15}{4} = \Box \dfrac{\Box}{4}$

   c $\dfrac{9}{5}$ → 9 ÷ 5 = ☐ remainder ☐ → $\dfrac{9}{5} = \Box \dfrac{\Box}{5}$

   d $\dfrac{7}{2}$ → 7 ÷ 2 = ☐ remainder ☐ → $\dfrac{7}{2} = \Box \dfrac{\Box}{2}$

Tip
= means 'is equal to'.
≠ means 'is not equal to'.

7.1 Ordering fractions

5   Write the correct inequality, < or >, between each pair of fractions.
    Use your answers to Question 4 to help you.

    a $\frac{7}{3} \square 2\frac{2}{3}$
    b $\frac{15}{4} \square 3\frac{1}{4}$
    c $\frac{9}{5} \square 1\frac{3}{5}$
    d $\frac{7}{2} \square 4\frac{1}{2}$

Tip

< means 'is less than'.

> means 'is greater than'.

6   Write the correct inequality, < or >, between each pair of fractions.
    The working for the first one has been done for you.

    a $\frac{2}{3} \square \frac{3}{5}$ Working: $\frac{2}{3} = \frac{2 \times 5}{3 \times 5} = \frac{10}{15}$ $\frac{3}{5} = \frac{3 \times 3}{5 \times 3} = \frac{9}{15}$
    b $\frac{2}{7} \square \frac{1}{4}$
    c $\frac{7}{8} \square \frac{5}{6}$
    d $\frac{7}{11} \square \frac{3}{4}$

Practice

Use the **common denominator** method to answer questions **7** to **10**.

7   Write the correct symbol, = or ≠, between each pair of fractions.

    a $\frac{1}{4} \square \frac{2}{8}$
    b $\frac{4}{5} \square \frac{9}{10}$
    c $\frac{2}{3} \square \frac{10}{15}$
    d $\frac{8}{20} \square \frac{3}{5}$
    e $\frac{20}{25} \square \frac{3}{5}$
    f $\frac{16}{24} \square \frac{2}{3}$

8   Write the correct inequality, < or >, between each pair of fractions.

    a $\frac{21}{4} \square 5\frac{3}{4}$
    b $4\frac{2}{7} \square \frac{27}{7}$
    c $\frac{29}{3} \square 9\frac{1}{3}$
    d $5\frac{1}{8} \square \frac{43}{8}$

Tip

First, write each improper fraction as a mixed number. Then use equivalent fractions.

9   Write the correct inequality, < or >, between each pair of fractions.

    a $\frac{17}{4} \square 4\frac{1}{2}$
    b $\frac{17}{6} \square 2\frac{2}{3}$
    c $2\frac{3}{5} \square \frac{38}{15}$
    d $7\frac{5}{6} \square \frac{95}{12}$

10 Work out which fraction is larger.

    a $\frac{9}{2}$ or $\frac{13}{3}$
    b $\frac{21}{4}$ or $\frac{16}{3}$
    c $\frac{43}{8}$ or $\frac{27}{5}$

Use the division method to answer questions **11** and **12**.

11 a Complete the workings to write each of these fractions as a decimal.

       i $\frac{11}{8}$
       ii $\frac{9}{7}$
       iii $\frac{15}{11}$

7 Fractions

i $\frac{11}{8} = 1\frac{3}{8}$ $8\overline{)3\ .\ ^30\ ^60\ 0}^{0\ .\ 3}$ $\frac{3}{8} = \underline{}$ $\frac{11}{8} = \underline{}$

ii $\frac{9}{7} = 1\frac{2}{7}$ $7\overline{)2\ .\ ^20\ ^60\ 0\ 0}^{0\ .\ }$ $\frac{2}{7} = \underline{}$ $\frac{9}{7} = \underline{}$

iii $\frac{15}{11} = 1\frac{4}{11}$ $11\overline{)4\ .\ ^40\ 0\ 0\ 0}^{0\ .\ }$ $\frac{4}{11} = \underline{}$ $\frac{15}{11} = \underline{}$

  b Use your answers to part **a** to write the fractions $\frac{11}{8}$, $\frac{9}{7}$, and $\frac{15}{11}$ in **order of size**, starting with the smallest.

12 Write the fractions $\frac{11}{3}$, $\frac{17}{5}$, $\frac{31}{9}$ and $\frac{47}{13}$ in order of size, starting with the smallest.

Challenge

13 Put these fraction cards in order of size, starting with the smallest. $\boxed{\frac{23}{6}}$ $\boxed{\frac{3}{5}}$ $\boxed{\frac{80}{21}}$ $\boxed{\frac{5}{9}}$

14 Amira has five improper fraction cards. She puts them in order, starting with the smallest. There are marks on two of the cards.

$\boxed{\frac{19}{4}}$ $\boxed{\frac{67}{14}}$ $\boxed{\frac{29}{6}}$

  a What fractions could be under the marks?
  b Give one example for each card.

 15 a Look at the fractions in this pattern: $\frac{1}{2}, \frac{2}{3}, \frac{3}{4}, \frac{4}{5}, \frac{5}{6}, \frac{6}{7}, \frac{7}{8}, \ldots$

    i Write down the next two fractions in the pattern.
    ii Are the fractions getting smaller or bigger as the pattern continues? Explain why.

  b Look at the fractions in this pattern: $\frac{1}{2}, \frac{2}{4}, \frac{4}{8}, \frac{8}{16}, \frac{16}{32}, \frac{32}{64}, \frac{64}{128}, \ldots$

    i Write down the next two fractions in the pattern.
    ii Are the fractions getting smaller or bigger as the pattern continues? Explain why.

  c Look at the fractions in this pattern: $\frac{1}{20}, \frac{2}{19}, \frac{3}{18}, \frac{4}{17}, \frac{5}{16}, \frac{6}{15}, \frac{7}{14}, \ldots$

    i Write down the next two fractions in the pattern.
    ii Are the fractions getting smaller or bigger as the pattern continues? Explain why.

> 7.2 Adding mixed numbers

Exercise 7.2

Focus

Look at this method for adding mixed numbers.

Key words
collecting like terms
simplest form

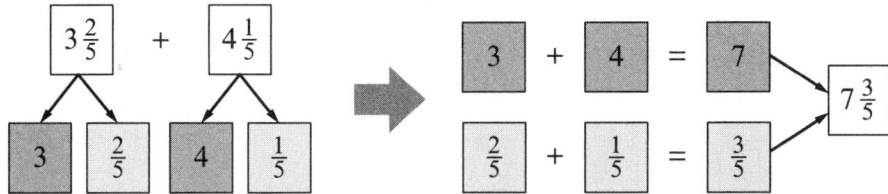

> **Tip**
>
> **Remember** to estimate first by adding the whole numbers.
> 3 + 4 = 7. Both of the fractions are less than a half so the answer
> will be between 7 and 8.

1 Use the method above to copy and complete the following.

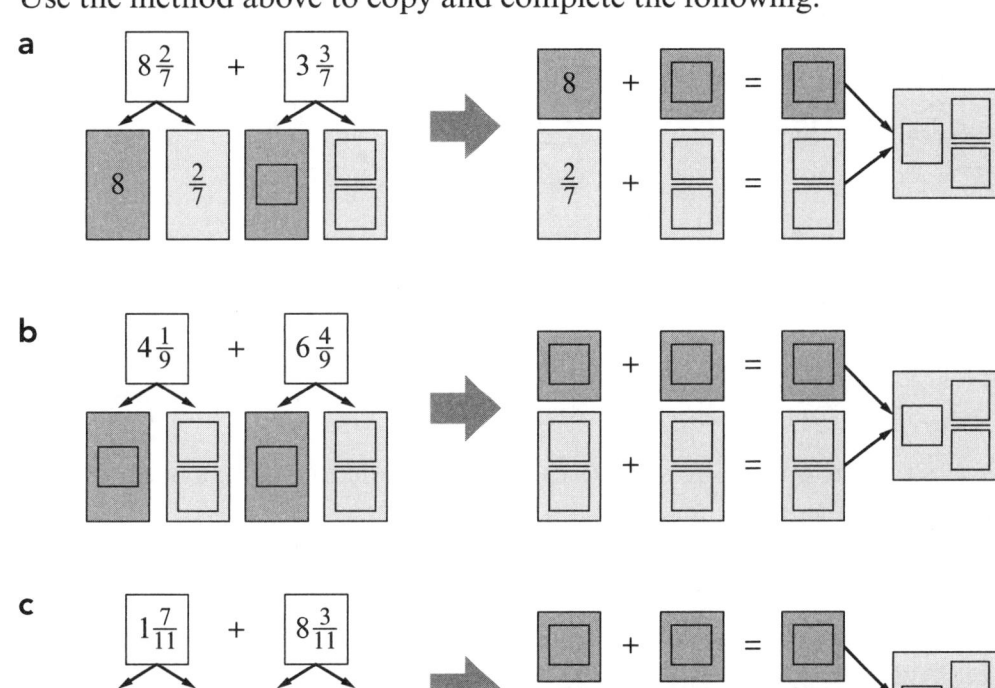

7 Fractions

2 Write each of these mixed numbers in its **simplest form**. The first one has been done for you.

a $1\dfrac{6}{9} = 1\dfrac{6 \div 3}{9 \div 3} = 1\dfrac{2}{3}$

b $3\dfrac{2}{4} = 3\dfrac{2 \div 2}{4 \div 2} = 3\dfrac{\square}{\square}$

c $6\dfrac{6}{8} = 6\dfrac{6 \div \square}{8 \div \square} = \square\dfrac{\square}{\square}$

d $9\dfrac{5}{15} = 9\dfrac{5 \div \square}{15 \div \square} = \square\dfrac{\square}{\square}$

3 Copy and complete the following additions. Write each answer in its simplest form.

a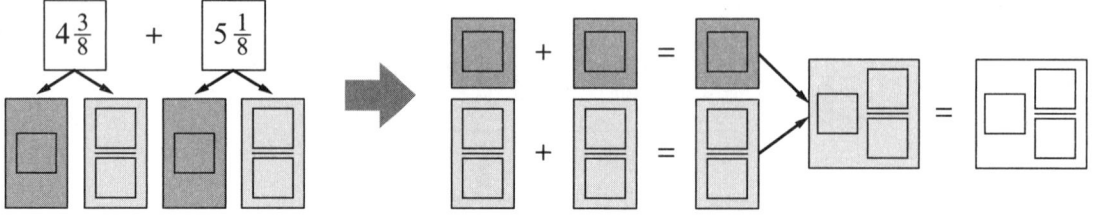

b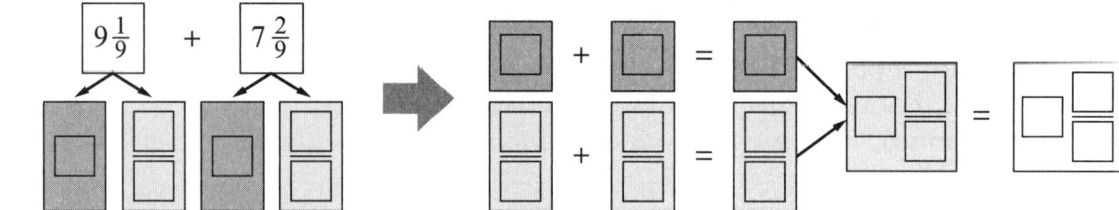

c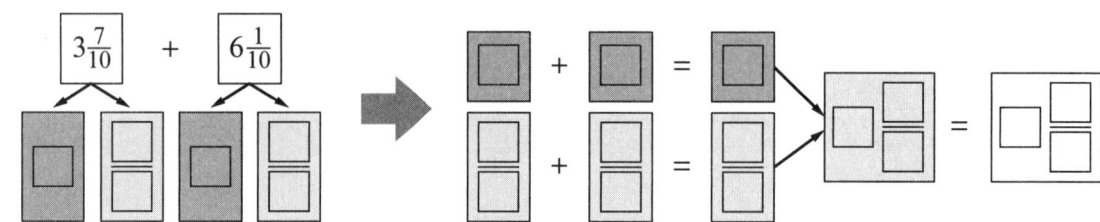

4 a Write each of these improper fractions as mixed numbers. The first one has been done for you.

i $\dfrac{4}{3} = 1\dfrac{1}{3}$

ii $\dfrac{3}{2} = \square\dfrac{\square}{\square}$

iii $\dfrac{7}{5} = \square\dfrac{\square}{\square}$

b Use your answers to part **a** to work out the following. The first one has been done for you.

i $4 + \dfrac{4}{3} = 4 + 1\dfrac{1}{3} = 5\dfrac{1}{3}$

ii $8 + \dfrac{3}{2} = 8 + \square\dfrac{\square}{\square} = \square\dfrac{\square}{\square}$

iii $3 + \dfrac{7}{5} = 3 + \square\dfrac{\square}{\square} = \square\dfrac{\square}{\square}$

7.2 Adding mixed numbers

5 Copy and complete the following.

a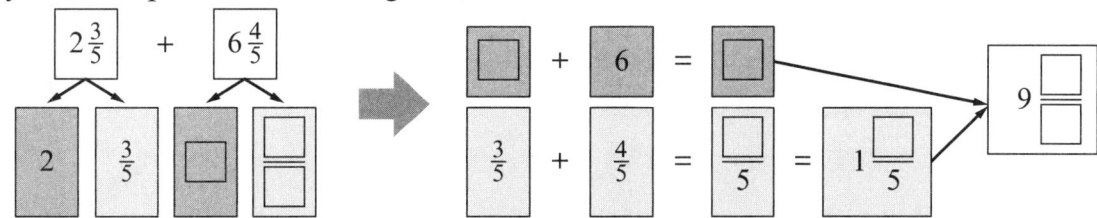

b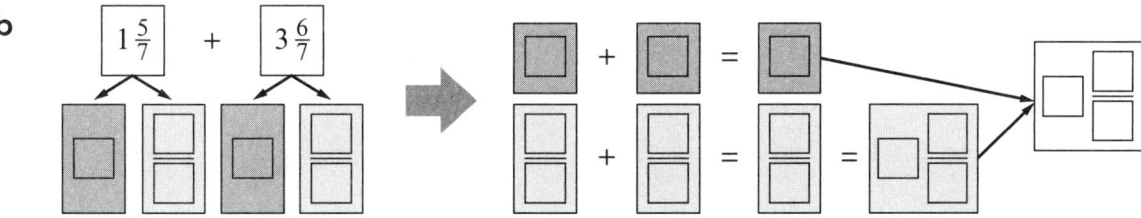

c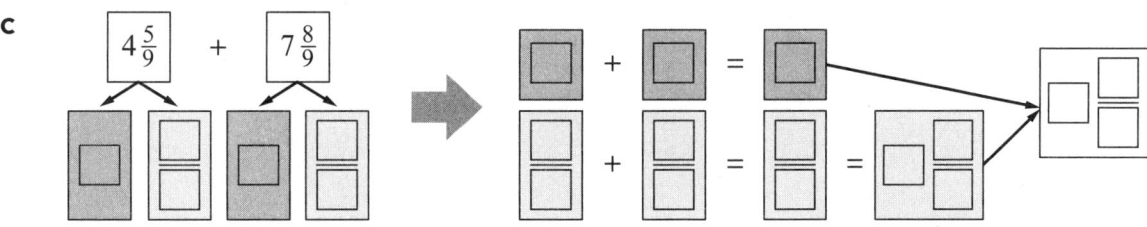

Practice

6 Copy and complete these additions.

a $5\frac{2}{9} + 2\frac{2}{9}$ ① $5 + 2 = \square$ ② $\frac{2}{9} + \frac{2}{9} = \frac{\square}{9}$ ③ $\square + \square\frac{\square}{9} = \square\frac{\square}{9}$

b $3\frac{1}{10} + 4\frac{3}{10}$ ① $3 + 4 = \square$ ② $\frac{1}{10} + \frac{3}{10} = \frac{\square}{10} = \frac{\square}{5}$ ③ $\square + \square\frac{\square}{5} = \square\frac{\square}{5}$

c $4\frac{5}{13} + 5\frac{9}{13}$ ① $4 + 5 = \square$ ② $\frac{5}{13} + \frac{9}{13} = \frac{\square}{13} = \square\frac{\square}{13}$ ③ $\square + \square\frac{\square}{13} = \square\frac{\square}{13}$

d $2\frac{3}{8} + 7\frac{7}{8}$ ① $2 + 7 = \square$ ② $\frac{3}{8} + \frac{7}{8} = \frac{\square}{8} = \frac{\square}{4} = \square\frac{\square}{4}$ ③ $\square + \square\frac{\square}{4} = \square\frac{\square}{4}$

7 The diagram shows the lengths of the three sides of a triangle. Work out the perimeter of the triangle. Write your answer as a mixed number in its simplest form.

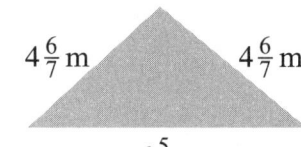

8 Work out the following additions. Write each answer as a mixed number in its simplest form. Write down an estimate for each of the additions first.

a $3\frac{1}{4} + 7\frac{1}{2}$ b $4\frac{1}{8} + 3\frac{3}{4}$ c $5\frac{2}{3} + 8\frac{5}{9}$ d $6\frac{5}{6} + 3\frac{5}{12}$

7 Fractions

9 Awen runs $17\frac{1}{2}$ km on Saturday and $14\frac{7}{8}$ km on Sunday.
   a What is the total distance that she runs?
   b Awen thinks that her total distance is more than $32\frac{1}{4}$ km. Is she correct? Explain your answer.

10 Kali cycles $8\frac{4}{5}$ km from home to her sister's house. She then cycles $7\frac{1}{2}$ km from her sister's house to work. What is the total distance that she cycles?

11 Zane has two boxes. The mass of one box is $8\frac{2}{3}$ kg. The mass of the other box is $5\frac{7}{8}$ kg. What is the total mass of the two boxes?

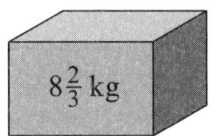 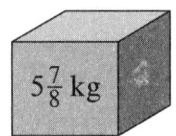

Challenge

12 This is part of Sorithy's homework. He has made some mistakes in his solution.

> Question
> Work out $4\frac{9}{13} + 3\frac{4}{5}$.
> Solution
> ① $4 + 3 = 7$
> ② $\frac{9}{13} + \frac{4}{5} = \frac{35}{65} + \frac{54}{65} = \frac{89}{65} = 1\frac{25}{65} = 1\frac{5}{13}$
> ③ $7 + 1\frac{5}{13} = 8\frac{5}{13}$

   a Explain the mistakes that Sorithy has made.
   b Work out the correct answer.

13 In this pyramid, you find the mixed number in each block by adding the mixed numbers in the two blocks below it.

Copy and complete the pyramid.

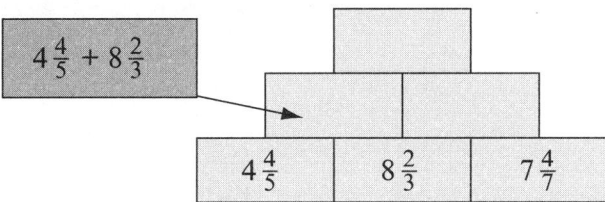

14 Simplify these expressions by **collecting like terms**.

a $\quad 2\frac{1}{4}x + 5\frac{1}{2}x$

b $\quad 4\frac{1}{3}y + 6\frac{1}{2}x + 5\frac{3}{4}y$

c $\quad 1\frac{5}{6}a + 3\frac{5}{8}b + 3\frac{1}{2}a + 4\frac{7}{12}b$

15 Minh measures the heights of some learners. The range in the height of the learners is $28\frac{1}{4}$ cm. The shortest learner is $122\frac{4}{5}$ cm. What is the height of the tallest learner?

Tip

Range = largest value − smallest value

16 Zara is looking at these two shapes.

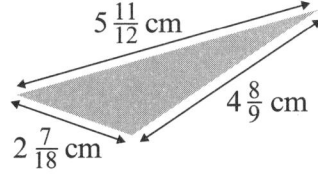

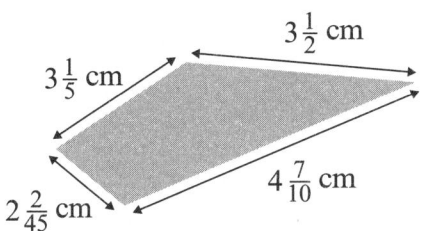

I think that the perimeter of the quadrilateral is exactly $\frac{1}{4}$ cm more than the perimeter of the triangle.

Is Zara correct? Show all your working.

7 Fractions

> 7.3 Multiplying fractions

Exercise 7.3

Key words
cancel
predict
proper fractions

Focus

1 Use the diagrams to complete these calculations.

a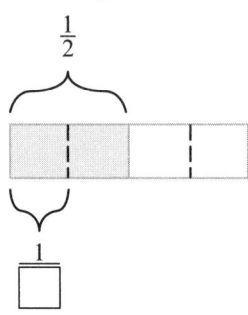

$\dfrac{1}{2} \times \dfrac{1}{2} = \dfrac{1 \times 1}{2 \times 2} = \dfrac{1}{\Box}$

b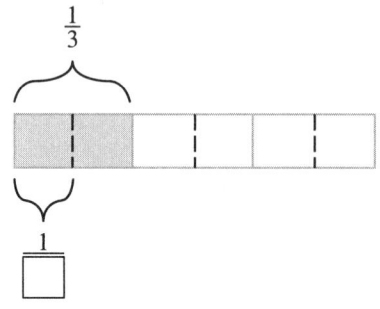

$\dfrac{1}{2} \times \dfrac{1}{3} = \dfrac{1 \times 1}{2 \times 3} = \dfrac{1}{\Box}$

c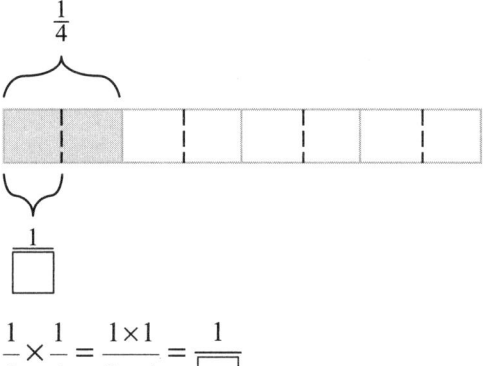

$\dfrac{1}{2} \times \dfrac{1}{4} = \dfrac{1 \times 1}{2 \times 4} = \dfrac{1}{\Box}$

2 Copy and complete:

a $\dfrac{1}{2} \times \dfrac{1}{5} = \dfrac{1 \times 1}{2 \times 5} = \dfrac{1}{\Box}$

b $\dfrac{1}{2} \times \dfrac{1}{6} = \dfrac{1 \times 1}{2 \times 6} = \dfrac{1}{\Box}$

c $\dfrac{1}{2} \times \dfrac{1}{7} = \dfrac{1 \times 1}{2 \times 7} = \dfrac{1}{\Box}$

d $\dfrac{1}{3} \times \dfrac{1}{5} = \dfrac{1 \times 1}{3 \times 5} = \dfrac{1}{\Box}$

e $\dfrac{1}{3} \times \dfrac{1}{6} = \dfrac{1 \times 1}{3 \times 6} = \dfrac{1}{\Box}$

f $\dfrac{1}{3} \times \dfrac{1}{7} = \dfrac{1 \times 1}{3 \times 7} = \dfrac{1}{\Box}$

3 Write true or false for each of these. If the answer is false, write down the correct answer.

a $\dfrac{1}{4} \times \dfrac{1}{4} = \dfrac{1}{16}$

b $\dfrac{1}{4} \times \dfrac{1}{5} = \dfrac{1}{9}$

c $\dfrac{1}{5} \times \dfrac{1}{5} = \dfrac{2}{25}$

d $\dfrac{1}{5} \times \dfrac{1}{6} = \dfrac{1}{30}$

4 Copy and complete:

a $\dfrac{1}{2} \times \dfrac{3}{4} = \dfrac{1 \times 3}{2 \times 4} = \dfrac{3}{\square}$

b $\dfrac{1}{2} \times \dfrac{5}{6} = \dfrac{1 \times 5}{2 \times 6} = \dfrac{\square}{12}$

c $\dfrac{1}{2} \times \dfrac{3}{5} = \dfrac{1 \times 3}{2 \times 5} = \dfrac{\square}{\square}$

d $\dfrac{1}{3} \times \dfrac{2}{5} = \dfrac{1 \times 2}{3 \times 5} = \dfrac{\square}{\square}$

e $\dfrac{1}{3} \times \dfrac{5}{6} = \dfrac{1 \times 5}{3 \times 6} = \dfrac{\square}{\square}$

f $\dfrac{1}{3} \times \dfrac{5}{7} = \dfrac{1 \times 5}{3 \times 7} = \dfrac{\square}{\square}$

5 Copy and complete the following. **Cancel** each answer to its simplest form.

All the answers are given in the cloud.

$\dfrac{1}{2} \quad \dfrac{5}{21} \quad \dfrac{2}{5} \quad \dfrac{6}{25}$

a $\dfrac{2}{3} \times \dfrac{3}{5} = \dfrac{2 \times 3}{3 \times 5} = \dfrac{6}{15} = \dfrac{\square}{\square}$

b $\dfrac{3}{4} \times \dfrac{2}{3} = \dfrac{3 \times 2}{4 \times 3} = \dfrac{\square}{\square} = \dfrac{\square}{\square}$

c $\dfrac{4}{5} \times \dfrac{3}{10} = \dfrac{4 \times 3}{5 \times 10} = \dfrac{\square}{\square} = \dfrac{\square}{\square}$

d $\dfrac{2}{7} \times \dfrac{5}{6} = \dfrac{2 \times 5}{7 \times 6} = \dfrac{\square}{\square} = \dfrac{\square}{\square}$

Practice

6 Work out:

a $\dfrac{1}{4} \times \dfrac{1}{3}$

b $\dfrac{3}{4} \times \dfrac{3}{4}$

c $\dfrac{5}{7} \times \dfrac{1}{6}$

d $\dfrac{3}{4} \times \dfrac{3}{5}$

e $\dfrac{3}{5} \times \dfrac{2}{7}$

f $\dfrac{5}{8} \times \dfrac{2}{3}$

7 Work these out. Write each answer in its simplest form.

a $\dfrac{4}{5} \times \dfrac{1}{2}$

b $\dfrac{2}{3} \times \dfrac{3}{5}$

c $\dfrac{3}{4} \times \dfrac{2}{5}$

d $\dfrac{3}{4} \times \dfrac{2}{3}$

e $\dfrac{7}{8} \times \dfrac{8}{11}$

f $\dfrac{5}{9} \times \dfrac{18}{25}$

8 Work out the area of this rectangle. Write your answer in its simplest form.

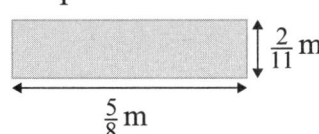

$\dfrac{2}{11}$ m

$\dfrac{5}{8}$ m

Tip
The formula for the area of a rectangle is: Area = length × width.

9 Work out the area of this square.

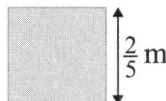

$\dfrac{2}{5}$ m

7 Fractions

10 In a shop, $\frac{5}{8}$ of the staff are male.

    a What fraction of the staff are not male?

Of the males, $\frac{2}{5}$ are from China.

    b What fraction of the males are not from China?
    c What fraction of the staff are males from China?
    d What fraction of the staff are males who are not from China?

> **Tip**
> In part **c**, you need to work out $\frac{2}{5}$ of $\frac{5}{8}$.

11 $\frac{2}{7}$ of the people watching a football game are children. $\frac{3}{8}$ of the children are girls.

    a What fraction of the people watching the football game are girls?
    b What fraction of the people watching the football game are boys?
    c What fraction of the people watching the football game are not children?

12 $\frac{2}{7}$ of the people at a concert are from Zimbabwe. The other people are from Zambia. $\frac{3}{5}$ of the people from Zambia are female.

    a What fraction of all the people at the concert are female and from Zambia?
    b What fraction of all the people at the concert are male and from Zambia?

Challenge

13 Work out both the estimate and the accurate answer to each of the following.

    a $\frac{5}{7} \times \frac{1}{10}$

> **Tip**
> Use the fact that $\frac{5}{7}$ is greater than $\frac{1}{2}$, but is less than 1.

    b $\frac{2}{5} \times \frac{1}{6}$

> **Tip**
> Use the fact that $\frac{2}{5}$ is greater than 0, but is less than $\frac{1}{2}$.

14 The diagram shows four fractions linked by lines.

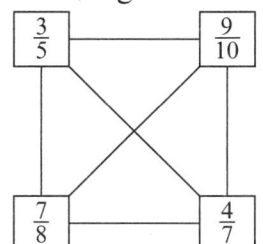

- **a** Choose any two of the linked fractions. Work out the product of the two fractions. Write your answer in its simplest form.
- **b** Which two fractions give the:
  - **i** largest product?
  - **ii** smallest product?
- **c** Without working out all the products, how can you decide, just by looking at the fractions, which two fractions give the:
  - **i** largest product?
  - **ii** smallest product?

Tip

To work out the product of two fractions, you multiply the two fractions together.

15 Work these out. Write each answer in its simplest form.

- **a** $\frac{1}{2} \times \frac{2}{3}$
- **b** your answer to part **a** $\times \frac{3}{4}$
- **c** your answer to part **b** $\times \frac{4}{5}$
- **d** your answer to part **c** $\times \frac{5}{6}$
- **e** your answer to part **d** $\times \frac{6}{7}$
- **f** Copy and complete this table.

Part	Question	Answer
i	$\frac{1}{2} \times \frac{2}{3}$	
ii	$\frac{1}{2} \times \frac{2}{3} \times \frac{3}{4}$	
iii	$\frac{1}{2} \times \frac{2}{3} \times \frac{3}{4} \times \frac{4}{5}$	
iv	$\frac{1}{2} \times \frac{2}{3} \times \frac{3}{4} \times \frac{4}{5} \times \frac{5}{6}$	
v	$\frac{1}{2} \times \frac{2}{3} \times \frac{3}{4} \times \frac{4}{5} \times \frac{5}{6} \times \frac{6}{7}$	

Tip

Your answers to parts **a** to **e** are the answers to parts **i** to **v** in the table.

7 Fractions

g Can you see a pattern in the answers to the questions in the table above?

How can you **predict** what the answer will be without working it out?

h Using the pattern in the table above, write down the answers to the following.

  i $\frac{1}{2} \times \frac{2}{3} \times \frac{3}{4} \times \frac{4}{5} \times \frac{5}{6} \times \frac{6}{7} \times \frac{7}{8}$

  ii $\frac{1}{2} \times \frac{2}{3} \times \frac{3}{4} \times \frac{4}{5} \times \frac{5}{6} \times \frac{6}{7} \times \frac{7}{8} \times \frac{8}{9} \times \frac{9}{10} \times \frac{10}{11}$

16 Jon multiplies two **proper fractions** and writes the answer in its simplest form. The answer is $\frac{1}{5}$.

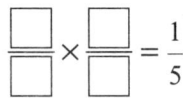
$\frac{\square}{\square} \times \frac{\square}{\square} = \frac{1}{5}$

Give three examples of two proper fractions that multiply to give $\frac{1}{5}$.

17 Kai eats $\frac{2}{5}$ of a pizza. Sam eats $\frac{3}{4}$ of the rest of the pizza.

Hari eats $\frac{3}{4}$ of the rest of the pizza after Kai and Sam have eaten.

What fraction of the pizza is left?

18 Work out the area of this rectangle. Write your answer as a mixed number in its simplest form.

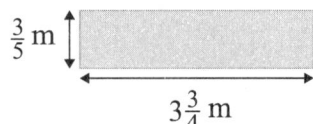
$\frac{3}{5}$ m
$3\frac{3}{4}$ m

Tip

The formula for the area of a rectangle is Area = length × width.

> 7.4 Dividing fractions

Exercise 7.4

Key words
reciprocal
upside down

Tip

Remember that when you turn a fraction upside down you get a **reciprocal** fraction. For example the reciprocal of $\frac{1}{3}$ is $\frac{3}{1}$ or just 3.

Focus

1 Copy and complete:

a $\quad \dfrac{1}{4} \div \dfrac{1}{3} = \dfrac{1}{4} \times \dfrac{3}{1}$
$\qquad = \dfrac{1 \times 3}{4 \times 1}$
$\qquad = \dfrac{\square}{\square}$

b $\quad \dfrac{1}{5} \div \dfrac{1}{4} = \dfrac{1}{5} \times \dfrac{4}{1}$
$\qquad = \dfrac{1 \times 4}{5 \times 1}$
$\qquad = \dfrac{\square}{\square}$

c $\quad \dfrac{1}{6} \div \dfrac{1}{5} = \dfrac{1}{6} \times \dfrac{5}{1}$
$\qquad = \dfrac{1 \times 5}{6 \times 1}$
$\qquad = \dfrac{\square}{\square}$

d $\quad \dfrac{1}{7} \div \dfrac{1}{6} = \dfrac{1}{7} \times \dfrac{6}{1}$
$\qquad = \dfrac{1 \times 6}{7 \times 1}$
$\qquad = \dfrac{\square}{\square}$

2 Write true or false for each of the following. If the answer is false, write down the correct answer.

a $\quad \dfrac{1}{8} \div \dfrac{1}{7} = \dfrac{7}{8}$
b $\quad \dfrac{1}{9} \div \dfrac{1}{8} = \dfrac{9}{8}$
c $\quad \dfrac{1}{10} \div \dfrac{1}{9} = \dfrac{9}{10}$

Tip

As shown in the working for Question 1, turn the second fraction **upside down**.

3 Copy and complete:

a $\quad \dfrac{1}{4} \div \dfrac{3}{5} = \dfrac{1}{4} \times \dfrac{5}{3}$
$\qquad = \dfrac{1 \times 5}{4 \times 3}$
$\qquad = \dfrac{\square}{\square}$

b $\quad \dfrac{1}{2} \div \dfrac{4}{5} = \dfrac{1}{2} \times \dfrac{5}{4}$
$\qquad = \dfrac{1 \times 5}{2 \times 4}$
$\qquad = \dfrac{\square}{\square}$

c $\quad \dfrac{5}{8} \div \dfrac{2}{3} = \dfrac{5}{8} \times \dfrac{3}{2}$
$\qquad = \dfrac{5 \times 3}{8 \times 2}$
$\qquad = \dfrac{\square}{\square}$

d $\quad \dfrac{3}{11} \div \dfrac{2}{3} = \dfrac{6}{11} \times \dfrac{3}{2}$
$\qquad = \dfrac{6 \times 3}{11 \times 2}$
$\qquad = \dfrac{\square}{\square}$

4 Write each of these fractions in its simplest form. The first one has been done for you.

a $\quad \dfrac{2}{4} = \dfrac{1}{2}$
b $\quad \dfrac{6}{15} = \dfrac{\square}{\square}$
c $\quad \dfrac{35}{40} = \dfrac{\square}{\square}$
d $\quad \dfrac{15}{20} = \dfrac{\square}{\square}$

7 Fractions

5 Copy and complete.

a) $\frac{1}{4} \div \frac{1}{2} = \frac{1}{4} \times \frac{2}{1}$
$= \frac{1 \times 2}{4 \times 1}$
$= \frac{2}{4}$
$= \frac{\square}{\square}$

b) $\frac{1}{3} \div \frac{5}{6} = \frac{1}{3} \times \frac{6}{5}$
$= \frac{1 \times 6}{3 \times 5}$
$= \frac{\square}{\square}$
$= \frac{\square}{\square}$

c) $\frac{5}{8} \div \frac{5}{7} = \frac{5}{8} \times \frac{7}{5}$
$= \frac{5 \times 7}{8 \times 5}$
$= \frac{\square}{\square}$
$= \frac{\square}{\square}$

d) $\frac{3}{10} \div \frac{2}{5} = \frac{3}{10} \times \frac{5}{2}$
$= \frac{3 \times 5}{10 \times 2}$
$= \frac{\square}{\square}$
$= \frac{\square}{\square}$

Tip

Use your answers to Question 4 to help you.

Practice

6 Work out:

a) $\frac{1}{2} \div \frac{2}{3}$
b) $\frac{1}{4} \div \frac{3}{5}$
c) $\frac{3}{7} \div \frac{1}{2}$
d) $\frac{5}{9} \div \frac{6}{7}$
e) $\frac{2}{5} \div \frac{5}{9}$
f) $\frac{1}{10} \div \frac{3}{7}$

7 Work these out. Write each answer as a mixed number.

a) $\frac{1}{2} \div \frac{1}{3}$
b) $\frac{3}{5} \div \frac{4}{7}$
c) $\frac{1}{3} \div \frac{2}{7}$
d) $\frac{7}{9} \div \frac{1}{2}$
e) $\frac{5}{6} \div \frac{2}{11}$
f) $\frac{4}{7} \div \frac{3}{13}$

8 Work these out. Write each answer in its simplest form and, when possible, as a mixed number.

a) $\frac{5}{8} \div \frac{1}{2}$
b) $\frac{4}{13} \div \frac{3}{13}$
c) $\frac{5}{8} \div \frac{5}{12}$
d) $\frac{1}{3} \div \frac{5}{9}$
e) $\frac{1}{4} \div \frac{1}{12}$
f) $\frac{7}{9} \div \frac{1}{6}$

7.4 Dividing fractions

9   This is part of Nova's homework. She has made a mistake in her solution.

> Question: Work out $\frac{7}{8} \div \frac{5}{6}$.
>
> Solution $\frac{7}{8} \div \frac{5}{6} = \frac{7}{8} \times \frac{5}{6} = \frac{35}{48}$

a   Explain the mistake Nova has made.
b   Work out the correct answer.

10 The area of this rectangle is $\frac{5}{6}$ m². The length is $\frac{15}{16}$ m. Work out the width of the rectangle.

Tip
The formula for the area of a rectangle is Area = length × width, so Width = area ÷ length.

11 In this pyramid, you find the fraction in each block by dividing (from left to right) the fractions in the two blocks below it. Copy and complete the pyramid.

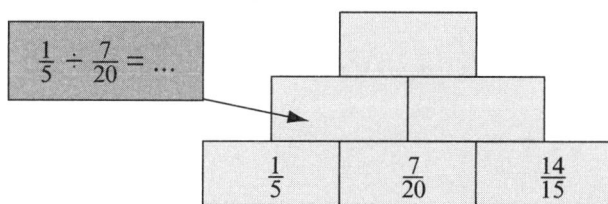

$\frac{1}{5} \div \frac{7}{20} = ...$

Challenge

12 Ramondo is using fraction cards to make correct calculations.

$\frac{3}{20} \div \boxed{} = \frac{4}{15}$

Work out the correct card for the division above. Write your answer in its simplest form.

Tip
Use the fact that if $a \div b = c$, then $a \div c = b$.

13 The grey triangle has an area of $\frac{1}{5}$ m². The base length of the triangle is $\frac{14}{15}$ m. Work out the height of the triangle.

7 Fractions

14 Look at this fractions pattern.

Pattern	Working	Answer
$\frac{1}{2} \div \frac{2}{3}$	$\frac{1}{2} \div \frac{2}{3} = \frac{1}{2} \times \frac{3}{2} = \frac{3}{4}$	$\frac{3}{4}$
$\frac{2}{3} \div \frac{3}{4}$	$\frac{2}{3} \div \frac{3}{4} = \frac{2}{3} \times \frac{4}{3} =$	
$\frac{3}{4} \div \frac{4}{5}$		
$\frac{4}{5} \div \frac{5}{6}$		
$\frac{5}{6} \div \frac{6}{7}$		

a Copy and complete the table.
b Are the answers in this pattern getting smaller or bigger?
c If the pattern continues, do you think that one of the answers will be 1? Explain why.

15 The shaded area in this shape is $\frac{13}{30}$ m². Work out the missing length.

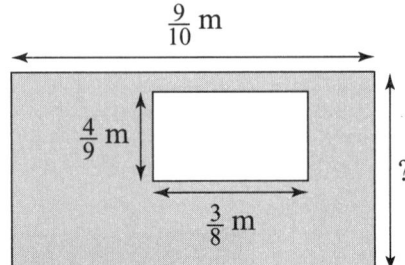

16 Darna uses this formula to work out the approximate length of the diameter of a circle.

Diameter = circumference ÷ $\frac{22}{7}$

Use the formula to work out the diameter when the circumference is:

a $\frac{1}{4}$ m

b $1\frac{11}{21}$ m

Tip

In part **b**, before you use the formula, change $1\frac{11}{21}$ to an improper fraction.

> 7.5 Making fraction calculations easier

Exercise 7.5

Key word

factor

Focus

1   a   Write each of these numbers as a product of two **factors**.
All the answers are given in the cloud. The first one has been done for you.

$3 \times 3 \quad 3 \times 5 \quad 2 \times 2$
$2 \times 7 \quad 2 \times 5$

   i $6 = 2 \times 3$
   ii $4 = \square \times \square$
   iii $10 = \square \times \square$
   iv $9 = \square \times \square$
   v $15 = \square \times \square$
   vi $14 = \square \times \square$

   b   Write each of these fractions as a product of two fractions.
Use your answers to part **a** to help you. The first one has been done for you.

   i $\dfrac{1}{6} = \dfrac{1}{2} \times \dfrac{1}{3}$
   ii $\dfrac{1}{4} = \dfrac{\square}{\square} \times \dfrac{\square}{\square}$
   iii $\dfrac{1}{10} = \dfrac{\square}{\square} \times \dfrac{\square}{\square}$
   iv $\dfrac{1}{9} = \dfrac{\square}{\square} \times \dfrac{\square}{\square}$
   v $\dfrac{1}{15} = \dfrac{\square}{\square} \times \dfrac{\square}{\square}$
   vi $\dfrac{1}{14} = \dfrac{\square}{\square} \times \dfrac{\square}{\square}$

2   Copy and complete the workings to make these calculations easier.
Use factors to change the fractions.

   a $\dfrac{1}{2} \times 18 \qquad 18 \div 2 = \ldots$

   b $\dfrac{1}{4} \times 120 = \dfrac{1}{2} \times \dfrac{1}{2} \times 120 \qquad 120 \div 2 = \boxed{60} \longrightarrow \boxed{60} \div 2 = \square$

   c $\dfrac{1}{6} \times 90 = \dfrac{1}{2} \times \dfrac{1}{3} \times 90 \qquad 90 \div 2 = \square \longrightarrow \square \div 3 = \square$

   d $\dfrac{1}{15} \times 210 = \dfrac{1}{3} \times \dfrac{1}{5} \times 210 \qquad 210 \div 3 = \square \longrightarrow \square \div 5 = \square$

   e $\dfrac{1}{14} \times 420 = \dfrac{1}{2} \times \dfrac{1}{7} \times 420 \qquad 420 \div 2 = \square \longrightarrow \square \div 7 = \square$

7 Fractions

3 Which of the divisions, **A** or **B**, would you find easier to do? Work out the answer.

    a   **A** $96 \div 3$ or   **B** $96 \div 2$

    b   **A** $84 \div 3$ or   **B** $84 \div 4$

    c   **A** $90 \div 3$ or   **B** $90 \div 5$

    d   **A** $126 \div 3$ or   **B** $126 \div 7$

4 Copy and complete the workings to make these calculations easier.

    a $\frac{1}{6} \times 96 = \frac{1}{3} \times \frac{1}{2} \times 96$ $96 \div \Box = \Box \longrightarrow \Box \div \Box = \Box$

    b $\frac{1}{12} \times 84 = \frac{1}{3} \times \frac{1}{4} \times 84$ $84 \div \Box = \Box \longrightarrow \Box \div \Box = \Box$

    c $\frac{1}{15} \times 90 = \frac{1}{3} \times \frac{1}{5} \times 90$ $90 \div \Box = \Box \longrightarrow \Box \div \Box = \Box$

    d $\frac{1}{21} \times 126 = \frac{1}{3} \times \frac{1}{7} \times 126$ $126 \div \Box = \Box \longrightarrow \Box \div \Box = \Box$

Tip

Use your answers to Question **3** to help you.

5 Match each fraction given in a rectangle with its equivalent fraction given in an oval.

     $\boxed{\frac{1}{5}}$ $\boxed{\frac{2}{5}}$ $\boxed{\frac{3}{5}}$ $\boxed{\frac{4}{5}}$ $\left(\frac{4}{10}\right)$ $\left(\frac{8}{10}\right)$ $\left(\frac{2}{10}\right)$ $\left(\frac{6}{10}\right)$

6 Copy and complete the workings to make these calculations easier. The first one has been done for you.

    a $\frac{1}{5} \times 90$ $\frac{1}{5} = \frac{2}{10}$ $90 \div 10 = \boxed{9} \longrightarrow \boxed{9} \times 2 = 18$

    b $\frac{2}{5} \times 80$ $\frac{2}{5} = \frac{\Box}{10}$ $80 \div 10 = \Box \longrightarrow \Box \times \Box = \Box$

    c $\frac{3}{5} \times 70$ $\frac{3}{5} = \frac{\Box}{10}$ $70 \div 10 = \Box \longrightarrow \Box \times \Box = \Box$

    d $\frac{4}{5} \times 60$ $\frac{4}{5} = \frac{\Box}{10}$ $60 \div 10 = \Box \longrightarrow \Box \times \Box = \Box$

Tip

Use your answers to Question **5** to help you.

Practice

7 Work these out. Use factors to change the fractions. Show all your working.

    a $\frac{1}{4} \times 104$ **b** $\frac{1}{6} \times 162$ **c** $\frac{1}{8} \times 216$ **d** $\frac{1}{15} \times 210$

Tip

For part **a**, use $\frac{1}{4} = \frac{1}{2} \times \frac{1}{2}$.

8 Zara reads this newspaper headline:

> ROUGHLY $\frac{1}{12}$ OF THE POPULATION ARE LEFT-HANDED

Work out roughly how many people in Zara's village are left-handed.

Use factors to change the fraction. Show all your working.

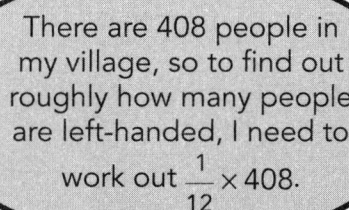

9 Zara wants to work out $\frac{1}{16}$ of a number.

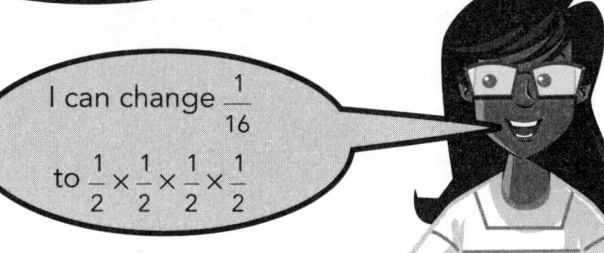

  a Is Zara correct? Explain your answer.

  b Use your answer to part **a** to work out $\frac{1}{16} \times 600$.

10 Work these out. Use equivalent fractions. The first one has been started for you.

  a $\frac{1}{5} \times 270$ $\frac{1}{5} = \frac{2}{10}$ $270 \div 10 = \Box$ $\Box \times 2 = \Box$

  b $\frac{2}{5} \times 320$ **c** $\frac{3}{5} \times 220$

11 $\frac{4}{5}$ of the girls at Asher's school have blue eyes. There are 820 girls enrolled at her school.

How many of the girls at Asher's school have blue eyes? Show all your working.

12 Work these out. Use equivalent fractions. The first one has been started for you.

  a $\frac{3}{20} \times 700$ $\frac{3}{20} = \frac{15}{100}$ $700 \div 100 = \Box$ $\Box \times 15 = \Box$

  b $\frac{9}{20} \times 500$ **c** $\frac{7}{20} \times 300$

7 Fractions

13 Work these out. Use the method of finding factors that are the same in the numerator and the denominator. The first two have been started for you.

a $\quad \dfrac{5}{8} \times \dfrac{7}{15} = \dfrac{5 \times 7}{8 \times 15} = \dfrac{5 \times 7}{8 \times 3 \times 5} = \dfrac{7 \times 5}{24 \times 5} = \dfrac{\square}{\square}$

b $\quad \dfrac{8}{11} \times \dfrac{3}{4} = \dfrac{8 \times 3}{11 \times 4} = \dfrac{4 \times 2 \times 3}{11 \times 4} = \dfrac{\square}{\square}$

c $\quad \dfrac{4}{9} \times \dfrac{18}{23}$

14 This is part of Seb's homework.

> Question: Work out $\dfrac{7}{25} \times \dfrac{9}{14}$.
>
> Solution $\quad \dfrac{7}{25} \times \dfrac{9}{14} = \dfrac{7 \times 9}{25 \times 14}$
>
> $\qquad = \dfrac{7 \times 9}{25 \times 7 \times 7} = \dfrac{9 \times 7}{25 \times 7 \times 7}$
>
> $\qquad = \dfrac{9 \times 7}{175 \times 7} = \dfrac{9}{175} \times \dfrac{7}{7}$
>
> $\qquad = \dfrac{9}{175} \times 1 = \dfrac{9}{175}$

Check every step of Seb's homework.

Is his homework correct? Explain your answer.

Challenge

15 Work these out. Show all your working.

a $\quad \dfrac{8}{9} \times 270$ b $\quad \dfrac{10}{11} \times 550$ c $\quad \dfrac{14}{15} \times 600$ d $\quad \dfrac{29}{30} \times 900$

16 Work these out. Give each answer in its simplest form. Show all your working.

a $\quad \dfrac{3}{5} + \dfrac{7}{8} \times \dfrac{4}{5}$ b $\quad \dfrac{8}{9} - \dfrac{3}{4} \times \dfrac{7}{9}$ c $\quad \dfrac{3}{5} \times \dfrac{2}{3} + \dfrac{11}{12} \times \dfrac{4}{5}$

> **Tip**
>
> Remember to use the method that makes the calculations the easiest.

7.5 Making fraction calculations easier

17 Here are three fraction cards and six number cards.

$\frac{8}{9}$ $\frac{11}{12}$ $\frac{19}{20}$

840   760   720   800   770   640

Use the cards to complete these calculations. Each card can be used only once.

a $\frac{\Box}{\Box} \times \Box = \Box$ b $\frac{\Box}{\Box} \times \Box = \Box$ c $\frac{\Box}{\Box} \times \Box = \Box$

18 Paloma uses this method to work out $\left(\frac{4}{5}\right)^2 \times 300$.

Solution $\left(\frac{4}{5}\right)^2 = \frac{4}{5} \times \frac{4}{5} = \frac{16}{25}$ and $\frac{16}{25} = \frac{16 \times 4}{25 \times 4} = \frac{64}{100}$

So, $\left(\frac{4}{5}\right)^2 \times 300 = \frac{64}{100} \times 300$

$300 \div 100 = 3$ and $3 \times 64 = 192$.

a Did you find Paloma's method easy to follow?
b Can you think of a better method you could use to work out $\left(\frac{4}{5}\right)^2 \times 300$?
c Use Paloma's method or your own method to work out:

   i $\left(\frac{2}{5}\right)^2 \times 400$ ii $\left(\frac{3}{5}\right)^2 \times 200$

d Use a method of your choice to work out:

   i $\left(\frac{2}{3}\right)^2 \times 720$ ii $\frac{3}{4} \times \frac{8}{13} \times 260$

8 Shapes and symmetry

> 8.1 Identifying the symmetry of 2D shapes

This shape has one **line of symmetry**.

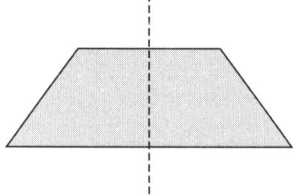

If you place a mirror along a line of symmetry, when you look in the mirror you will see an exact reflection of the shape.

The order of **rotational symmetry** is the number of times a shape looks the same in one **full turn**.

The easiest way to work this out is using tracing paper.

Follow these steps to work out the order of rotation of a shape. This example shows a rectangle:

1   Trace the shape.

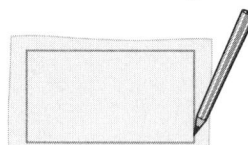

2   Put your pencil on the centre of the shape.

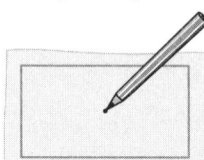

Key words
full turn
horizontal line
line symmetry
once
rotational symmetry
twice
vertical line

Tip
A line of symmetry is sometimes called a mirror line.

3 Turn the tracing paper one full turn and count the number of times the shape fits on itself.

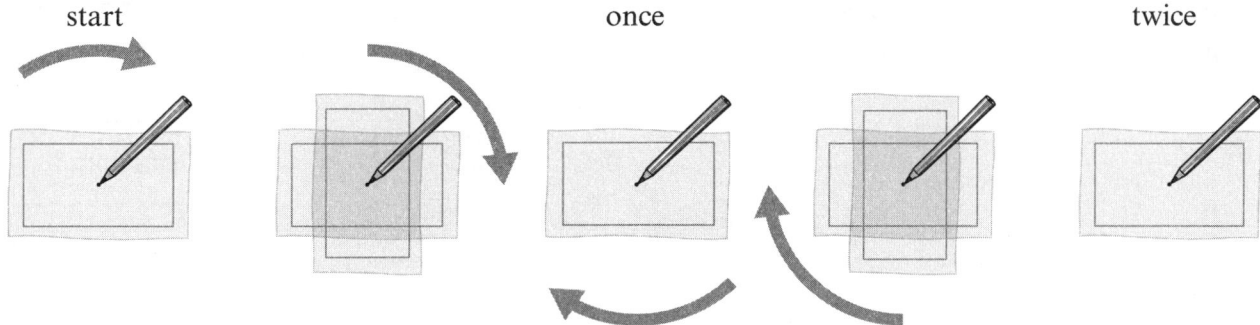

The rectangle fits on itself **twice**, so it has an order of rotation 2.

Exercise 8.1

Focus

1 This is part of Marcus's homework. He thinks he has drawn the correct line of symmetry on each of these letters.

Write 'C' if the line of symmetry is correct or write 'N' if the line of symmetry is not correct.

If the line of symmetry is not correct, draw the letter with the line of symmetry in the correct place.

> **Tip**
> Use a mirror to help you.

2 Each of these shapes has one line of symmetry. Copy the shapes and draw the line of symmetry on each of your diagrams.

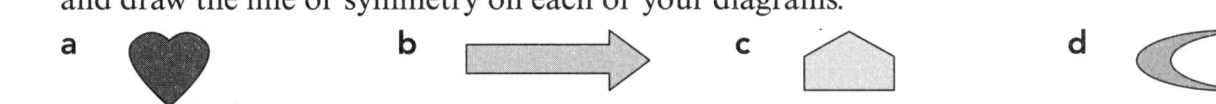

3 Each of these shapes has two lines of symmetry. Copy the shapes and draw the lines of symmetry on each of your diagrams.

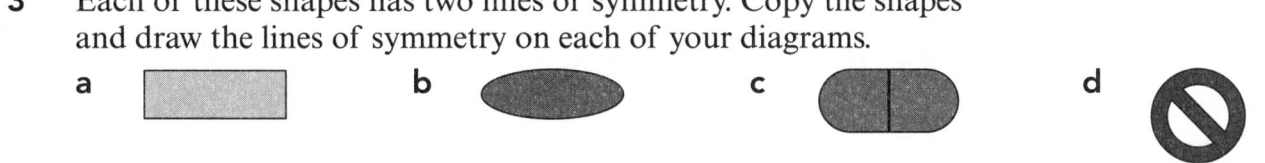

8 Shapes and symmetry

4 Follow the steps shown in the introduction of this section to work out the order of rotational symmetry of these shapes.

> **Tip**
> A shape that fits on to itself only **once** has an order of rotation 1.

a 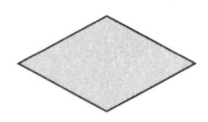 b 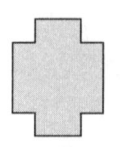 c

d  e 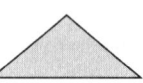 f

g  h 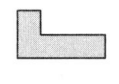 i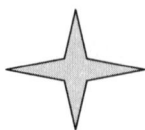

5 Match each shape (**A** to **E**) to its order of rotational symmetry (**i** to **v**). The first one has been done for you: **A** and **iii**.

A  B 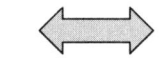 C 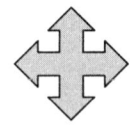 D 

A ...

A B C D E

i   order 1   ii   order 4   iii   order 5   iv   order 3   v   order 2

Practice

6 Copy each of these shapes. On each copy, draw the line(s) of symmetry.

a  b  c 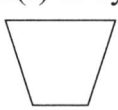 d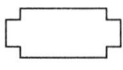

e 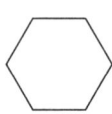 f 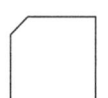 g  h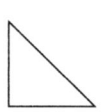

i 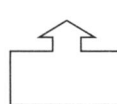 j 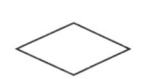 k  l

7 For each of the shapes in Question **6**, write down the order of rotational symmetry.

8   Write down the number of lines of symmetry for each of these shapes.

   a 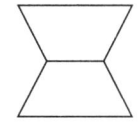   b    c 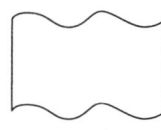   d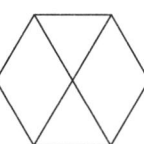

   e 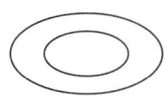   f 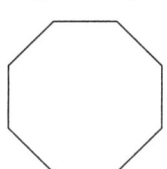   g 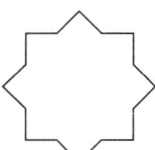   h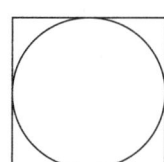

9   For each of the shapes in Question **8**, write down the order of rotational symmetry.

10 In each diagram, the dotted lines are lines of symmetry.

   a   Copy and complete each diagram by shading squares.

   Tip

   Shade only as many squares as you need to make the diagram symmetrical.

   i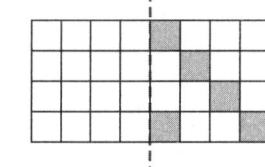

   ii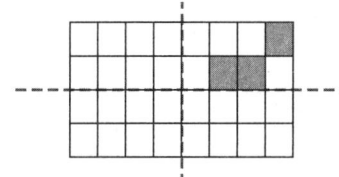

   iii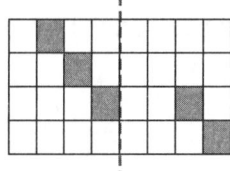

   b   Write down the order of rotational symmetry of each of the patterns in part **a**.

11 Copy these patterns onto squared paper.

   i 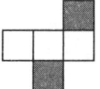   ii 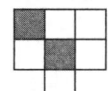   iii 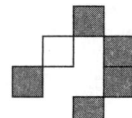   iv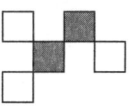

   a   Look at each pattern. Decide how you can change each pattern to give the pattern exactly one line of symmetry.

   You may add only one more grey square.

   You must make only one change for each diagram.

   b   Draw the line of symmetry onto each of your patterns.

   c   Write down whether your shape has a **horizontal**, **vertical** or **diagonal** line of symmetry.

8 Shapes and symmetry

 12   Jason has six white tiles and three grey tiles. Each tile is an equilateral triangle.

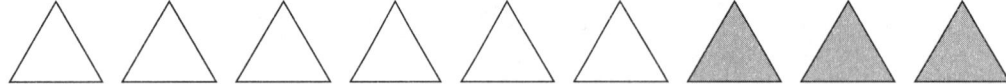

Jason wants to arrange the tiles to form a pattern with order 3 rotational symmetry.

a   Draw two patterns to show how he could arrange the tiles.

b   For the patterns of tiles you drew in part **a**, how many lines of symmetry does each pattern have?

Challenge

 13   Marcus has made this pattern from grey and black tiles. He has two spare black tiles.

There are six different ways I can add the two black tiles to the pattern to make a pattern with only one line of symmetry.

There is only one way I can add the two black tiles to the pattern to make a pattern with two lines of symmetry.

Show that Marcus is correct.

You can only join the tiles side-to-side like this ▢▢, not corner to corner like this ⌐▢.

 14   Josephine has a box of tiles.
All the tiles have the same pattern.
The pattern on the tile is shown in the diagram.
Josephine uses four of the tiles to make a square pattern.
Her pattern has four lines of symmetry.
Draw two different patterns that Josephine could make.

 15   Toby is making a pattern from grey and white squares.
This is what he has drawn so far.
Make four copies of the diagram.

a   Start with three of your copies of the diagram. In each diagram, shade three more squares so that the pattern has rotational symmetry of order 2. Each pattern must be different.

How many lines of symmetry does each pattern have?

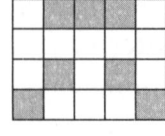

b In your fourth copy of the diagram, shade three more squares so that the pattern has rotational symmetry of order 4. How many lines of symmetry does this pattern have?

16 On isometric paper, copy the following shapes.

In each of the diagrams, shade two more triangles to make the shapes have the order of rotational symmetry as follows:

a order 1 b order 2
c order 3 d order 6

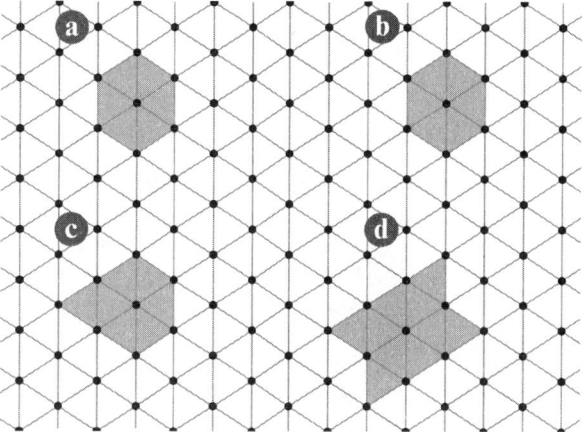

17 On squared paper draw a:
a five-sided shape with one line of symmetry
b six-sided shape with order 2 rotational symmetry.

> 8.2 Circles and polygons

A **chord** of a circle is a straight line that starts and finishes on the circumference of the circle.

A **tangent** to a circle is a straight line that touches the circumference of the circle at only one point.

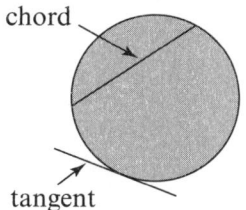

Key words
chord
polygon
sketch
tangent

Exercise 8.2

Focus

1 Write down whether each of these diagrams shows a chord or a tangent.

a 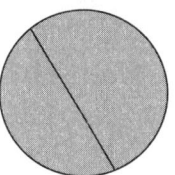 b 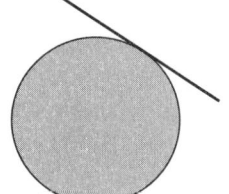 c 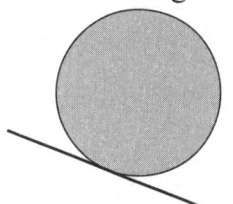 d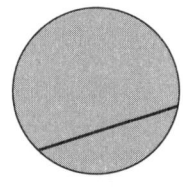

8 Shapes and symmetry

2 Alun draws this diagram of a circle with a chord and a tangent.

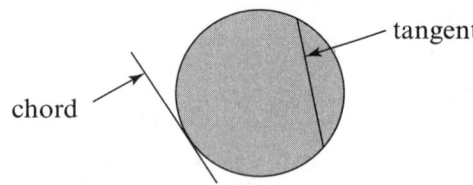

What is incorrect about Alun's diagram?

3 Ffion draws this diagram of a circle with a chord and a tangent.

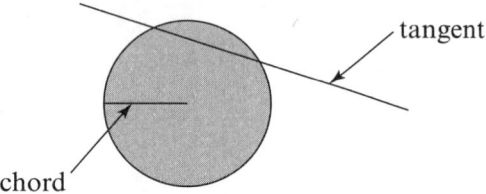

What is incorrect about Ffion's diagram?

4 Draw a circle. On your circle draw two different chords of the circle.

5 Draw a circle. On your circle draw two different tangents to the circle.

6 Copy and complete this statement:

A tangent to a circle and the radius of a circle always meet at ☐°.

7 Match each of the following **polygons** to its correct name and number of sides. Write a sentence for each shape. The first one has been done for you: **A** is a pentagon and has 5 sides.

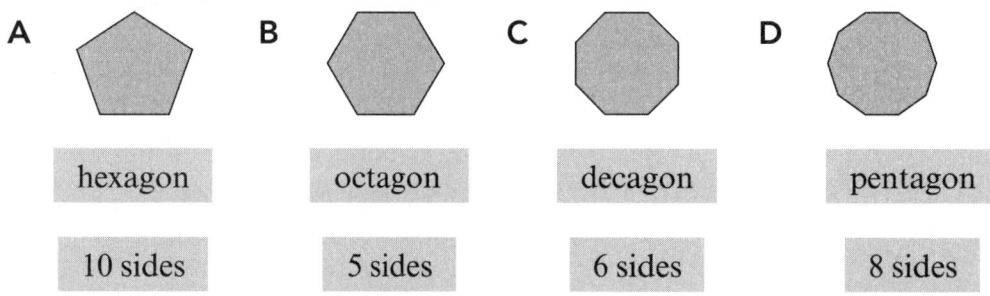

Practice

8 Copy the diagram and label the parts of the circle.

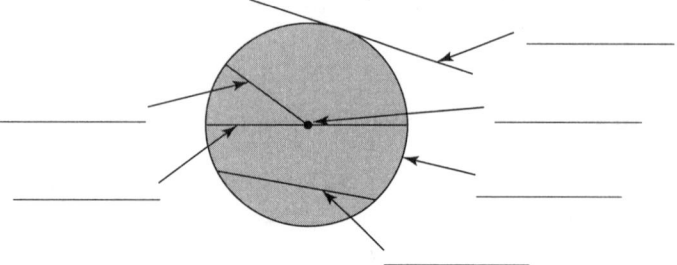

8.2 Circles and polygons

9 Sofia draws this diagram.

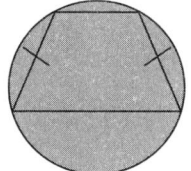

> Inside a circle I can draw four chords that make an isosceles trapezium.

Draw three circles.

a Inside the first circle draw four chords that make a rectangle.
b Inside the second circle draw four chords that make a square.
c Inside the third circle draw four chords that make a kite.

10 a Draw a small circle. Draw three tangents to the circle that make a triangle.

b Copy each of these sentences and choose the correct word or number for the triangle you have drawn in part **a**.

My triangle is called a scalene/isosceles/equilateral triangle.

My triangle has 0/2/3 sides the same length.

My triangle has 0/2/3 angles the same size.

My triangle has 0/1/3 lines of symmetry.

My triangle has order 1/3 rotational symmetry.

11 a **Sketch** a regular pentagon.

b Describe the properties that characterise a regular pentagon.

12 The diagram shows a regular dodecagon (12 sides).

Copy and complete the properties that characterise a regular dodecagon.

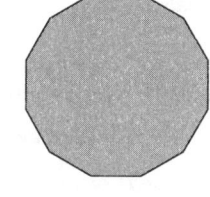

A regular dodecagon has:

- …… sides the same length
- …… angles the same size
- …… lines of symmetry
- rotational symmetry of order …….

Challenge

13 The diagram shows a circle with centre C.

A tangent touches the circle at D.

A line from C meets the tangent at E.

CDE is a triangle. $\angle CED = 32°$.

a Copy and complete this sentence:

The line CD is a ………… of the circle.

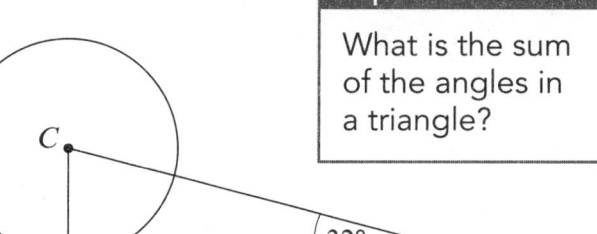

> **Tip**
> What is the sum of the angles in a triangle?

8 Shapes and symmetry

b Write down the size of ∠CDE.

c Work out the size of ∠DCE.

 14 The diagram shows a regular hexagon with side length 5 cm.

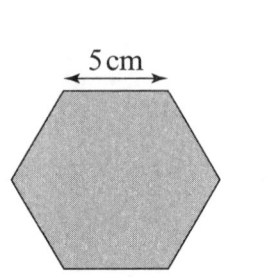 

I think the perimeter of the hexagon is 35 cm.

Is Arun correct? Explain your answer.

15 The diagram shows a regular octagon and a regular decagon.
The perimeters of the shapes are the same.
Work out the side length of the decagon.

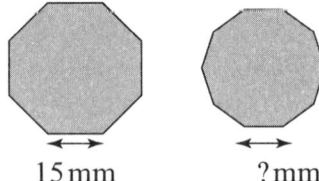

 16 Look at Belinda's method for working out the angles inside a pentagon.

> *There are five identical triangles inside the pentagon.*
> *Angles around a point add up to 360°.*
> $x = 360° \div 5 = 72°$
> *Each triangle is isosceles.*
> *Angles in a triangle add up to 180°.*
> $2y = 180° - 72° = 108°$
> $y = 108° \div 2 = 54°$
> *Angle z is the same as y + y.*
> $z = 54° + 54° = 108°$

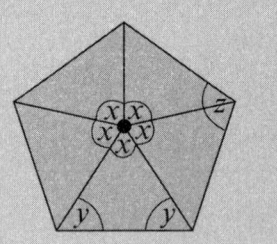

Tip

Look back at Unit 2 for a reminder on using algebra.

a Use Belinda's method to work out the value of angles x, y and z in this hexagon.

Show all your working.

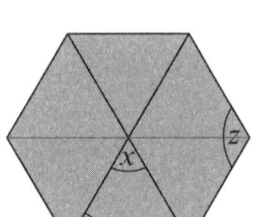

110

b Without drawing any more shapes, copy and complete this table.

Show how you worked out the answers.

Name of regular polygon	Number of triangles	x	y	z
pentagon	5	72°	54°	108°
hexagon	6			
octagon				
nonagon				
decagon				

c What do you notice about the answers for angles *x*, *y* and *z* in your table in part **b**?

Copy and complete the following rules:

$z = \boxed{} \times y$ $\qquad x + z = \boxed{}°$

> 8.3 Recognising congruent shapes

Exercise 8.3

Key word
congruent

Focus

 1 Which of the shapes, A, B or C, is not exactly the same size as the other two shapes?

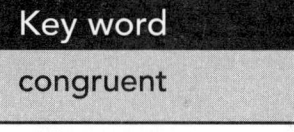

Tip

If you are not sure, use some tracing paper. Trace triangle **A**, then see which other triangles your tracing fits onto exactly. Remember you can turn or flip the paper.

a A  B  C

b A  B 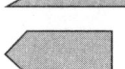 C

c A  B 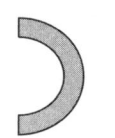 C

d A B C

8 Shapes and symmetry

2 Which of these triangles are **congruent** to triangle A?

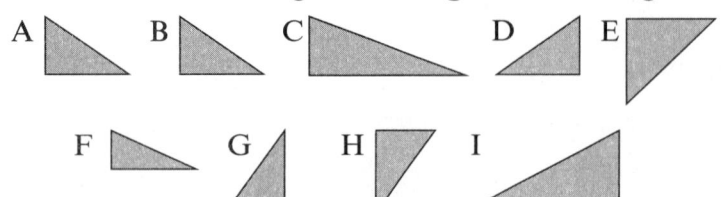

Tip

Remember: Congruent shapes are <u>identical</u> in <u>shape</u> and <u>size</u>. Use tracing paper to trace triangle A, then place your tracing on top of the other triangles. If it fits exactly, it is a congruent triangle.

3 Explain why these two squares are <u>not</u> congruent.

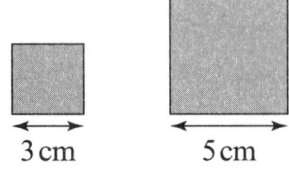

4 These two rectangles are congruent.
Write down the length of:
a   EH   b   HG

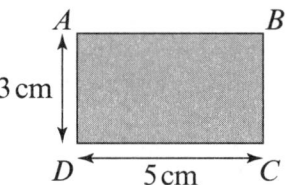

5 These two rectangles are congruent.
Write down the length of:
a   KL   b   ML

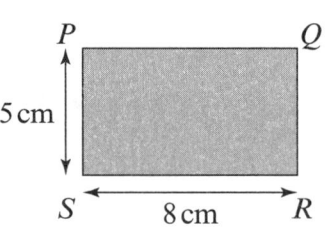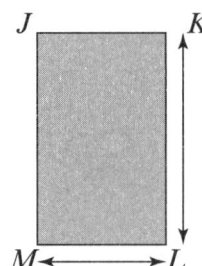

Practice

6 Which of the following shapes are congruent to shape A?

7 Parallelogram PQRS is congruent to parallelogram WXYZ.
     a   Write down the length of the side WX.
     b   Write down the length of the side WZ.

8 Triangle KLM is congruent to triangle DEF.

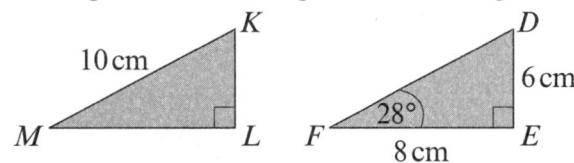

     a   Write down the length of the side:
         i   DF   ii   KL   iii   LM
     b   Work out the size of ∠EDF.

Tip

Remember that the angles in a triangle add up to 180°.

8.3 Recognising congruent shapes

   c Write down the size of:
      i ∠KML   **ii** ∠LKM

   d Copy and complete these sentences. The first one has been done for you.
      i Side *KM* corresponds to side *DF*.   **ii** Side *KL* corresponds to side ....
      iii Side *LM* corresponds to side ....   **iv** ∠KLM corresponds to ∠.......
      v ∠KML corresponds to ∠.......   **vi** ∠LKM corresponds to ∠.......

9 These two triangles are congruent.

   a Write down the length of:
      i AC   **ii** QR   **iii** BC

   b Write down the size of:
      i ∠BAC   **ii** ∠RPQ   **iii** ∠PQR

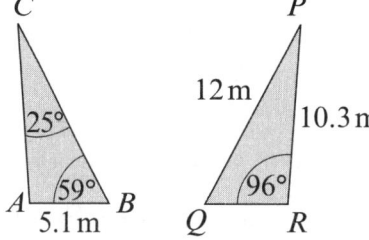

10 These quadrilaterals are congruent.

   a Write down the side that corresponds to:
      i SR   **ii** QR
      iii YZ   **iv** WZ

   b Write down the angle that corresponds to:
      i ∠PQR   **ii** ∠QRS   **iii** ∠XWZ   **iv** ∠WZY

Challenge

11 Copy each of these shapes.

Show how you can split each shape into the number of congruent shapes stated. The first one has been done for you.

   a Two pairs of congruent triangles.

   b Two pairs of congruent triangles.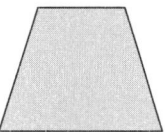

   c Two pairs of congruent triangles.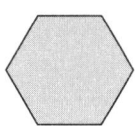

   d One pair of congruent triangles and two congruent trapezia.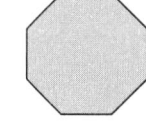

   e Five congruent triangles.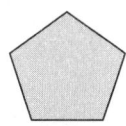

12 Triangles ABC and CDE are congruent. ACD is a straight line.

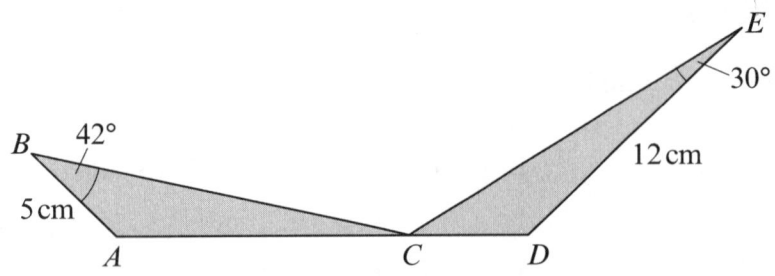

a Write down the length of AC.
b Work out the length of AD.
c Write down the size of:
   i ∠BCA   ii ∠DCE
d Work out the size of ∠BCE.

13 In the diagram, the dotted line represents a line of symmetry.

ADE and CDG are straight lines.

∠ABC = 115°, ∠DGF = 70° and ∠BCD = 120°.

Work out the value of ∠CDE.

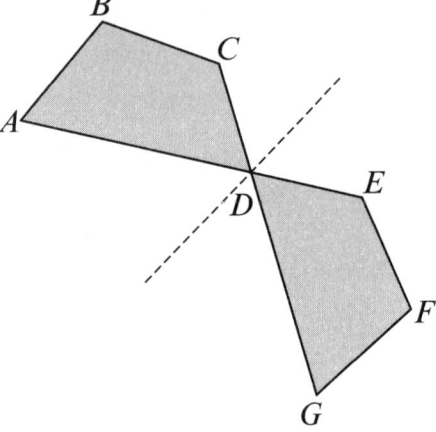

14 Sol draws quadrilateral ABCD on a coordinate grid. The coordinates of the vertices are A(−4, 0), B(−2, 3), C(−1, −1) and D(−2, −2).

Sol starts to draw the congruent quadrilateral, PQRS, on the same grid. He plots the points P(1, 1) and R(4, 0).

a What are the coordinates of the vertices Q and S?
b Sol changes the coordinates of P and Q so that P is at (4, 0) and R is at (1, 1). What are the new coordinates of the vertices Q and S?

Tip

Draw a coordinate grid to help you.

> 8.4 3D shapes

Exercise 8.4

Focus

Key words
front view
side view
top view

1 You use the words faces, edges and vertices to describe solid shapes.
   Match each word to its correct description.

Faces are...	...the corners of a solid shape.
Edges are...	...the flat sides of a solid shape.
Vertices are...	...the lines where two faces meet.

2 Copy and complete these properties of a cuboid.
   All the numbers you need are given in the cloud.

   A cuboid has:
   - ☐ rectangular faces
   - ☐ vertices
   - ☐ edges
   - all angles are ☐°.

   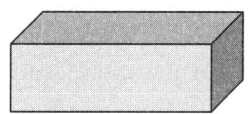

   90   8
      6   12

3 Copy and complete these properties of a tetrahedron.
   All the numbers you need are given in the cloud.

   A tetrahedron has:
   - ☐ triangular faces
   - ☐ vertices
   - ☐ edges
   - all angles are ☐°.

   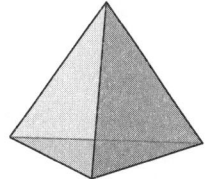

   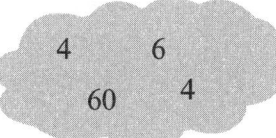
   4   6
     60   4

4 Here is a list of 3D shapes.

   cube   sphere   cuboid   cone
         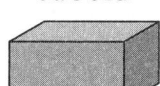

   cylinder   triangular prism   square-based pyramid
      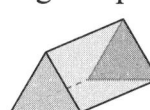   

8 Shapes and symmetry

    a Which of the shapes in the list have at least one circular face?
    b Which of the shapes in the list have a curved surface?
    c Which of the shapes in the list have no vertices?

5 This is a pentagonal pyramid. Copy and complete this description:

I have a total of …… faces.

One of my faces is a pentagon and the other …… faces are congruent triangles.

I have …… edges and …… vertices.

Practice

6 Match the properties (**a–d**) of each 3D shape with its name (**A–D**) and picture (**i–iv**).

	Properties		Name of shape		Picture of shape
a	I have six congruent square faces. I have 12 edges and eight vertices.	A	square-based pyramid	i	(cone)
b	I have five faces. One face is a square and four faces are congruent triangles. I have eight edges and five vertices.	B	hexagonal prism	ii	(cube)
c	I have eight faces. Two faces are congruent hexagons and the rest are congruent rectangles. I have 18 edges and 12 vertices.	C	cone	iii	(square-based pyramid)
d	I have two faces. One face is a circle and the other face is a curved surface. I have one edge and one vertex.	D	cube	iv	(hexagonal prism)

7 Write down the properties of a cylinder. You must include information about the faces, edges and vertices.

8   Arun is describing this shape to Zara.

Arun says: Zara says:

Arun: The shape has five faces. Two of the faces are triangles and three of the faces are rectangles.

Zara: I think it is an isosceles triangular prism.

a   Is Zara correct?
b   What piece of information is missing from Arun's description?

9   Put each of these shapes through this classification flow chart.
    Write down the letter where each shape comes out.

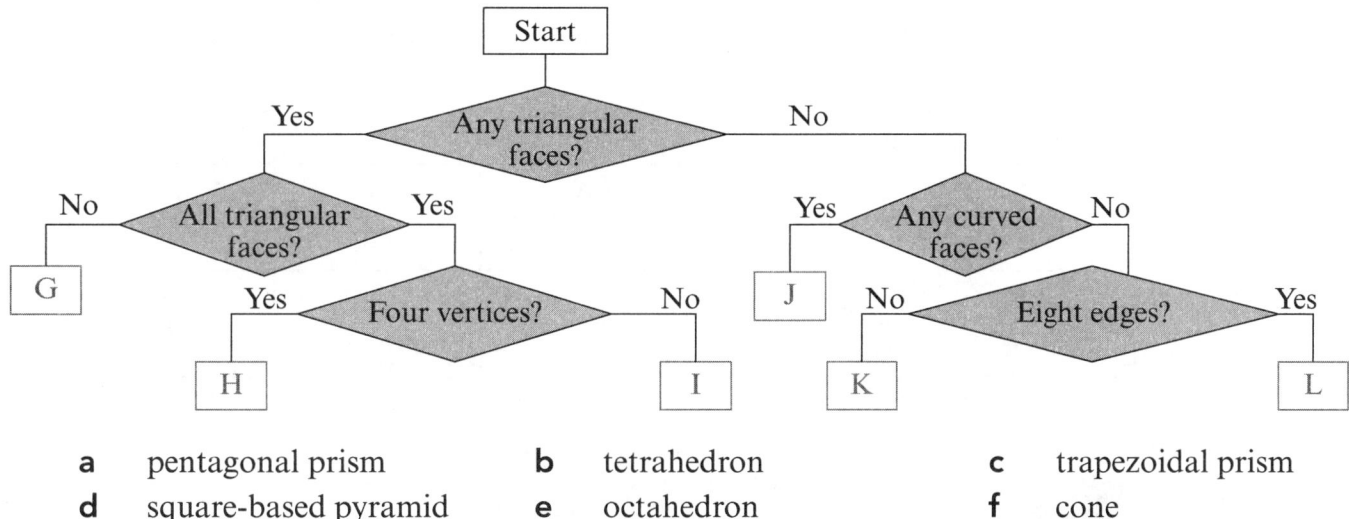

a   pentagonal prism   b   tetrahedron   c   trapezoidal prism
d   square-based pyramid   e   octahedron   f   cone

8 Shapes and symmetry

10 The table shows the **top view**, **front view** and **side view** of some 3D shapes. The names of the 3D shapes are missing. Write the missing names of the 3D shapes.

Name of 3D shape	Top view	Front view	Side view
a	square	square	square
b	rectangle	triangle	rectangle
c	circle	circle	circle
d	triangle (with lines from centre)	triangle	triangle

Tip

Remember that the top view can also be called the plan view or just plan. The side and front views can also be called the side and front elevations.

11 Draw the top view, front view and side view of a cylinder.

Challenge

 12 Arun makes a table showing the number of faces, vertices and edges of different pyramids. This is what he has done so far.

Original shape	Number of sides	Shape of base of pyramid	Number of faces	Number of vertices	Number of edges
triangle	3	triangular	4	4	6
square	4	square	5	5	8
pentagon	5	pentagonal	6	6	10
hexagon		hexagonal			
heptagon		heptagonal			
octagon		octagonal			

a Copy and complete the table.

b Arun says:

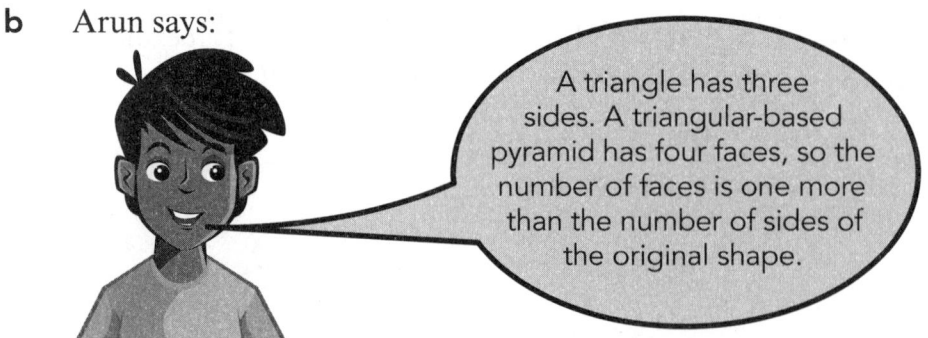

A triangle has three sides. A triangular-based pyramid has four faces, so the number of faces is one more than the number of sides of the original shape.

Is this true for every pyramid? Explain your answer.

118

c   Look back at the table. Compare the number of sides of the original shapes with the number of vertices of the pyramids. What do you notice?

Write down a general rule that connects the number of sides of the original shape with the number of vertices of the pyramid.

d   Look back at the table. Compare the number of sides of the original shape with the number of edges of the pyramid. What do you notice?

Write down a general rule that connects the number of sides of the original shape with the number of edges of the pyramid.

e   Use your answer to part **d** to copy and complete this statement:

The number of edges of a pyramid is always a multiple of ....

13 a   Andrea makes this new shape from a cube and a square-based pyramid. How many faces, edges and vertices does the new shape have?

b   Copy and complete this table.

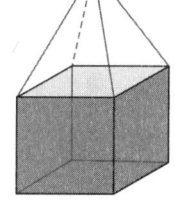

Shape	Number of faces	Number of edges	Number of vertices
cube			
pyramid			
new shape			

c   Jun makes this new shape from a pentagonal prism and a pentagonal-based pyramid. How many faces, edges and vertices does the new shape have?

d   Copy and complete this table.

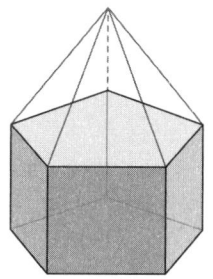

Shape	Number of faces	Number of edges	Number of vertices
pentagonal prism			
pentagonal pyramid			
new shape			

Sofia looks at the tables in parts **b** and **d**. She finds a rule to work out the number of faces on the new shape when she knows the number of faces on the two starting shapes.

When I add together the number of faces on the two starting shapes and then subtract 2, I get the number of faces on the new shape.

8 Shapes and symmetry

  e i Explain why this rule works.
     ii Find a general rule to work out the number of edges on the new shape when you know the number of edges on the two starting shapes.
     iii Find a general rule to work out the number of vertices on the new shape when you know the number of vertices on the two starting shapes.
  f Check that your rules in part e work if you make a new shape from a hexagonal prism and a hexagonal-based pyramid.

14 Draw the front view, side view and top view for each of these shapes.

The arrows show the direction that you must look at the shape for the front view (F), side view (S) and top view (T).

a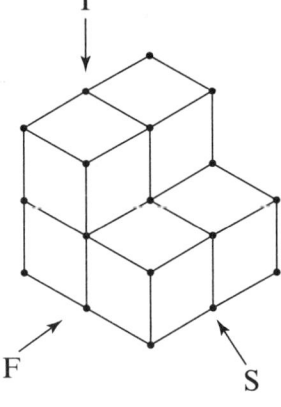

b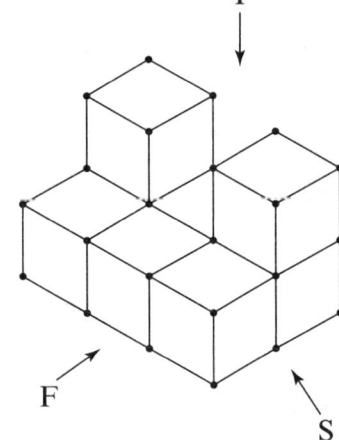

c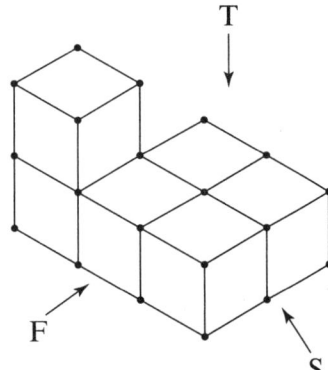

d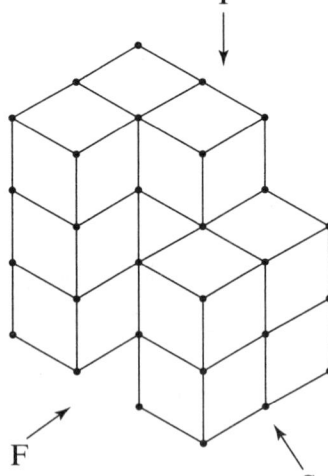

9 Sequences and functions

> 9.1 Generating sequences 1

Here is a **sequence** of numbers:
4, 6, 8, 10, 12, …
The first **term** of the sequence is 4.
The **term-to-term rule** is 'Add 2'.
4 + 2 = 6, 6 + 2 = 8, 8 + 2 = 10, etc.

> **Key words**
>
> finite sequence
> infinite sequence
> sequence
> term
> term-to-term rule

Exercise 9.1

Focus

1   Write down the next two terms in each of these sequences.
    Also write down the term-to-term rule.

   a   5, 10, 15, 20, ☐, ☐
       Term-to-term rule: …………
   b   1, 3, 5, 7, ☐, ☐
       Term-to-term rule: …………
   c   6, 10, 14, 18, ☐, ☐
       Term-to-term rule: …………
   d   20, 28, 36, 44, ☐, ☐
       Term-to-term rule: …………
   e   10, 9, 8, 7, ☐, ☐
       Term-to-term rule: …………
   f   16, 13, 10, 7, ☐, ☐
       Term-to-term rule: …………

> **Tip**
>
> The first term is the first number in the list.

> **Tips**
>
> 5 + 5 = 10,
> 10 + 5 = 15,
> 15 + 5 = 20, …
> The rule is 'Add 5'.
>
> 1 + ? = 3,
> 3 + ? = 5,
> 5 + ? = 7,
> 7 + ? = ?
> The rule is 'Add ?'.

9 Sequences and functions

g 20, 18, 16, 14, ☐, ☐
Term-to-term rule: ....

h 50, 45, 40, 35, ☐, ☐
Term-to-term rule: ....

2 Use the given first term and term-to-term rule to write down the next four terms of each sequence.

a Add 3   5, ☐, ☐, ☐, ☐
b Add 6   2, ☐, ☐, ☐, ☐
c Add 10   12, ☐, ☐, ☐, ☐
d Add 7   0, ☐, ☐, ☐, ☐
e Subtract 2   12, ☐, ☐, ☐, ☐
f Subtract 5   25, ☐, ☐, ☐, ☐
g Subtract 1   13, ☐, ☐, ☐, ☐
h Subtract 20 100, ☐, ☐, ☐, ☐

Tip

For the sequence in part **a**, the first term is 5, then
5 + 3 = 8,
8 + 3 = 11,
11 + 3 = ?, etc.

3 Write down the missing terms in each of these sequences.

a 4, 10, 16, ☐, 28, ☐, 40, 46
b 45, 43, ☐, 39, 37, ☐, 33

Tip

For the sequence in part **a**:
4 + ? = 10,
10 + ? = 16, so the rule is 'Add ?'.

Practice

4 For each of these **infinite sequences**, write down:
   i   the term-to-term rule
   ii the next two terms
   iii the tenth term

a 12, 14, 16, 18, ☐   b 5, 8, 11, 14, ☐   c 46, 42, 38, 34, ☐

5 Write down the first three terms of each of these sequences. Show your working.

	First term	Term-to-term rule
a	4	add 3
b	30	subtract 5
c	4	multiply by 2
d	80	divide by 2

6 Copy these **finite sequences**. Fill in the missing terms.

a 6, 9, ☐, 15, ☐, 21, 24   b 3, 10, 17, ☐, ☐, 38, ☐
c 45, ☐, ☐, 27, 21, ☐, 9   d ☐, ☐, 17, 14, ☐, ☐, ☐

7 Write down whether each of these sequences is finite or infinite.
   a 5, 10, 15, 20   b 3, 5, 7, 9, ☐   c 585, 575, 565, 555

8 Write down the first three terms of each of these sequences. The first one has been started for you.
   a First term is 5. Term-to-term rule is: Multiply by 2 then add 3.

   > First term = 5
   > Second term = 5 × 2 + 3 = 10 + 3 = 13
   > Third term = 13 × 2 + 3 = ☐ + 3 = ☐

   b First term is 7. Term-to-term rule is: Subtract 4 then multiply by 3.
   c First term is 30. Term-to-term rule is: Divide by 2 then subtract 1.

9 Hari invests $100. At the end of each month $15 is added to his investment, but he must pay a $3 fee.
   a How much money does Hari have at the end of the first month?

   During the next three months exactly the same happens. $15 is added to Hari's investment and he pays a $3 fee.

   b Work out how much money he has at the end of the second, third and fourth months.

10 Marcus and Zara are looking at this number sequence.

    3, 6, 17, 42, 87, 158, ☐, ☐

Marcus: I think the term-to-term rule is: 'Add 3.'

Zara: I think the term-to-term rule is: 'Multiply by 2.'

Is either of them correct? Explain your answer.

9 Sequences and functions

Challenge

11 Write down three possible term-to-term rules for each of these sequences and work out the next two terms for each rule. The first one has been started for you.

  a 1, 3, ☐ ① Add 2 would give 1, 3, 5, 7, ☐

  ② Multiply by 4 and subtract 1 would give 1, 3, 11, 43, ☐

  ③ ☐

  b 3, 6, ☐   c 1, 8, ☐   d 5, 11, ☐

12 The second term of a sequence is 10. The term-to-term rule is: Multiply by 4 then subtract 2. What is the first term of the sequence?

13 The fourth term of a sequence is 18. The term-to-term rule is: Subtract 3 then multiply by 3. What is the first term of the sequence?

14 What is the term-to-term rule for this sequence?

  2, 4, 10, 28, ☐

15 Write two sequences containing the numbers 4 and 12. There must be at least one term in between 4 and 12. For each sequence, write down the term-to-term rule that you use.

16 For each of these sequences, write down the:

  i   term-to-term rule   ii next two terms

  a 4, 1, −2, −5, ☐   b −50, −44, −38, −32, ☐
  c −2, −3, −5, −9, ☐   d −50, −26, −14, −8, ☐

> 9.2 Generating sequences 2

Exercise 9.2

> **Key words**
>
> sequence of patterns
> term-to-term rule

Focus

1 Look at this **sequence of patterns** of squares.

  pattern 1   pattern 2   pattern 3

  a Write down the number of squares in:

    i pattern 1   ii pattern 2   iii pattern 3

b Zara and Sofia look at this sequence of patterns.

Zara says: I think the term-to-term rule for this pattern is: 'Add 2.'

Sofia says: I think the term-to-term rule for this pattern is: 'Add 4.'

Who is correct?

c Draw pattern 4 and pattern 5.

d Copy and complete this table.

Pattern number	1	2	3	4	5
Number of squares	2	4	6		

e Copy and complete the sequence of the number of squares in each pattern:

2, 4, 6, ☐, ☐, ☐

2 Look at this sequence of patterns of triangles.

pattern 1   pattern 2   pattern 3

a Write down the number of triangles in:

i pattern 1   **ii** pattern 2   **iii** pattern 3

b What is the **term-to-term rule** for this sequence of patterns?

Choose the correct rule from the box shown.

| add 3 | add 1 | add 2 | add 4 |

c Draw pattern 4 and pattern 5.

d Copy and complete this table.

Pattern number	1	2	3	4	5
Number of triangles	3	4			

e Copy and complete the sequence of the number of triangles in each pattern:

3, 4, ☐, ☐, ☐, ☐

9 Sequences and functions

3 This sequence of patterns is made from dots.
  a Draw the next two patterns in the sequence.
  b Write down the number sequence of the dots.
  c Write down the term-to-term rule.
  d Explain how the sequence is formed.

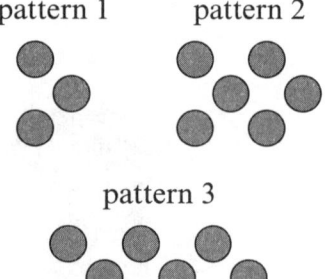

Practice

4 This sequence of patterns is made from squares.
  a Draw the next two patterns in the sequence.
  b Copy and complete the table to show the number of squares in each pattern.

Pattern number	1	2	3	4	5
Number of squares	3	5			

  c Write down the term-to-term rule.
  d How many squares will there be in:
   i pattern 6? ii pattern 8?

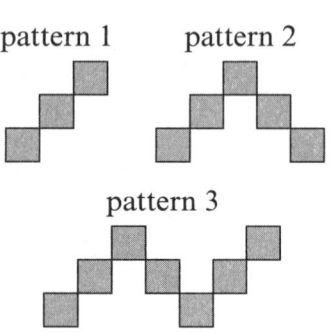

5 This sequence of patterns is made from blocks.
  a Draw the next two patterns in the sequence.
  b Copy and complete the table to show the number of blocks in each pattern.

Pattern number	1	2	3	4	5
Number of blocks					

  c Write down the term-to-term rule.
  d How many blocks will there be in:
   i pattern 6? ii pattern 9?

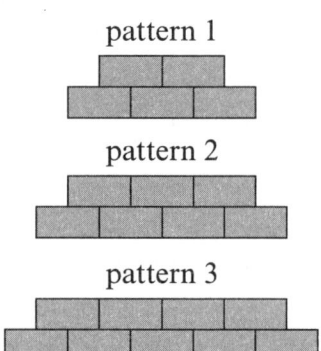

6 This sequence of patterns is made from dots.
  a Copy and complete the table to show the number of dots in each pattern.

Pattern number	1	2	3	4	5
Number of dots					

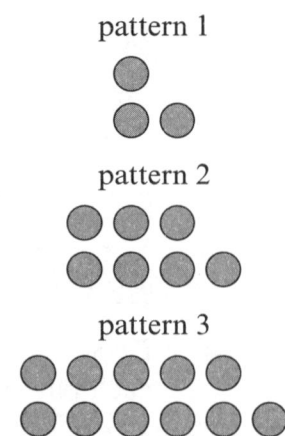

b How many dots will there be in:

  i pattern 10?   **ii** pattern 18?

  Show how you worked out your answers.

7 This sequence of patterns is made from hexagons.

  a Copy and complete the table to show the number of hexagons in each pattern.

Pattern number	1	2	3	4	5
Number of hexagons					

pattern 1

pattern 2

pattern 3

  b Irena thinks that one of the patterns will have 51 hexagons in it.

  Is she correct? Explain your answer.

  c Sion thinks that one of the patterns will have 92 hexagons in it.

  Without doing any calculations, explain how you can tell that he is incorrect.

  d What can you say about the number of hexagons used in this sequence of patterns?

8 Sesane is using dots to draw a sequence of patterns. There are marks over the first and third patterns in her sequence.

  pattern 1   pattern 2   pattern 3   pattern 4

  a Draw the first and the third patterns of Sesane's sequence.

  b How many dots will there be in pattern 6?

9 Zara and Sofia are looking at this sequence of patterns made from squares.

  pattern 1   pattern 2   pattern 3   pattern 4

  5 squares   8 squares   11 squares   14 squares

9 Sequences and functions

Zara says:

Sofia says:

Who is correct? Explain your answer.

Challenge

10 Draw patterns to show these sequences. You can use a shape of your choice for each pattern.

Draw the first three patterns in each sequence.

a 4, 6, 8, ☐   b 1, 4, 7, ☐   c 3, 8, 13, ☐

11 This sequence of patterns is made from grey and white triangles.

pattern 1

pattern 2

pattern 3

a Copy and complete the table to show the number of grey and white triangles in each pattern. Also write down the total number of triangles in each pattern.

Pattern number	1	2	3	4	5
Number of grey triangles					
Number of white triangles					
Total number of triangles					

b Write down the term-to-term rule for the:
  i   number of grey triangles
  ii number of white triangles
  iii total number of triangles

What do you notice about your answers to parts **i**, **ii** and **iii**?

c How many grey triangles will there be in pattern 10?
d How many white triangles will there be in pattern 12?
e What is the total number of triangles in pattern 21?

12 This sequence of patterns is made from grey octagons and white squares.

a Copy and complete the table to show the number of grey octagons and white squares in each pattern. Also write down the total number of shapes in each pattern.

Pattern number	1	2	3	4	5
Number of grey octagons					
Number of white squares					
Total number of shapes					

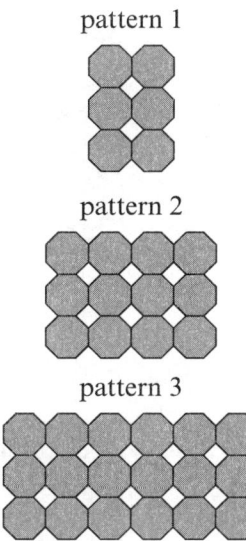

pattern 1

pattern 2

pattern 3

b Write down the term-to-term rule for the:
  i   number of grey octagons
  ii number of white squares
  iii total number of shapes
  What do you notice about your answers to parts **i**, **ii** and **iii**?
c How many grey octagons will there be in pattern 12?
d How many white squares will there be in pattern 20?
e What is the total number of shapes in pattern 50?

> 9.3 Using the *n*th term

Exercise 9.3

Focus

1 Copy and complete the tables to find out the ***n*th term** rule for these sequences.

The first one has been started for you.

a 2, 4, 6, 8, 10, ☐

Position number	1	2	3	4	5
×2	×2	×2	×☐	×☐	×☐
Term	2	4	6	8	10

Term = ☐ × **position number**, so *n*th term rule is: *n*th term = $2n$.

Key words

fewest

*n*th term

position number

Tip

The sequence 2, 4, 6, 8, 10, ☐ is the 2 times table, so the rule is $n \times 2$.

9 Sequences and functions

b 3, 6, 9, 12, 15, ☐

Position number	1	2	3	4	5
×☐	×☐	×☐	×☐	×☐	×☐
Term	3	6	9	12	15

Term = ☐ × position number, so nth term rule is: nth term = ☐n.

c 4, 8, 12, 16, 20, ☐

Position number	1	2	3	4	5
×☐	×☐	×☐	×☐	×☐	×☐
Term	4	8	12	16	20

Term = ☐ × position number, so nth term rule is: nth term = ☐n.

2 Copy and complete the tables to find out the nth term rule for these sequences.

The first one has been started for you.

a 2, 3, 4, 5, 6, ☐

Position number	1	2	3	4	5
+1	+1	+1	+☐	+☐	+☐
Term	2	3	4	5	6

Term = position number + ☐, so nth term rule is:
nth term = $n + 1$.

b 3, 4, 5, 6, 7, ☐

Position number	1	2	3	4	5
+☐	+☐	+☐	+☐	+☐	+☐
Term	3	4	5	6	7

Term = position number + ☐, so nth term rule is:
nth term = n + ☐.

> **Tip**
>
> The numbers 2, 3, 4, 5, 6, ☐ are always one more than the position number, so the rule is $n + 1$.

c 7, 8, 9, 10, 11, ☐

Position number	1	2	3	4	5
+☐	+☐	+☐	+☐	+☐	+☐
Term	7	8	9	10	11

Term = position number + ☐, so nth term rule is:
nth term = n + ☐.

3 Copy and complete the workings to find the first four terms of these sequences.

a nth term = $5n$
When $n = 1$, $5 \times 1 = 5$.
When $n = 2$, $5 \times 2 = 10$.
When $n = 3$, $5 \times 3 = $ ☐
When $n = 4$, $5 \times 4 = $ ☐

First four terms of this sequence are 5, 10, ☐, ☐

b nth term = $n + 3$
When $n = 1$, $1 + 3 = 4$.
When $n = 2$, $2 + 3 = $ ☐
When $n = 3$, $3 + 3 = $ ☐
When $n = 4$, $4 + 3 = $ ☐

First four terms of this sequence are 4, ☐, ☐, ☐

4 Copy and complete the workings to find the 10th term of these sequences.

a nth term = $4n$ When $n = 10$, $4 \times 10 = $ ☐
b nth term = $8n$ When $n = 10$, $8 \times 10 = $ ☐
c nth term = $n + 4$ When $n = 10$, $10 + 4 = $ ☐
d nth term = $n + 8$ When $n = 10$, $10 + 8 = $ ☐

Practice

5 Work out the nth term rule for each of these sequences.

a 9, 18, 27, 36, 45, ☐
b 10, 20, 30, 40, 50, ☐
c 12, 24, 36, 48, 60, ☐
d 30, 60, 90, 120, 150, ☐

> **Tip**
> All these sequences have the rule nth term = ☐ × n.

6 For each of the sequences in Question 5, use its nth term rule to work out the:

i 10th term
ii 20th term

9 Sequences and functions

7 Work out the *n*th term rule for each of these sequences.
   a 8, 9, 10, 11, 12, ☐
   b 11, 12, 13, 14, 15, ☐
   c 14, 15, 16, 17, 18, ☐
   d 20, 21, 22, 23, 24, ☐

   Tip
   All these sequences have the rule *n*th term = *n* + ☐

8 For each of the sequences in Question **7**, use its *n*th term rule to work out the:
   i 12th term
   ii 25th term

9 Sofia is looking at the sequence −6, −5, −4, −3, ☐

I think the *n*th rule is: *n*th term = *n* − 7.

   Tip
   You could start by writing the sequence in a table.

   Is Sofia correct? Explain your answer and show all your working.

10 Work out the first five terms of each of these sequences.
   a *n*th term = *n* − 8
   b *n*th term = *n* + 24
   c *n*th term = 50*n*
   d *n*th term = *n* − 10

   Tip
   Substitute *n* = 1, 2, 3, 4 and 5 into each *n*th term rule.

11 Copy and complete this table.

*n*th term rule	5th term in sequence	10th term in sequence	20th term in sequence
*n*th term = *n* + 30	35		
*n*th term = *n* − 12		−2	
*n*th term = 5*n*	25		
*n*th term = *n* + 14			34
*n*th term = *n* − 20		−10	
*n*th term = 40*n*			800

9.3 Using the *n*th term

Challenge

12 Match each sequence given in a rectangle (**A** to **E**) to its correct *n*th term rule given in an oval (**i** to **v**).

A 17, 34, 51, 68, ☐

B 17, 18, 19, 20, ☐

C 17, 16, 15, 14, ☐

D −17, −18, −19, −20, ☐

E −17, −16, −15, −14, ☐

i $n - 18$ **ii** $18 - n$ **iii** $17n$

iv $n + 16$ **v** $-16 - n$

13 **a** Work out the first five terms of these sequences.
   i *n*th term = $n - 5$ **ii** *n*th term = $5 - n$
 b Work out the first five terms of these sequences.
   i *n*th term = $n - 11$ **ii** *n*th term = $11 - n$
 c What do you notice about your answers to parts **a** and **b**? What can you say about the two sequences with *n*th term = n − 'a number' and *n*th term = 'a number' − n, where 'a number' is the same number?

14 Here are some number cards.

| −24 | −20 | −12 | −10 | −7 | 0 | 1 |

Here are some *n*th rule cards for four sequences.

| Sequence A: *n*th term = $-4n$ | Sequence B: *n*th term = $n - 22$ |
| Sequence C: *n*th term = $2 - n$ | Sequence D: *n*th term = $-5n$ |

 a All of the numbers can be in only one of the sequences. Is the sequence A, B, C or D?
   Show that all of the numbers are in the sequence by working out their positions in the sequence.
 b Which number is in all of the sequences? Show that it is in all the sequences.
 c Two of the numbers can be used in three of the sequences. Show that this is true.
 d Which sequence uses the **fewest** of these numbers? Explain how you worked out your answer.

Tip

Work out the value of *n* that gives each number on the cards.

9 Sequences and functions

> 9.4 Representing simple functions

Here is a **function machine**.

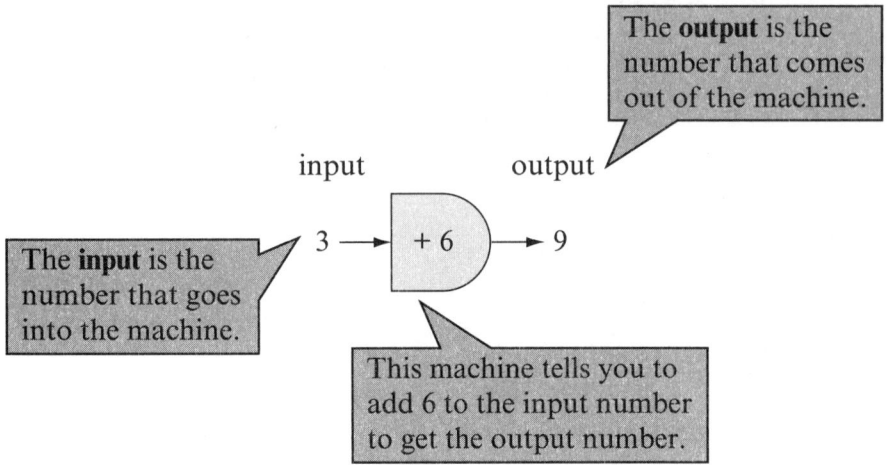

The **input** is the number that goes into the machine.

The **output** is the number that comes out of the machine.

This machine tells you to add 6 to the input number to get the output number.

Key words
- function
- function machine
- input
- mapping diagram
- output

Exercise 9.4

Focus

1   Find the missing **output** numbers in each of these function machines.

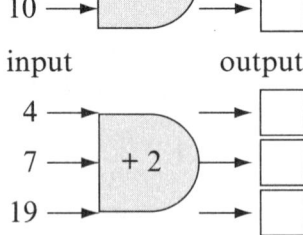

Tip

For part **a**:
output number =
input number × 2,
so 3 × 2 = ?

Tips

For part **b**:
15 ÷ 3 = ?

There can be more than one input number, so in part **c** work out both output numbers:
8 − 8 = ? and
10 − 8 = ?

9.4 Representing simple functions

2 Find the missing input numbers in each of these function machines.

a input   output
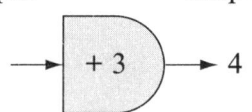

b input   output
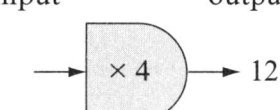

c input   output
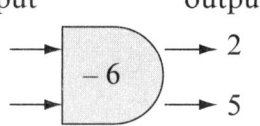

d input   output
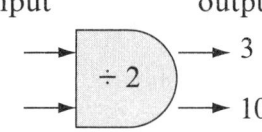

e input   output

→ +7 → 10
→   → 14
→   → 30

> **Tips**
>
> Find the input number by working backwards. For part **a**:
>
> Input + 3 = output, so 4 − 3 = ?
>
> For part **b**:
>
> 12 ÷ 4 = ?

Practice

3 Copy these function machines and find the missing inputs and outputs.

a input   output
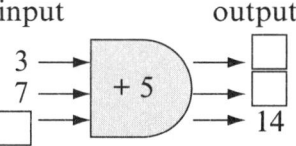

b input   output
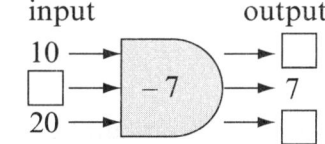

c input   output
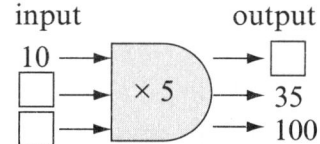

4 Copy and complete these inverse function machines and tables of values.

a
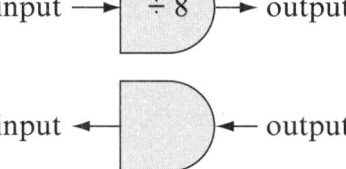

input → [ ] → output

Input			
Output	3	8	10

b
input → ×2 → output

input ← [ ] ← output

Input			
Output	16	26	60

c
input → −9 → output

input ← [ ] ← output

Input			
Output	1	14	25

9 Sequences and functions

5 Work out the rule to complete these function machines.

a input → [ ] → output: 3→6, 7→10, 11→14

b input → [ ] → output: 15→5, 21→7, 30→10

c input → [ ] → output: 3→21, 5→35, 7→49

6 Copy and complete the **mapping diagram** below for this function machine.

input → +4 → output: 3→7, 5→9, 6→10

input 0 1 2 3 4 5 6 7 8 9 10

output 0 1 2 3 4 5 6 7 8 9 10

Challenge

7 Shen draws this mapping diagram for a function.

input 0 1 2 3 4 5 6 7 8 9 10

output 0 1 2 3 4 5 6 7 8 9 10

Copy and complete this function machine and table of values for the same function.

Explain how you worked out your answer.

Input			
Output			

input → ( ) → output

8 This function machine shows only one input and one output.

20 → ( ) → 5

Write down two possible functions for this function machine. Justify your answers.

9 This is part of Marcus's homework. There are marks covering some of the numbers.

6 → ● → 12
9 → ● → ●
17 → ● → 23
● → ● → ●

a Work out the numbers that are covered by the marks.

b Is it possible to work out all the numbers? If not, what numbers could the missing numbers be? Explain your answer.

10 Percentages

> 10.1 Fractions, decimals and percentages

Exercise 10.1

Key words
fraction
percentage

Focus

1   a   List all the **percentages** less than 100 that are multiples of 10.
     b   Write each percentage in part **a** as a **fraction** in its simplest form.

2   Write these percentages as fractions, in their simplest form.
     a   72%   b   73%   c   74%   d   75%   e   76%

3   Arun says:

6% is equivalent to 0.6.

Write two statements to show that Arun is incorrect.

4   Write these in order, listing the smallest first.

     77%   0.8 $\frac{3}{4}$ 0.71 $\frac{38}{50}$ 70% $\frac{17}{25}$

Practice

5   Write these fractions as percentages.
     a $\frac{3}{5}$ b $\frac{3}{10}$ c $\frac{13}{50}$ d $\frac{23}{25}$ e $\frac{33}{50}$

10 Percentages

6 Here is a circle divided into 20 equal sectors.
  a What percentage of the circle is grey?
  b The area of the circle is 120 cm². Find the area of the grey part.

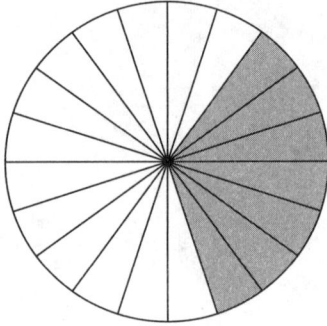

7 a Work out:
  i 30% of $240
  ii 70% of $240
  iii 5% of $240
  iv 95% of $240

  b Did you use the answer to part **a iii** to find the answer to part **a iv**?
  If not, how could you use the answer to part **a iii** to find the answer to part **a iv**?

Challenge

8 a Copy and complete this diagram.

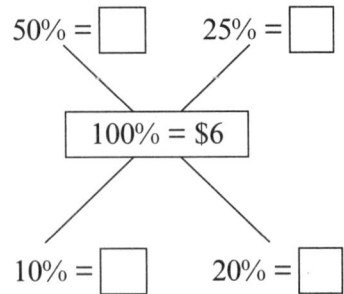

  b Add four more branches to the diagram.

9 Describe three different methods to work out 45% of 800 kg.

10 14% of 58 m = 8.12 m

  Show how to use this fact to work out:
  a 28% of 58 m
  b 7% of 58 m
  c 14% of 174 m

11 a Show that 20% of 50 is the same as 50% of 20.
  b Explain why 70% of 30 must be the same as 30% of 70.

12 Copy and complete this table. Use the pattern to fill in the last column.

Fraction	$\frac{3}{5}$	$\frac{3}{10}$	$\frac{3}{20}$	$\frac{3}{40}$	
Percentage		30%			

> 10.2 Percentages large and small

Exercise 10.2

> **Key word**
> mixed number

Focus

1. Write these percentages as fractions, in their simplest form.
   a 0.1%   b 0.2%   c 0.3%   d 0.4%   e 0.5%

2. Work out:
   a 80% of $45   b 8% of $45   c 0.8% of $45

3. a Work out 1% of 240.
   b Use your answer to part **a** to work out:
      i 0.5% of 240   ii 0.1% of 240   iii 0.2% of 240

4. Write each percentage as a fraction, in its simplest form.
   a 2.5%   b 7.5%   c 12.5%   d 17.5%

5. Work out the percentage of $200 of the following amounts.
   a $40   b $112   c $185

Practice

6. Here are some statements. Write whether each statement is possible or impossible. If the statement is impossible, give a reason why.
   a The price of an apartment increases by 120%.
   b The population of a town decreases by 120%.
   c My salary is 120% of my brother's salary.

7. Write these as decimals and as percentages.
   a $\frac{13}{10}$ b $1\frac{4}{5}$ c $\frac{107}{100}$ d $1\frac{1}{20}$ e $2\frac{3}{25}$

8. Copy and complete this table.

Percentage	20%	40%	65%	130%		
Fraction					$1\frac{3}{4}$	
Decimal						1.9

10 Percentages

9 Write these percentages as **mixed numbers**.
  a 110%   b 180%   c 135%   d 215%

10 Copy this table and add some of your own values to the empty columns.

Percentage		45%	60%	75%	90%			
Fraction			$\frac{3}{5}$	$\frac{3}{4}$				

11 There are 40 apartments in a block. 26 have been sold.
Work out the percentage that are:
  a sold   b not sold

Challenge

12 Hayley's height is 140 cm. Hayley has a sister and a brother.
  a Her sister's height is 95% of Hayley's height. Work out Hayley's sister's height.
  b Her brother's height is 115% of Hayley's height. Work out Hayley's brother's height.

13 a Write 37.5% as a fraction, in its simplest form.
  b Find 137.5% of $400.   c Find 187.5% of $400.

14 Describe two different methods to work out 140% of 60. Show that both methods give the same answer.

15 Copy this diagram. Fill in the missing numbers.

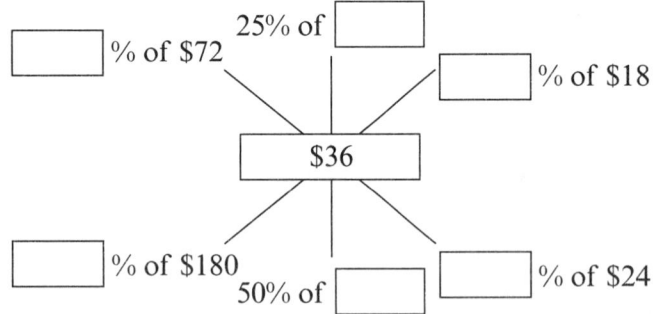

16 The price of a ticket is increased from $32 to $96.
  a What percentage of $32 is $96?
  b What is the percentage increase?

11 Graphs

> 11.1 Functions

Exercise 11.1

> **Key words**
> function
> variable

Focus

1. In a test Arun scored 3 marks fewer than Sofia.
   a. If Sofia scored 30 marks, how many marks did Arun score?
   b. If Sofia scored 12.5 marks, how many marks did Arun score?
   c. If Arun scored 19 marks, how many marks did Sofia score?
   d. Sofia scores x marks and Arun scores y marks.
      Copy and complete this **function**: $y = $ …………

2. The length of a rectangle is four times its width.
   a. If the width of the rectangle is 11 cm, what is its length?
   b. If the length of the rectangle is 100 cm, what is its width?
   c. The width is w cm and the length is l cm. Write down a function that gives l in terms of w.

3. The price of a train ticket is $12 more than the price of a bus ticket.
   a. Find the price of the train ticket if the price of the bus ticket is $9.
   b. The price of the bus ticket is $$b$. What is the price of the train ticket?
   c. If the price of the train ticket is $$t$, write a function for t.

4. Zara's mass is half the mass of Sofia.
   a. Together, Zara and Sofia have a mass of more than 20 kg. Give an example of the possible masses of Zara and Sofia.
   b. Sofia is x kg and Zara is y kg. Write a formula for y in terms of x.

11 Graphs

Practice

5   Marcus and Zara walk to school. Marcus takes 10 minutes longer than Zara.

  a Copy and complete this table of possible times.

Zara (minutes)	10	15	23		
Marcus (minutes)				17	41

  b Zara takes x minutes and Marcus takes y minutes. Write a function for y in terms of x.

6   Zara has two plates. The diameter of one plate is 1.5 times the diameter of the other plate.

  a If the diameter of the small plate is 15 cm, work out the diameter of the large plate.
  b Copy and complete this table of possible diameters.

Small plate (x cm)	15	16	17	18		
Large plate (y cm)					30	31.5

  c Write a function connecting x and y.

 7   All the sides of this pentagon are the same length.
  a If the length of each side is 7 cm, work out the perimeter.
  b If the perimeter is 120 cm, work out the length of each side.
  c If the perimeter is x cm and the length of each side is y cm, which of these functions (**A** to **D**) is correct?

  A $y = 5x$ B $y = 0.2x$
  C $y = x \div 5$ D $y = x + 5$

8   The length of this rectangle is twice its width.
  a If the width is 5 cm, work out the: i length   ii perimeter
  b If the width is 6.5 cm, work out the: i length   ii perimeter
  c If the width is w cm and the length is l cm, work out a function for l in terms of w.
  d If the width is w cm and the perimeter is p cm, work out a function for p in terms of w.

11.1 Functions

9   Fadi buys a book online. The postage is $6.
    a   Copy and complete this table to show the total cost for five books of different prices.

Price of book ($)					
Total including postage ($)					

    b   If the total cost, including postage, is $17.95, work out the price of the book.
    c   If the book costs $x and the total cost is $y, which of these functions (**A** to **E**) is correct?
        A $y=6x$ **B** $y=6+x$ **C** $y=x\div 6$ **D** $y=x+6$ **E** $y=x-6$

Challenge

10 Twenty books cost $340.
    a   Work out the cost of 10 books.
    b   Work out a function for the cost, c, in dollars, of n books.
    c   Use your function to find the cost of 36 books.
    d   How many books can you buy for $1000?

11 At an airport, a price is shown in two currencies:
    a   Work out a similar price ticket that shows these two currencies for an item that costs 10 dollars.
    b   Work out a formula that you can use to convert dollars to crowns. Explain the **variables** you use.

    20 dollars
    270 crowns

12 The mass of 100 A5 sheets of paper is 250 g.
    a   Work out the mass of 10 A5 sheets of paper.
    b   Work out a function to the find the mass (y kg) of n A5 sheets of paper.
    c   An A3 sheet of paper is four times the area of an A5 sheet of paper. Work out a function for the mass (z kg) of n A3 sheets of paper.

    > **Tip**
    > Paper is sold in different sizes: A3, A4, A5, and so on.

13 The cost of 40 litres of petrol is $120.
    a   Work out the cost of:
        i   20 litres   ii   10 litres   iii   1 litre
    b   Write a formula for the cost (c), in dollars, of x litres of petrol.
    c   Use your formula to work out the cost of 33.5 litres of petrol.

11 Graphs

> 11.2 Graphs of functions

Exercise 11.2

Key words
- axes
- coordinates
- graph

Focus

1. **a** Copy and complete this table of values.

x	−4	−2	0	2	4	6
x + 3				5		

   b Use the table from part **a** to draw a **graph** of $y = x + 3$.

   c The following points are on the line. Copy and complete the missing **coordinates**.

   i (3, ☐)   **ii** (8, ☐)   **iii** (−3, ☐)   **iv** (−9, ☐)

2. The equation of a line is $y = x + 1$.

   a Copy and complete this table of values.

x	−3	−2	−1	0	1	2	3	4
x + 1					2		4	

   b Use the table to draw a graph of $y = x + 1$.

   c Which of the following points are on the line?

   (6, 7)   (−6, −7)   (10, 9)   (−10, −9)   (−0.5, 0.5)

3. **a** Copy and complete this table of values.

x	−4	−2	0	2	4
1.5x	−6				

   b Draw a graph of the line $y = 1.5x$.

   c The point (8, ☐) is on the line. Work out the missing coordinate.

   d The point (☐, −15) is on the line. Work out the missing coordinate.

Practice

4. **a** Create a table of values for points on the line $y = x + 7$. Choose x values between −4 and 4.

   b Use your table from part **a** to draw a graph of $y = x + 7$.

   c If you extend your graph, where will it cross the x-axis?

   d Find the point where the line crosses the line $y = −7$.

5   a   Copy and complete this table of values.

x	−6	−3	0	3	6
x − 5		−8			

   b   Use the table from part **a** to draw a graph of the line $y = x − 5$.
   c   On the same **axes** draw the line $y = x + 5$.

6   a   One kilogram of fruit costs $12.
       Copy and complete this table of values.

Mass (kg)	1	2	3	4	5	6
Cost ($)						

   b   Use the table from part **a** to draw a graph.
   c   Copy and complete this name for the line: $y = $ ....
   d   Work out the cost of: i   2.5 kg of fruit   ii   9 kg of fruit

7   Most countries measure distances in kilometres.
    Some countries, such as the USA, use miles.
    This graph shows how to change miles
    to kilometres.

   a   Use the graph to copy and complete this
       table of values.

Miles	10	20	30	40	50
Kilometres		32			80

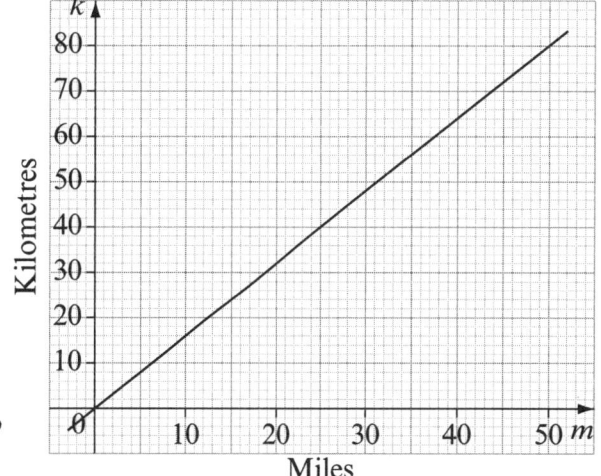

   b   How many miles are the same as 40 km?
   c   How many kilometres are the same as 1 mile?
   d m miles is the same as k kilometres. Write a
       function to show the connection between m and k.

Challenge

8   You can exchange 100 dollars for 250 riyals.
   a   Draw a graph to help convert from dollars to riyals.
   b   How many riyals can you get in exchange for 40 dollars?
   c   Copy and complete this table of values.

Dollars (d)	20	40	60	80	100
Riyals (r)					250

   d   Find a function to change from dollars to riyals.

11 Graphs

9 a Describe the graph of $y = x + 20$.
   b A graph is $y = x + a$, where a is a positive number. Where does the graph cross the coordinate axes?
   c The point $(5, k)$ is on the line $y = x - 12$. Work out the value of k.

10 a Draw the straight line that passes through $(0, 0)$, $(3, 6)$ and $(-2, -4)$.
   b Work out the name of the line.
   c On the same axes draw the line that passes through $(0, 0)$, $(3, 7.5)$ and $(-2, -5)$.
   d Work out the name of the second line.

> 11.3 Lines parallel to the axes

Exercise 11.3

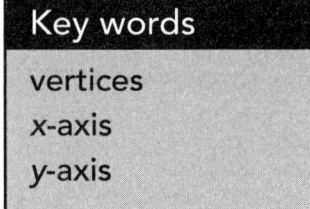

Focus

1 Three **vertices** of a square are $(2, 3)$, $(2, -3)$ and $(-4, -3)$.
   a Draw the square.
   b Write the coordinates of the other vertex.
   c Find the coordinates of the centre of the square.
   d One side of the square is on the line $x = 2$. Write a line for each of the other three sides.

2 Here are two sides of rectangle $ABCD$.
   a Draw the rectangle and find the coordinates of D.
   b Work out the coordinates of the centre of BC.
   c Work out the coordinates of the centre of the rectangle.
   d Work out the equation of the straight line through C that is parallel to the **x-axis**.
   e Work out the equation of the straight line through C that is parallel to the **y-axis**.

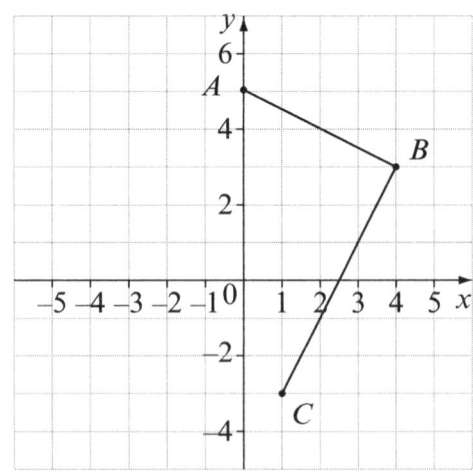

3   The lines $x = -5$ and $y = 4$ divide this grid into four regions: A, B, C and D.

    In which region is each of these points?
    a   (5, 5)   b   (10, −10)
    c   (−7, 2)   d   (−10, 10)
    e   (25, 3)

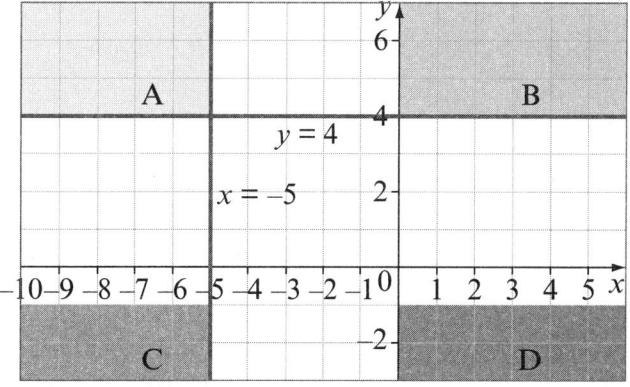

Practice

4   Point A has coordinates (2, 6), point B has coordinates (−4, 6) and point C has coordinates (−4, −4).
    a   Draw the triangle ABC.
    b   Write the equation of the line through A and B.
    c   Write the equation of the line through B and C.
    d   Find the equation of the line through (−1, 6) that is perpendicular to AB.
    e   Find the equation of the line through (−4, 1) that is perpendicular to BC.

5   EFG is a triangle. E is (5, 2) and F is (1, −4) and $x = 1$ is a line of symmetry.
    a   Work out the coordinates of G.
    b   Work out the name of the line through G and E.

6   Here are four lines: $x = -2.8$ $y = 5.3$ $x = -4.5$ $y = -0.7$
    Write the coordinates of the points where the lines meet.

Challenge

7   The lines $x = 6$, $x = -12$, $y = 10$ and $y = 3$ make a rectangle. Work out the lengths of the sides of the rectangle.

8   a   A line is perpendicular to $x = -4$ and passes through (0, 6). Find the equation of the line.
    b   A line is parallel to $y = -2$ and passes through (5, 3). Find the equation of the line.

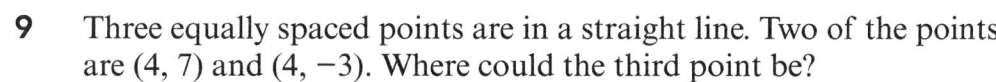

9   Three equally spaced points are in a straight line. Two of the points are (4, 7) and (4, −3). Where could the third point be?

10 The lines $y = x$, $x = -2$ and $y = 6$ enclose a triangle. Find the coordinates of the vertices.

11 Graphs

11 The four lines $x = 0$, $x = -4$, $y = x + 1$ and $y = x + 4$ enclose a shape.
   a   What is the name of the shape?
   b   Find the coordinates of the vertices of the shape.

12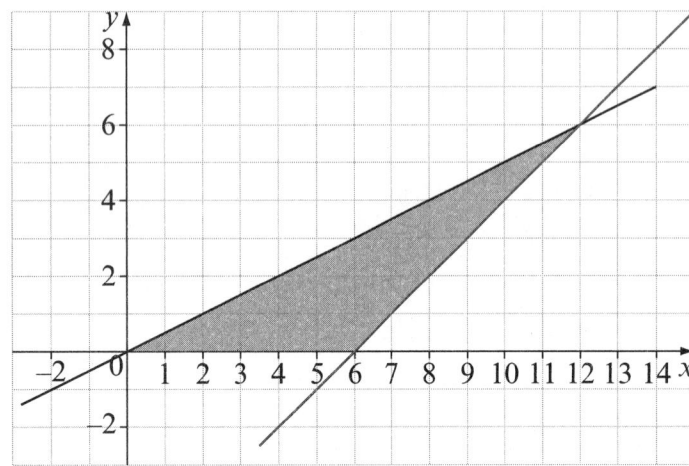

The triangle is enclosed by three lines.
Work out the equation of each line.

> 11.4 Interpreting graphs

Exercise 11.4

Key word
rate

Focus

1 This is a graph of distance against time for Erica as she runs.

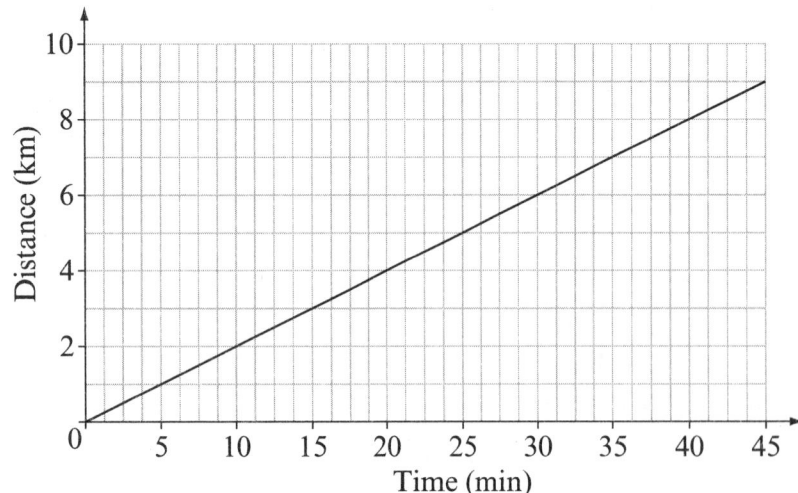

a How far does Erica run in 10 minutes?
b How long does Erica take to run 6 km?
c Use the graph to copy and complete this table of values.

Time (min)	5	10	15	20	25
Distance (km)					

d The graph is a straight line. What does that tell you about Erica's speed?
e How far will Erica run in 1 hour if she continues at the same speed?
f A marathon is 42 km. How long will it take Erica to run a marathon at this speed?

2 Bilal is reading a book. The graph shows how fast he is reading.
   a How many pages does he read in 4 hours?
   b How long does he take to read 100 pages?
   c What is his **rate** of reading, in pages per hour?
   d The book has 240 pages. How long will it take Bilal to read the book?
   e Choose the correct word for the gradient.
      positive   negative   zero

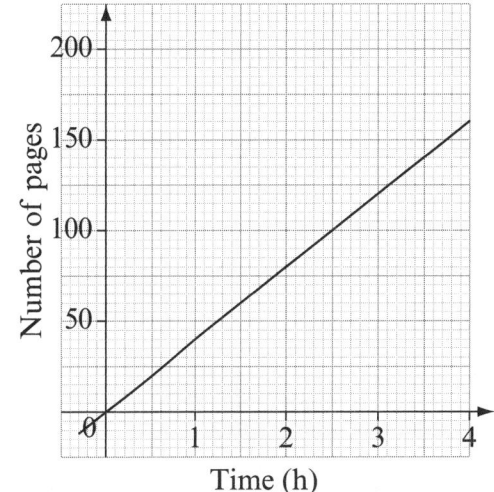

3 Zara is walking home from school. The graph shows her the distance from her home.
   a How far from home is she after 15 minutes?
   b How far is it from Zara's school to her home?
   c How does the graph show that she is walking at a constant speed?
   d Which word describes the gradient?
      positive   negative   zero

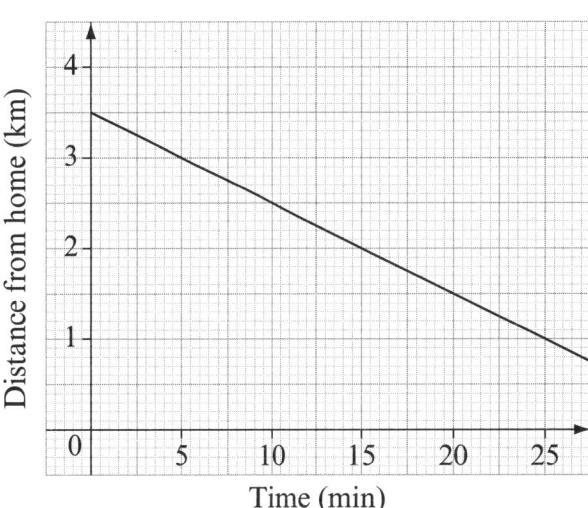

e Copy and complete this table of values.

Time (min)	0	5	10	15	20
Distance from home (km)		3			

f If Zara continues to walk at the same rate, how long will it take her to walk home from school?

Practice

4 This graph shows the cost of a long-distance phone call.

a Find the cost of a call that lasts 8 minutes.

b A call costs $4. How long does the call last?

c Describe in words how the cost of a call is calculated.

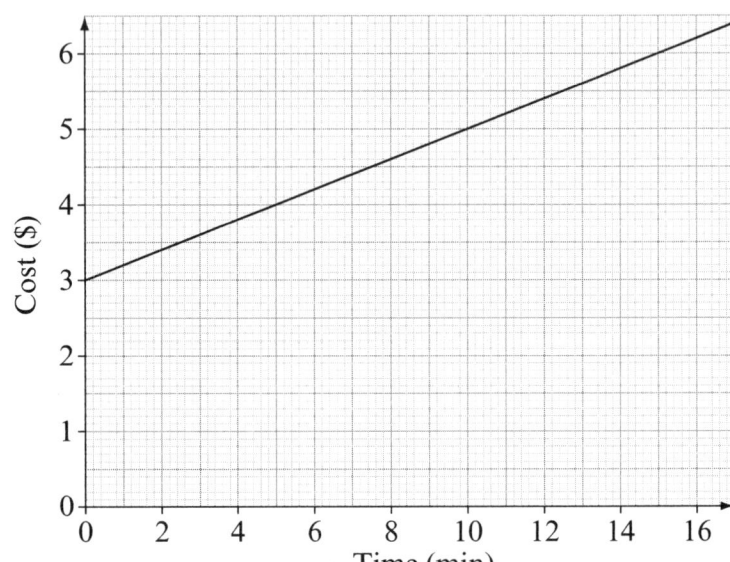

d Marcus says:

A 10 minute call costs $5 so a 20 minute call costs twice as much, which is $10.

Explain why Marcus is incorrect. Can you write a better explanation of the cost?

5 The graph shows how the charge on the battery of an electronic device decreases as the device is being used.

a What is the initial charge?

b Copy and complete this table.

Time (h)	0	1	2	3	4
Charge (%)			60		

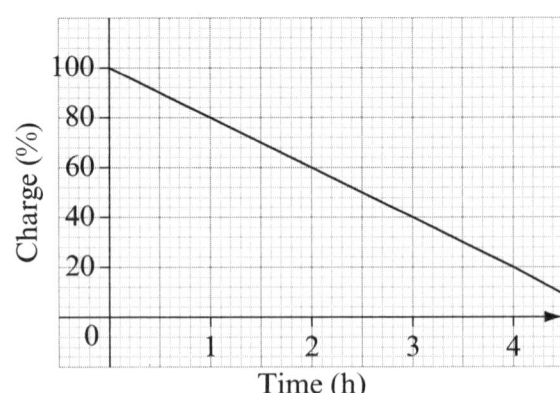

c If the charge continues to decrease at the same rate, when will the battery have no charge?
d What is the rate at which the charge is decreasing, in percentage points per hour?
e Suppose the initial charge was only 70%. Draw a graph to show how the charge changes in this case.

6 A cable car takes passengers to the top of a hill. The graph shows the height of the cable car above sea level.

a What is the height of the starting point above sea level?
b How long does it take the cable car to reach the top?
c How fast does the cable car climb, in metres per minute?
d Draw a graph to show the journey when the cable car travels twice as fast.

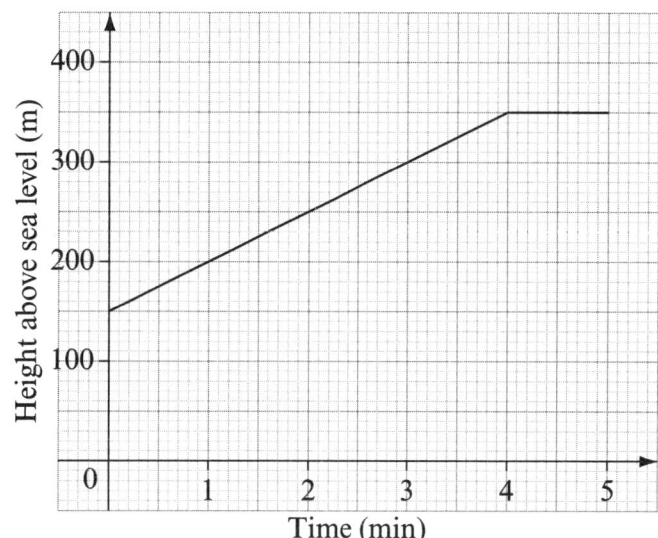

Challenge

7 This graph shows how the temperature of a liquid is changing.

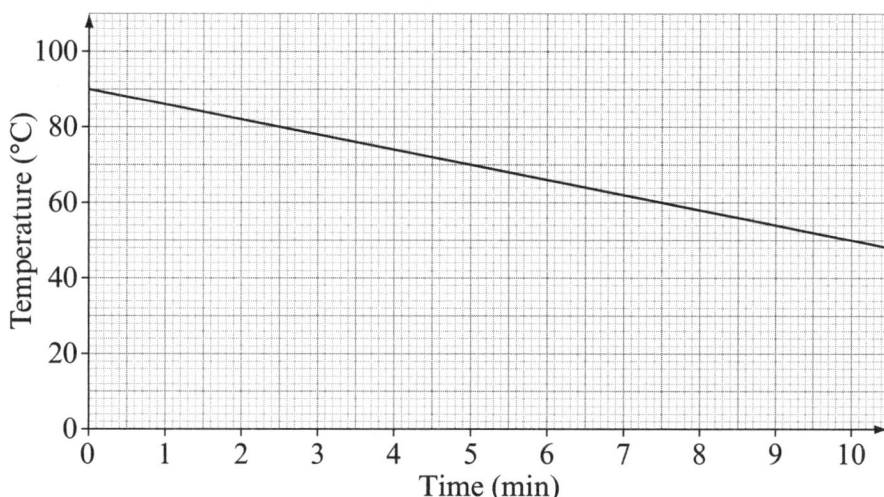

a What does the shape of the graph tell you?
b What is the initial temperature?
c What is the temperature after 5 minutes?
d How many degrees does the temperature change each minute?
e How long will it take for the temperature to reach 30 °C? What assumption did you make to answer this question?

11 Graphs

8 A tap is slowly filling a barrel with water. This graph shows the depth of water in the barrel.

  a What is the initial depth?

  b How long does it take for the depth to be 3 metres?

  c How much does the depth change each minute?

  d What would the graph look like if the water flowed into the tank twice as quickly?

  e Zara says:

  "If the water flowed into the tank twice as quickly, the depth would be 3 metres in 12 minutes."

  Is Zara's statement true or false? Give evidence to justify your answer.

9 This graph shows how the speed of a car changes during 70 seconds.

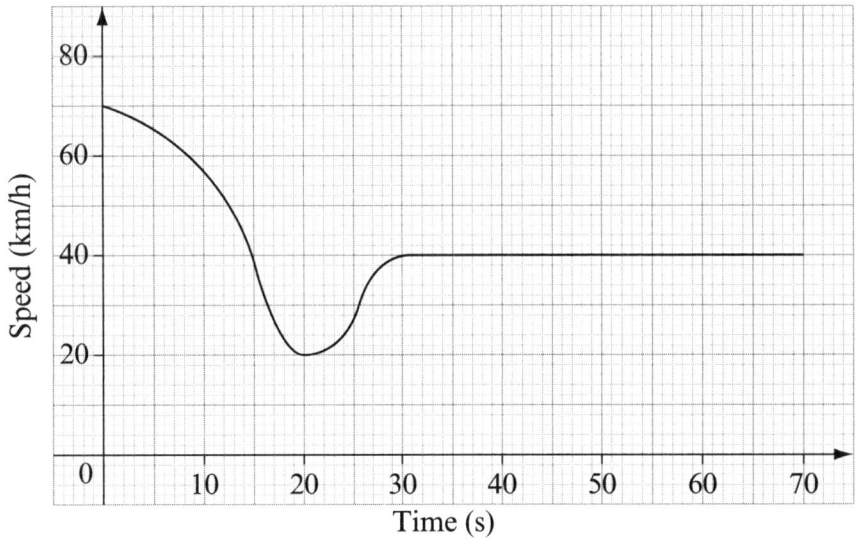

  a Describe how the speed changes.

  b When is the speed changing at the fastest rate?

  c Describe when the gradient is:

   i positive   **ii** negative   **iii** zero

10 The diagram shows a vase.

The vase is filled with water at a constant rate.

Sketch a graph to show how the depth of water in the vase changes with time.

12 Ratio and proportion

> 12.1 Simplifying ratios

A **ratio** compares one amount to another.
In this diagram, there are two black squares and three white squares.

■■□□□

The ratio of black squares : white squares is 2 : 3
The ratio of white squares : black squares is 3 : 2

In this diagram, there are two black squares and six white squares.

■■□□□□□□

The ratio of black squares : white squares is 2 : 6.

You can redraw the diagram like this:

■□□□ ■□□□

You can see that for every black square there are three white squares, so the ratio 2 : 6 is the same as the ratio 1 : 3.
You say that the ratio 2 : 6 in its **simplest form** is 1 : 3.

> **Key words**
>
> proportion
> ratio
> simplest form

> **Tip**
>
> For every two black squares there are three white squares.

> **Tip**
>
> For every two black squares there are six white squares.

Exercise 12.1

Focus

1 Look at this diagram.

   ■□□

   a Write the number of black squares.
   b Write the number of white squares.

12 Ratio and proportion

    c   Write the ratio of black squares : white squares.

    d   Write the ratio of white squares : black squares.

2   Copy and complete the workings to find the ratio of black squares : white squares in this diagram.

> **Tip**
>
> You can redraw the diagram like this:

There are two black squares and …… white squares.

The ratio of black squares : white squares is 2 : ☐, which simplifies to 1 : ☐.

3   Copy and complete the workings to find the ratio of black squares : white squares in this diagram.

There are two black squares and …… white squares.

The ratio of black squares : white squares is 2 : ☐, which simplifies to 1 : ☐.

> **Tip**
>
> You can redraw the diagram like this:

4   Copy and complete the workings to find the ratio of black squares : white squares in this diagram.

There are …… black squares and …… white squares.

The ratio of black squares : white squares is ☐ : ☐, which simplifies to 2 : ☐.

> **Tip**
>
> You can redraw the diagram like this:

Practice

5 For each of these necklaces, write down the ratio of white beads to black beads. Give each ratio in its simplest form.

a 　　b 　　c 　　d

6 For each of the following, choose **A**, **B** or **C** as the correct answer.
- **a** 2 : 8 written in its simplest form is: **A** 1 : 6　**B** 1 : 4　**C** 1 : 2
- **b** 5 : 15 written in its simplest form is: **A** 1 : 10　**B** 1 : 5　**C** 1 : 3
- **c** 24 : 4 written in its simplest form is: **A** 12 : 2　**B** 1 : 6　**C** 6 : 1
- **d** 18 : 9 written in its simplest form is: **A** 2 : 1　**B** 9 : 1　**C** 1 : 2

7 Write each of these ratios in its simplest form.
- **a** 2 : 4
- **b** 2 : 20
- **c** 3 : 9
- **d** 3 km : 21 km
- **e** 4 L : 16 L
- **f** 4 m : 20 m
- **g** 24 : 4
- **h** 60 : 10
- **i** 60 : 3
- **j** 21 kg : 7 kg
- **k** 40 t : 8 t
- **l** 64 cm : 8 cm

8 Write each of these ratios in its simplest form.
- **a** 4 : 18
- **b** 4 : 30
- **c** 16 : 18
- **d** 6 h : 15 h
- **e** 8 m : 18 m
- **f** 8 °C : 30 °C
- **g** 15 : 12
- **h** 32 : 12
- **i** 55 : 10
- **j** 16 days : 10 days
- **k** 24 mL : 15 mL
- **l** 21 mm : 6 mm

9 Look at this number sequence:　　50, 45, ☐, 35, 30, ☐, 20, 15

Two of the numbers are missing.

Write the ratio of the first missing number : the second missing number, in its simplest form.

10 Greg sees this recipe for Irish soda bread. He says, 'The ratio of white flour to porridge oats is 2 : 5.'

> **Irish soda bread**
> 250 g white flour　　1 tsp salt
> 250 g wholemeal flour　1 tsp soda
> 100 g porridge oats　　25 g butter
> 500 mL buttermilk

- **a** Explain the mistake that Greg has made.
- **b** Copy and complete this statement correctly for Greg:
  The ratio of .... to .... is ....

12 Ratio and proportion

11 Katrina makes a model of a house. The house is 550 cm tall. Her model is 66 cm tall.

Write the ratio of the height of the house to the height of the model, in its simplest form.

12 Azul makes a drink by mixing mango juice with water in the ratio 3 : 4.

Belen makes a drink by mixing mango juice with water in the ratio 2 : 3.

Who has the drink with the higher **proportion** of mango juice?

Explain how you worked out your answer.

> **Tip**
>
> The drink with the higher proportion of mango juice is the drink that has more mango juice.

Challenge

13 a At a Harare swimming club, there are 35 girls and 25 boys. Write the ratio of girls : boys, in its simplest form.

b In a Bulawayo swimming club, there are 22 girls and 14 boys. Write the ratio of girls : boys, in its simplest form.

c Which swimming club has the greatest proportion of girls? Explain how you worked out your answer.

d Five girls and five boys join the Harare swimming club. Two girls and seven boys join the Bulawayo swimming club.

Which swimming club now has the greatest proportion of girls?

14 Write each of these ratios in its simplest form. The first one has been done for you.

a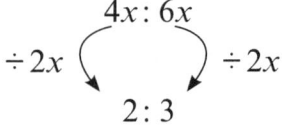

b $12y : 15y$

c $30k : 65k$

d $14n : 63n$

15 You can write a ratio with more than two numbers in its simplest form, like this.

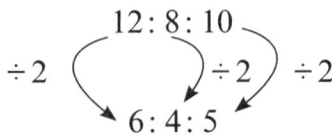

Write each of these ratios in its simplest form.

a 15 : 10 : 20   b 6 : 9 : 12   c 20 : 8 : 32   d 60 : 96 : 48

16 Sarelia makes bread using 800 g of flour. She uses 300 g of rye flour, 150 g of gram flour and the rest is white flour.

Write down the ratio of rye : gram : white flour, in its simplest form.

17 The bar chart shows the number of red, green and blue T-shirts sold in a shop in one week. Write the ratio of red T-shirts : green T-shirts : blue T-shirts sold, in its simplest form.

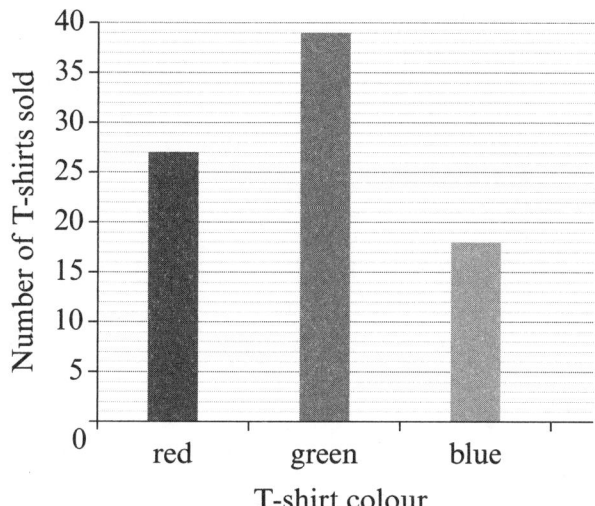

> 12.2 Sharing in a ratio

Key words
conjecture
divide
share

This diagram shows how you can **share** an amount in a ratio.

Absko and Barasa share six sweets in the ratio 1 : 2.

For every one sweet Absko gets, Barasa gets two sweets.

So, in total, Absko gets two sweets and Barasa gets four sweets.

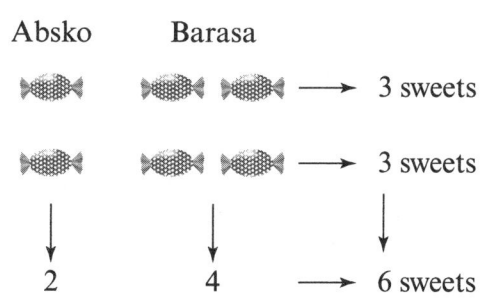

This is how you can share an amount in a ratio, without drawing a diagram.

Carla and Mitch share $48 in the ratio 1 : 3.

Carla gets one part of the money and Mitch gets three parts, so the total number of parts is 1 + 3 = 4.

Value of one part is $48 ÷ 4 = $12.

Carla gets 1 × $12 = $12.

Mitch gets 3 × $12 = $36.

Check: $12 + $36 = $48 ✓

Tip
To find the value of one part, you **divide** the amount to be shared by the total number of parts.

12 Ratio and proportion

Exercise 12.2

Focus

1. Tudza and Pepi share 12 sweets in the ratio 1 : 3. How many sweets do they each get?

   Use the diagram to help you.

2. Sassi and Mimi share 15 sweets in the ratio 2 : 3. How many sweets do they each get?
   Use the diagram to help you.

3. Copy and complete the working to share $48 between Nigel and Pamela in the ratio 1 : 2.

   Total number of parts is 1 + 2 = ☐

   Value of one part is $48 ÷ 3 = ☐

   Nigel gets 1 × ☐ = ☐

   Pamela gets 2 × ☐ = ☐

4. Copy and complete the working to share $45 between Ben and Kir in the ratio 4 : 1.

   Total number of parts is 1 + 4 = ☐

   Value of one part is $45 ÷ ☐ = ☐

   Ben gets 4 × ☐ = ☐

   Kir gets 1 × ☐ = ☐

5. Copy and complete the working to share $60 between Danai and Maita in the ratio 2 : 3.

   Total number of parts is 2 + 3 = ☐

   Value of one part is $60 ÷ ☐ = ☐

   Danai gets 2 × ☐ = ☐

   Maita gets 3 × ☐ = ☐

Practice

6. Share these amounts between Migina and Tadi in the ratios given.

   a $24 in the ratio 1 : 3
   b $45 in the ratio 1 : 4
   c $49 in the ratio 1 : 6
   d $32 in the ratio 3 : 1
   e $36 in the ratio 5 : 1
   f $32 in the ratio 7 : 1

7   Share these amounts between Yakecan and Nantan in the ratios given.
    a $55 in the ratio 2 : 3
    b $49 in the ratio 3 : 4
    c $64 in the ratio 3 : 5
    d $28 in the ratio 5 : 2
    e $48 in the ratio 7 : 5
    f $28 in the ratio 11 : 3

8   A box of fruit contains oranges and apples in the ratio 4 : 3. The box contains 35 pieces of fruit.
    a   How many oranges are there in the box?
    b   What fraction of the fruit in the box are oranges?

9   A factory makes orange paint by mixing red paint and yellow paint in the ratio 7 : 2. The factory makes 2700 litres of orange paint every day.
    a   How many litres of yellow paint does the factory use every day?
    b   What fraction of the orange paint is:
        i   red paint?
        ii yellow paint?

10 Cheng and Amira buy an apartment for $36 000. Cheng pays $12 000 and Amira pays the rest.
    a   Write the ratio of the amount they each pay, in its simplest form.
    b   Two years later they sell the apartment for $42 000. How much money should Amira get?

Challenge

11 There are two types of fish in a lake. The two types are carp and pike. In a netted area of the lake 120 carp and 16 pike are caught. In the whole lake it is estimated that there are 34 000 fish.

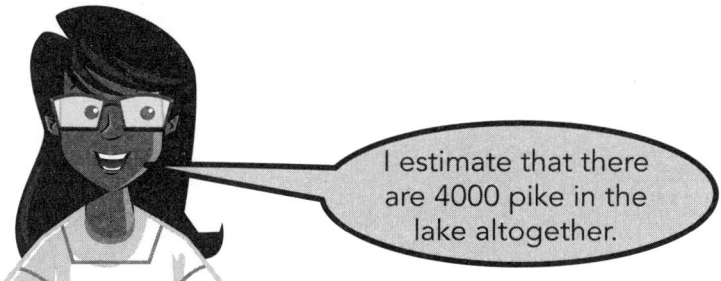

I estimate that there are 4000 pike in the lake altogether.

Show how Zara has worked out this estimate.

12 Ratio and proportion

 12 Estela and Luiza are going to share 35 dolls <u>either</u> in the ratio of their ages <u>or</u> in the ratio of the number of dolls they have already.

Estela is 9 years old and already has 24 dolls. Luiza is 12 years old and already has 36 dolls.

    a Without working out the answer, **conjecture** which ratio, age <u>or</u> dolls they have already, do you think will be better for Estela? Explain your decision.

    b Work out whether your decision is correct.

 13 Arun has 72 coins. He has 5-cent and 10-cent coins in the ratio 5 : 3.

Is Arun correct? Explain your answer. Show your working.

14 Feng spends $\frac{1}{2}$ of his wages on rent. He keeps $\frac{1}{3}$ of what is left.

He shares the rest of his wages between his mother and his brother in the ratio 5 : 4.

Feng earns $648 each month. How much does he give his brother in one year?

15 Purple gold is made from two metals, gold and aluminium, in the ratio 4 : 1.

A purple gold necklace weighs 20 g. If 1 g of gold costs $41.40 and 1 g of aluminium costs $4.25, what is the total value of the metals in the necklace?

> 12.3 Using direct proportion

One bag of chips costs $1.20.
Two bags of chips cost $2.40.
Three bags of chips cost $3.60.
The number of bags of chips and the cost are said to be in **direct proportion**.

You can use direct proportion to solve problems like this:

The mass of two water bottles is 600 g. What is the mass of five water bottles?

The mass of two bottles is 600 g.
The mass of one bottle is $600 \div 2 = 300$ g.
The mass of five bottles is $300 \times 5 = 1500$ g.

Key words
direct proportion
unitary method

Tip

As the number of bags of chips increases, the total cost increases in the same proportion.

Tip

Find the mass of one item first, then find the mass of the number of items needed.

Exercise 12.3

Focus

1 Copy and complete the following.

One shirt costs $30.　　　　　Four shirts cost: ☐ × 30 = $☐
Two shirts cost: 2 × 30 = $☐　Ten shirts cost: ☐ × 30 = $☐
Three shirts cost: 3 × 30 = $☐

2 Copy and complete the following.

One chair weighs 8 kg.　　　　Five chairs weigh: ☐ × ☐ = ☐ kg
Two chairs weigh: 2 × 8 = ☐ kg　Eight chairs weigh: ☐ × ☐ = ☐ kg
Three chairs weigh: ☐ × ☐ = ☐ kg

3 Copy and complete the following.

Two drinks cost $3. How much do seven drinks cost?
Two drinks cost $3
One drink costs $3 \div 2 = \$$☐
Seven drinks cost $7 \times$ ☐ $= \$$☐

Tip

Use the **unitary method**.

$3 \div 2 = 1.5$.
In dollars, this is $1.50.

12 Ratio and proportion

4   Copy and complete the following.
    Five grapes weigh 60 g. How much do four grapes weigh?
    Five grapes weigh 60 g.
    One grapes weighs: 60 g ÷ ☐ = ☐ g
    Four grapes weigh: ☐ × ☐ = ☐ g

Practice

5   Tara goes to the gym three times a week. Work out how many times she goes to the gym in:
    a   three weeks
    b   one year

Tip
Remember that there are 52 weeks in a year.

6   Copy and complete the workings to find the mass of seven potatoes.
    The mass of four potatoes is 500 g.

    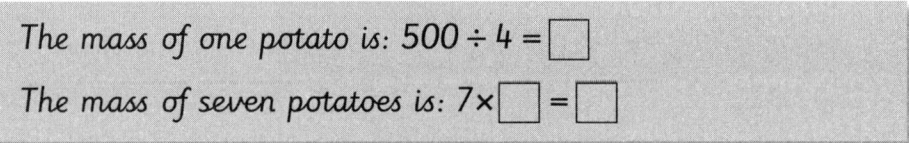

    The mass of one potato is: 500 ÷ 4 = ☐
    The mass of seven potatoes is: 7 × ☐ = ☐

7   The mass of five pieces of bacalhau is 900 g. Work out the mass of:
    a   one piece of bacalhau
    b   seven pieces of bacalhau

Tip
Bacalhau is salted cod.

8   Hank pays $22.50 for five people to go 10-pin bowling. How much does it cost for seven people to go 10-pin bowling?

9   A recipe uses 400 g of onion for five people. How many grams of onion is needed for three people?

10 Melissa is paid $56 for 8 hours of work. How much does she earn when she works for:
    a   4 hours?
    b   12 hours?

11 A money exchange shop exchanges £100 for €166. How many euros does it exchange for:
    a   £50?
    b   £250?

Challenge

12 This is part of Eduardo's homework.

> Question: A recipe for four people uses 280 g of potatoes.
>
> How much potato does the recipe need for 10 people?
>
> Solution: The recipe is for four people: 4 + 6 = 10
>
> Four people need 280 g of potatoes.
>
> Two people need: 280 g ÷ 2 = 140 g potatoes
>
> 4 + 2 = 6, so 280 + 140 = 420 g
>
> Altogether, the recipe needs 420 g of potato.

Explain Eduardo's mistake and write the correct solution.

13 A carpenter buys 40 identical pieces of wood. The total value of the wood is $300.

The carpenter makes a mistake in his measuring, so he then buys eight extra pieces of wood. He works out that the total value of the wood is now $375.

Is he correct? Explain your answer.

If the carpenter is not correct, what mistake do you think he has made?

14 A shop has bags of chips on offer.

Offer 1	Offer 2	Offer 3
3 bags for 85 cents	7 bags for $1.75	15 bags for $3.99

Which offer is the best value for money? Explain your answer.

15 A businessman buys 3 tonnes of rice for $3600.
He sells the rice for $1.60 per kg. How much profit does he make per kilogram?

16 A washing machine is made from plastic and metal.
The ratio of plastic to metal is 4 : 5.

The mass of five washing machines is 360 kg. What is the mass of metal in eight washing machines?

13 Probability

> 13.1 The probability scale

Exercise 13.1

Key words
- event
- even chance
- likely
- likelihood
- probability
- unlikely

Focus

1. **a** Write three **events** that are very **unlikely** to happen.
   b Write two events that are **likely** to happen.

2. Suppose you spin three coins at the same time. Describe the **likelihood** of getting:
   a three heads
   b at least one head
   c three tails or fewer

3. Look at these events on this **probability** scale.

   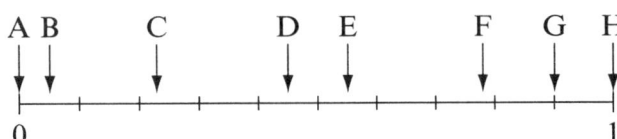

   Which event is best described as:
   a impossible?
   b very likely?
   c a little bit less than an **even chance**?

4. Match each probability (**a** to **e**) to a description (**i** to **vii**).

a	0.7		**i**	even chance
b	$\frac{8}{15}$		**ii**	impossible
c	4%		**iii**	very unlikely
d	$\frac{247}{250}$		**iv**	certain
e	50%		**v**	likely
			vi	more likely than not
			vii	extremely likely

5 Put these probabilities in order, with the smallest first.

$\frac{5}{8}$ 60% 0.9 46.7% $\frac{17}{20}$

Practice

6 Here is the probability scale from Question **3**.

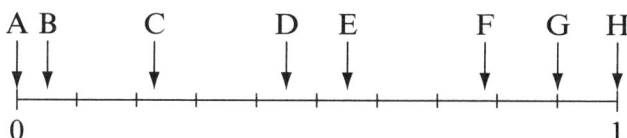

Which event has a probability of:

a about 23%?   b just over $\frac{3}{4}$?   c 0.55?

7 The probability of rain tomorrow is 30%.

a The likelihood of sunshine is half the likelihood of rain. What is the probability of sunshine?

b The likelihood of strong winds is twice the likelihood of rain. Show that strong winds have a more than even chance.

8 Show these events on a probability scale.

A The probability the team will win is $\frac{2}{3}$.

B The probability the train will be late is 15%.

C Hasini will definitely be late.

D The chance I will win the game is 0.2.

9 Here are some probabilities when you spin a coin three times. Mark the probabilities on a probability scale.

A: Getting three heads $\frac{1}{8}$

B: Not getting three heads $\frac{7}{8}$

C: Getting two or three heads even chance

Challenge

10 Arun says:

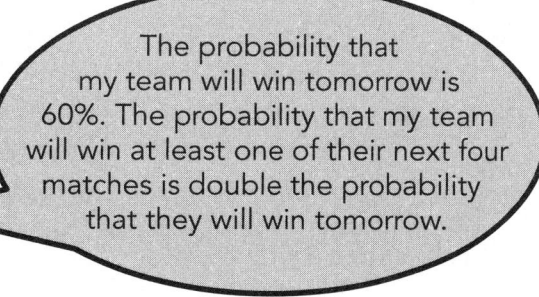

The probability that my team will win tomorrow is 60%. The probability that my team will win at least one of their next four matches is double the probability that they will win tomorrow.

Arun must be incorrect. Explain why.

13 Probability

11 Marcus' sister is taking a driving test. He says:

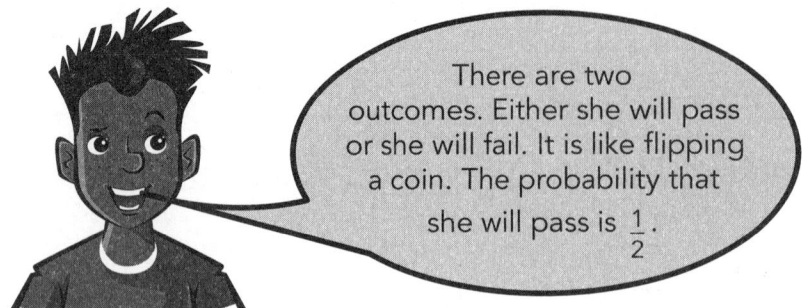

There are two outcomes. Either she will pass or she will fail. It is like flipping a coin. The probability that she will pass is $\frac{1}{2}$.

Do you agree with Marcus? If not, how would you convince him that he is incorrect?

12 a The probability that a train will be late is 10%. What is the probability that the train will not be late?

   b The probability that a basketball team will win a game is 60%. What can you say about the probability that the team will lose?

> 13.2 Mutually exclusive outcomes

Exercise 13.2

Key words

mutually exclusive outcome

Focus

1 Five cards have letters on them, as shown.

X   Y   X   Y   X

A card is taken without looking. Find the probability that the letter is:

a X   b Y   c Z

2 Here is a spinner with seven equal sectors.

Work out the probability that the spinner lands on:

a 2
b a number that is more than 2
c an even number
d an odd number
e a number that is less than 10
f a prime number

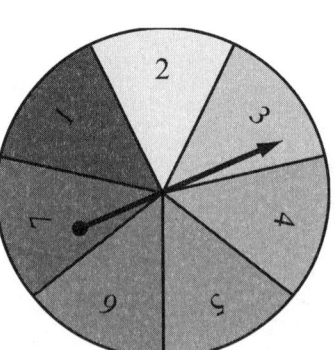

3   Look at the spinner in Question **2**. Describe three **mutually exclusive** outcomes that have different probabilities.

4   There are 10 balls in a bag. There are 4 red balls, 3 blue balls, 2 green balls and 1 yellow ball. A ball is taken without looking.

   a   Work out the probability that the ball taken is:
       i   blue   ii   red   iii   green
       iv yellow   v   purple
   b   Work out the probability that the ball taken is not red.
   c   The yellow ball is removed. What is the probability now for taking each of the three remaining colours?

Practice

5   Ushi throws a fair 6-sided dice.
   a   Find an **outcome** that has a probability of:
       i   50%   ii $\frac{1}{6}$ iii $\frac{5}{6}$ iv $\frac{1}{3}$ v $\frac{2}{3}$
   b   Explain why it is impossible to find an outcome with a probability of 25%.

6   A teacher has a class of 20 students. Of these students, 12 are boys.
   a   How can the teacher choose one name at random?
   b   Find the probability that the student chosen is a girl.

7   There are some coloured counters in a bag. One counter is removed without looking. The probability that the counter is red is 60%. The probability that the counter is blue is 30%.
   a   How do you know that there are other coloured counters in the bag?
   b   What can you say about the probability that the counter is green?

8   This fair dice has 20 faces, which are numbered from 1 to 20. The dice is thrown once.

   Find the probability that the outcome is:
   a   a multiple of 3   b   a multiple of 8
   c   a prime number   d   a square number
   e   a two-digit number   f   not 20
   g   not less than 5

13 Probability

Challenge

 9   Vidun has a set of lettered cards. He takes one card without looking. The probability that the letter is A is 20%. The probability that the letter is B is 30%.

  a   Work out the probability that the letter is not A or B.

  b   Explain why there must be an even number of cards in the set. Give a reason for your answer.

  c   What is the smallest possible number of cards in the set? Give a reason for your answer.

 10   Dice can have more than six faces.

Genji throws an unbiased dice with more than six faces. The faces are numbered 1, 2, 3, …

  a   The probability of an odd number is 50%. What can you say about the number of faces?

  b   The probability of a multiple of 3 is 30%. Work out the number of faces. Is there more than one answer possible?

11   A student puts each letter of her name on a separate card. She asks a friend to take one card without looking. The probability that the letter is A is 40%. The probability that the letter is S is 20%. The probability that the letter is E is zero.

What could the student's name be?

> 13.3 Experimental probabilities

Exercise 13.3

> **Key words**
>
> experimental probability
> theoretical probability
> trial

Focus

1   A gardener plants 45 seeds and 31 of the seeds grow successfully. Work out the **experimental probability** that a seed will:

  a   grow successfully   b   not grow successfully

2   A total of 378 babies are weighed when they are born. Of these, 125 babies have a mass of less than 3 kg.

Work out the experimental probability that a baby has a mass of:

  a   less than 3 kg   b   at least 3 kg

3   A call centre receives 200 calls. This table shows how long a caller must wait before speaking to a customer service officer.

Time	less than 1 minute	less than 2 minutes	less than 3 minutes	less than 4 minutes	less than 5 minutes
Frequency	21	43	110	148	200

Work out the experimental probability that a caller will wait:
a   less than 2 minutes   b   between 2 and 3 minutes   c   at least 3 minutes

Practice

4   The heights of 234 young men, aged 20 to 29 years, are measured. Here are the results.

Height	less than 165 cm	between 165 cm and 180 cm	over 180 cm
Frequency	28	160	46

Work out the experimental probability that the height of a man aged 20 to 29 years is:
a   less than 165 cm   b   180 cm or less   c   165 cm or more

5   The lights of 20 cars are tested. The car could pass (P) or fail (F).

Here are the results: PPPPP PPPPF PFPPPP PPPP
a   Work out the experimental probability that a car will:
    i   pass   ii   fail
Here are the results for another 20 cars: PPFPP FPPPP PPPPF FPPPP
b   Recalculate the probabilities in part a based on all 40 cars.
c   Why are the second experimental probabilities more reliable?

6   A woman travels to work on a bus each morning. She keeps a record for 30 days. The bus is late nine times.
a   Work out the experimental probability that the bus will be:
    i   late   ii   on time
In the next 25 days the bus is late four times.
b   Use all the results to find the experimental probability that the bus will be:
    i   late   ii   on time
c   The woman predicts that the bus will be late 24 times in the next 100 days. How did she work out this number?

13 Probability

Challenge

7 A computer simulates spinning three coins 160 times and records the number of heads. Here are the results.

Number of heads	0	1	2	3
Frequency	17	61	68	14

a Work out the experimental probability of getting:
  i three heads
  ii three tails
  iii at least two heads

A teacher says: 'The **theoretical probability** of getting three heads is $\frac{1}{8}$.'

b How does the theoretical probability compare to the experimental probability of getting three heads?

c What can you say about the theoretical and experimental probabilities for getting zero heads?

8 A computer simulates throwing two dice and adding the scores together. It does this 100 times. Here are the results.

8	10	7	8	10	9	9	5	3	7	7	7	6	7	6	5	9	10	7	8
10	7	9	5	4	7	10	4	6	4	5	7	4	12	9	10	10	6	6	5
5	7	7	3	8	6	5	9	6	10	7	6	12	5	8	9	4	6	8	11
10	5	4	6	4	8	5	7	5	4	7	5	8	5	5	8	6	8	4	10
2	3	6	2	3	6	4	10	8	7	4	8	8	6	3	7	5	7	9	10

a Work out the experimental probability of getting:
  i 7
  ii more than 7
  iii less than 7
  iv 12

b Do you think that 100 **trials** is enough to get reliable results? Give a reason for your answer.

9 A coin is spun until a head appears. The number of spins is recorded. This is repeated 100 times. The results are shown in this table.

Number of spins	1	2	3	4	5	6	7	8	9	10
Frequency	48	24	13	8	2	0	2	1	0	1

a Work out the experimental probability of:
  i getting a head on the first spin
  ii needing exactly three spins until a head appears
  iii needing more than three spins until a head appears

b Does 100 trials give a good estimate of the experimental probabilities of needing different number of spins? Explain your answer.

10 Some students are asked if they want to be engineers, lawyers or accountants. The results are shown in this table.

	Total number of students surveyed	Want to be an engineer	Want to be a lawyer	Want to be an accountant
Female	80	12	20	16
Male	120	48	21	19

Find the probability that:
a a female student wants to be an engineer
b a male student wants to be a lawyer
c a female student does not want to be an accountant

14 Position and transformation

> 14.1 Maps and plans

A **scale drawing** is a drawing that represents an object in real life.
The **scale** gives the relationship between the lengths on the drawing and the real-life lengths.
An example of a scale is:
1 cm represents 10 m.
So, 2 cm on the drawing represents 2 × 10 = 20 m in real life.
3 cm on the drawing represents 3 × 10 = 30 m in real life, etc.

Key words
scale
scale drawing

Tip
This means that 1 cm on the drawing represents 10 m in real life.

Exercise 14.1

Focus

1 Complete these workings using a scale of 1 cm represents 5 m.
   a 2 cm on the drawing represents 2 × 5 = ☐ m in real life.
   b 3 cm on the drawing represents 3 × 5 = ☐ m in real life.
   c 8 cm on the drawing represents ☐ × 5 = ☐ m in real life.

2 Complete these workings using a scale of 1 cm represents 20 cm.
   a 2 cm on the drawing represents 2 × 20 = ☐ cm in real life.
   b 3 cm on the drawing represents ☐ × 20 = ☐ cm in real life.
   c 6 cm on the drawing represents ☐ × ☐ = ☐ cm in real life.

3 Complete these workings using a scale of 1 cm represents 10 m.
   a 20 m in real life represents 20 ÷ 10 = ☐ cm on the drawing.
   b 30 m in real life represents 30 ÷ 10 = ☐ cm on the drawing.
   c 70 m in real life represents ☐ ÷ 10 = ☐ cm on the drawing.

Tip
To go from the drawing to real life, you <u>multiply</u> by the scale.

Tip
To go from real life to the drawing, you <u>divide</u> by the scale.

14.1 Maps and plans

4 Complete these workings using a scale of 1 cm represents 50 cm.

  a 100 cm in real life represents 100 ÷ 50 = ☐ cm on the drawing.

  b 150 cm in real life represents ☐ ÷ 50 = ☐ cm on the drawing.

  c 300 cm in real life represents ☐ ÷ ☐ = ☐ cm on the drawing.

5 Look at the cards shown. The white cards are scale drawing measurements. The grey cards are real-life measurements.

Match each white card (**A** to **G**) to the correct grey card (**i** to **vii**).

Scale: 1 cm represents 2 m.

The first one has been done for you: **A** and **iv**.

A	B	C	D	E	F	G
2 cm	6 cm	5 cm	2.5 cm	12 cm	3.5 cm	9.5 cm

i	ii	iii	iv	v	vi	vii
10 m	12 m	7 m	4 m	19 m	5 m	24 m

Practice

6 Zara makes a scale drawing of the front of a large building. She uses a scale of 1 cm represents 5 m.

  a On her drawing the building is 16 cm long. How long is the building in real life?

  b The building in real life is 120 m tall. How tall is the building on the scale drawing?

7 Sofia makes a scale drawing of a window. She uses a scale of 1 cm represents 20 cm.

  a On her drawing the window is 6 cm wide. How wide is the window in real life? Give your answer in metres.

  b The window in real life is 2.2 m tall. How tall is the window on the scale drawing? Give your answer in centimetres.

8 The map shows part of Spain.

The scale of the map is 1 cm represents 30 km.

  a Use a ruler to measure the distance, in cm, from Madrid to Toledo.

  b Work out the distance, in km, from Madrid to Toledo in real life.

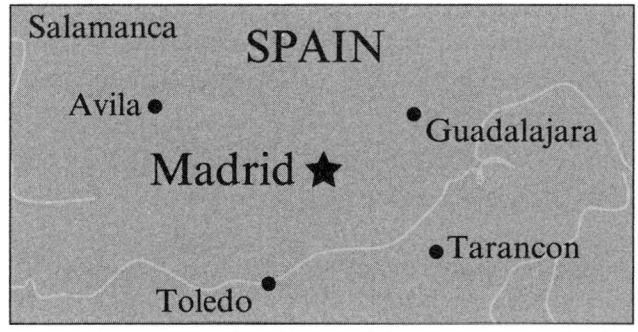

14 Position and transformation

9 Arun makes a scale drawing of his garden. He uses centimetre-squared paper. He uses a scale of 1 to 200.

  a Calculate the distance in real life of each of these lengths. Give your answers in metres.

    i   AB   ii   BC
    iii CD   iv   DE
    v   EF   vi   AF

  b The path in Arun's garden is 11 m long. How long will the path be on the scale drawing? Give your answer in centimetres.

  c The flowerbed in Arun's garden is 3 m wide. How wide will the flowerbed be on the scale drawing? Give your answer in centimetres.

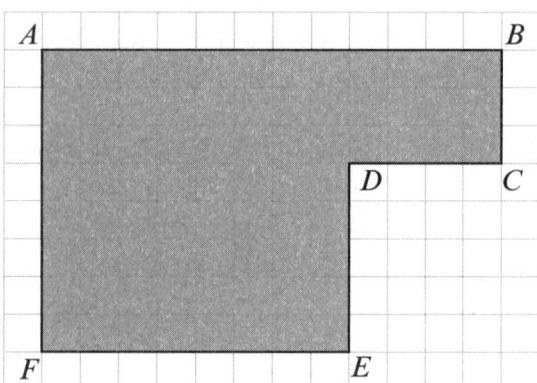

10 A map has a scale of 1 : 12 000.

  a On the map the distance between two shops is 20 cm. What is the distance, in km, between the two shops in real life?

  b The distance between two buildings is 6 km in real life. What is the distance, in cm, between the two buildings on the map?

Challenge

11 This map has a scale of 1 : 90 000.

  a Use a ruler to measure the distance, in cm, from St. Patrick to Six Cross Roads.

  b Work out the distance, in km, from St. Patrick to Six Cross Roads in real life.

  c The distance from St. Patrick to Pothouse is 10.35 km in real life. Work out how far this is, in cm, on the map.

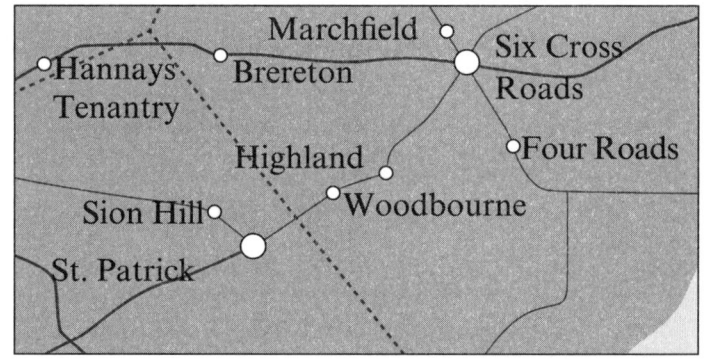

12 Rihanna takes part in a triathlon. She is given a map of the route for each part of the triathlon. Each map has a different scale.

Rihanna measures the distance of the route on each map. The table shows the distances on each map and each map's scale.

> **Tip**
>
> A triathlon is a competition in three parts. In the first part you must swim, in the second part you must cycle and in the third part you must run.

Part of triathlon	Map scale	Distance on map (cm)	Distance in reallife (km)
swim	1 : 15 000	18	
cycle	1 : 400 000	16	
run	1 : 80 000	20.5	

   a   Copy and complete the table.
   b   What is the total distance, in km, of the triathlon?

13   Sven takes part in a 56 km cycle ride. The distance of the route on a map is 32 cm.

   Work out if **A**, **B** or **C** is the correct map scale. Show your working.

   A   1 : 125 000   **B**   1 : 150 000   **C**   1 : 175 000

14   The distance from town A to town B is 18 cm on the map, and is 27 km in real life. The distance from town B to town C is 35 cm on the map.

   How far is the distance from town B to town C in real life? Show how you worked out your answer.

15   A police officer uses the length of a footprint to estimate the height of a criminal. The scale they use is 2 : 13.

   Estimate the height, in metres, of the criminals who have left these footprints. Show all your working.

   a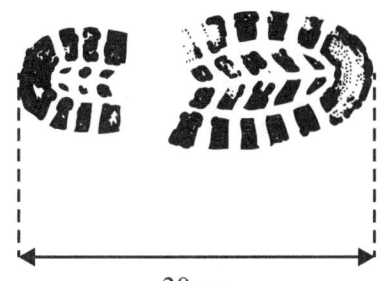
   30 cm

   b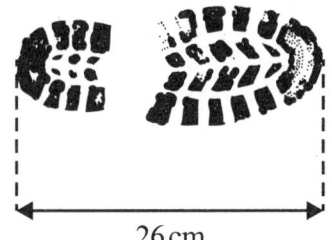
   26 cm

   c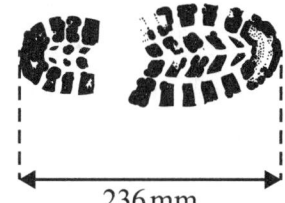
   236 mm

14 Position and transformation

> 14.2 Distance between two points

Azra uses this method to work out the **distance between the two points** (8, 4) and (3, 4).

Step 1 Write the coordinates underneath each other.   (8, 4)
                                                        (3, 4)

Step 2 Put your finger over the numbers that are the same.   (8, ▢)
                                                               (3, ▢)

Step 3 There are two numbers left, so work out biggest number − smallest number.
8 − 3 = 5 units

Key words
- distance between two points
- x-coordinate
- y-coordinate

Exercise 14.2

Focus

1   Work out the distance between these pairs of points. Use Azra's method, which is shown in the introduction. The first one has been started for you.

    a   (9, 2) and (6, 2)   (9, 2)
                               (6, 2)

    b   (12, 7) and (2, 7)   **c**   (1, 0) and (8, 0)   **d**   (12, 11) and (20, 11)

2   Work out the distance between these pairs of points. Use Azra's method, which is shown in the introduction. The first one has been started for you.

    a   (1, 5) and (1, 9)   (▢, 5)   9 − 5 = ▢ units
                                 (▢, 9)

    b   (2, 8) and (2, 3)   **c**   (9, 15) and (9, 10)   **d**   (11, 18) and (11, 28)

14.2 Distance between two points

3 Look at the cards shown. The white cards show pairs of points. The grey cards show the distances between the points.

Match each white card (**A** to **G**) to the correct grey card (**i** to **vii**). The first one has been done for you: **A** and **iii**.

A	B	C	D	E	F	G
(1, 8)	(8, 10)	(1, 5)	(13, 7)	(15, 15)	(18, 2)	(0, 27)
(1, 3)	(8, 12)	(7, 5)	(9, 7)	(15, 14)	(21, 2)	(0, 20)

i	ii	iii	iv	v	vi	vii
2 units	4 units	5 units	7 units	3 units	1 unit	6 units

Practice

4 Work out the distance between these pairs of points. Each pair of points has the same *y*-coordinate.

    a (14, 2) and (18, 2)   **b** (10, 8) and (5, 8)   **c** (2, 0) and (10, 0)

5 Work out the distance between these pairs of points. Each pair of points has the same *x*-coordinate.

    a (3, 17) and (3, 5)   **b** (18, 15) and (18, 25)   **c** (9, 19) and (9, 21)

6 Work out the distance between each pair of points. Choose the correct answer: **A**, **B** or **C**.

    a (9, 14) and (9, 23)
        A 5 units   **B** 7 units   **C** 9 units

    b (16, 4) and (0, 4)
        A 12 units   **B** 16 units   **C** 0 units

    c (3, 17) and (3, 16)
        A 1 unit   **B** 13 units   **C** 14 units

    d (8, 8) and (19, 8)
        A 12 units   **B** 0 units   **C** 11 units

7 This selection of cards show the coordinates of the points *A* to *J*.

A (14, 9)	B (17, 18)	C (21, 9)	D (17, 27)
E (14, 16)	F (26, 18)	G (14, 2)	H (8, 18)
I (7, 9)	J (17, 9)		

Classify the cards into these two groups:
Group 1: Points that are 7 units from *A*.
Group 2: Points that are 9 units from *B*.

14 Position and transformation

Challenge

8   Quadrilateral ABCD has vertices at the points A(4, 7), B(9, 7), C(9, 11) and D(4, 11).

Arun and Zara are discussing the quadrilateral.

Arun says: Zara says:

I think ABCD is a square.

I think ABCD is a rectangle.

Who is correct? Show your working and explain your answer.

9   The grey cards show pairs of points on a coordinate grid.
The white cards show the distances between two points.
Match each grey card (**A** to **D**) to its correct white card (**i** to **iv**).

A	(−9, 5) and (−4, 5)		B	(8, −3) and (8, −9)
C	(−5, −4) and (−5, −12)		D	(−3, 0) and (−10, 0)

i	6		ii	7		iii	5		iv	8

10 Work out the distance between each pair of points.
   a   (7, 4) and (7, −4)   b   (−3, 2) and (6, 2)
   c   (−8, 10) and (−8, −2)   d   (20, −1) and (−12, −1)

11 Quadrilateral EFGH has vertices at the points E(−4, 1), F(−1, 3), G(2, 1) and H(−1, −5).
   a   Work out the lengths of the diagonals:
      i   EG   ii   FH
   b   Use your answers to part **a** to explain why:
      i   EFGH is not a square   ii   EFGH is not a rectangle
   c   The diagonals EG and FH cross at the point X. Mair thinks that X has coordinates (−1, 1). Explain how you can tell, by looking at the coordinates of E, F, G and H, that Mair is correct.
   d   Work out the lengths of:
      i   EX   ii   XG   iii   FX   iv   XH
   e   Use your answers to part **d** to explain why:
      i   EFGH is not a rhombus   ii   EFGH is a kite

12 P is the point (2, 3). The distance PQ is 9 units. Work out four possible coordinates for the point Q. Show your working.

> 14.3 Translating 2D shapes

The diagram shows triangles ABC and $A'B'C'$.
$A'B'C'$ is the **image** of ABC.
The vertices of ABC have coordinates $A(3, 3)$, $B(3, 1)$ and $C(4, 1)$.
ABC is **translate**d 2 squares right, to become $A'B'C'$.
The vertices of $A'B'C'$ have coordinates $A'(5, 3)$, $B'(5, 1)$ and $C'(6, 1)$.
You **add 2** to the x-coordinates of ABC to get the coordinates of $A'B'C'$.

A	(3, 3)	B	(3, 1)	C	(4, 1)
↓	↓ + 2	↓	↓ + 2	↓	↓ + 2
A'	(5, 3)	B'	(5, 1)	C'	(6, 1)

> **Key words**
> image
> object
> translate

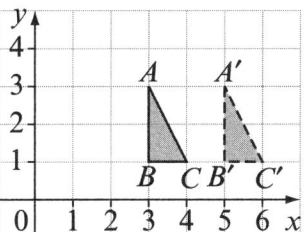

The diagram shows triangles DEF and $D'E'F'$.
$D'E'F'$ is the image of DEF.
The vertices of DEF have coordinates $D(2, 5)$, $E(2, 3)$ and $F(3, 3)$.
DEF is translated **3 squares up**, to become $D'E'F'$.
The vertices of $D'E'F'$ have coordinates $D'(2, 8)$, $E'(2, 6)$ and $F'(3, 6)$.
You **add 3** to the y-coordinates of DEF to get the coordinates of $D'E'F'$.

D	(2, 5)	E	(2, 3)	F	(3, 3)
↓	↓ + 3	↓	↓ + 3	↓	↓ + 3
D'	(2, 8)	E'	(2, 6)	F'	(3, 6)

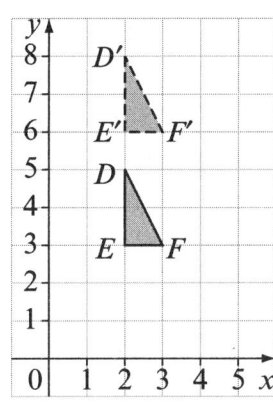

14 Position and transformation

Exercise 14.3

Focus

1 Triangle *ABC* from the first example in the introduction, is translated **5 squares right**.

Copy and complete the workings to find the coordinates of the vertices of the image *A'B'C'*.

A	(3,	3)	*B*	(3,	1)	*C*	(4,	1)
↓	↓ +5		↓	↓ +5		↓	↓ +5	
A'	(8,	3)	*B'*	(☐,	1)	*C'*	(☐,	1)

2 Triangle *ABC* from the first example in the introduction, is translated **3 squares left**.

Copy and complete the workings to find the coordinates of the vertices of the image *A'B'C'*.

A	(3,	3)	*B*	(3,	1)	*C*	(4,	1)
↓	↓ -3		↓	↓ -3		↓	↓ -3	
A'	(0,	3)	*B'*	(☐,	1)	*C'*	(☐,	1)

> **Tip**
> When you translate a shape 3 squares left, you **subtract 3** from the **x-coordinates** of *ABC* to get the coordinates of *A'B'C'*.

3 A square, *ABCD*, has vertices at the points *A*(5, 3), *B*(8, 3), *C*(8, 6) and *D*(5, 6).

ABCD is translated 4 squares left. The image of *ABCD* is *A'B'C'D'*.

Copy and complete the workings to find the coordinates of the vertices of *A'B'C'D'*.

A	(5, 3)	*B*	(8, 3)	*C*	(8, 6)	*D*	(5, 6)
↓	↓ -4	↓	↓ -4	↓	↓ -4	↓	↓ -4
A'	(1, 3)	*B'*	(☐, 3)	*C'*	(☐, 6)	*D'*	(☐, 6)

4 Triangle *DEF* from the second example in the introduction, is translated **1 square up**.

Copy and complete the workings to find the coordinates of the vertices of the image *D'E'F'*.

D	(2,	5)	*E*	(2,	3)	*F*	(3,	3)
↓	↓ +1		↓	↓ +1		↓	↓ +1	
D'	(2,	6)	*E'*	(2,	☐)	*F'*	(3,	☐)

14.3 Translating 2D shapes

5 Triangle *DEF* from the second example in the introduction, is translated **2 squares down**.

Copy and complete the workings to find the coordinates of the vertices of the image *D'E'F'*.

D	(2,	5)	E	(2,	3)	F	(3,	3)
↓	↓ -2	↓	↓ -2	↓	↓ -2
D'	(2,	3)	E'	(2,	☐)	F'	(3,	☐)

> **Tip**
> When you translate a shape 2 squares down, you **subtract 2** from the **y-coordinates** of *DEF* to get the coordinates of *D'E'F'*.

6 A rectangle, *ABCD*, has vertices at the points *A*(2, 7), *B*(6, 7), *C*(6, 9) and *D*(2, 9).

ABCD is translated **4 squares down**. The image of *ABCD* is *A'B'C'D'*.

Copy and complete the workings to find the coordinates of the vertices of *A'B'C'D'*.

A (2,   7)   B (6,   7)   C (6,   9)   D (2,   9)
↓   ↓ -4   ↓   ↓ -4   ↓   ↓ -4   ↓   ↓ -4
A' (2,   3)   B' (6,   ☐)   C' (6,   ☐)   D' (2,   ☐)

Practice

7 A triangle, *PQR*, has vertices at the points *P*(4, 5), *Q*(7, 5) and *R*(6, 9).

PQR is translated 3 squares right and 4 squares up. The image of *PQR* is *P'Q'R'*.

Copy and complete the workings to find the coordinates of the vertices of *P'Q'R'*.

P (2,   5)   Q (7,   1)   R (2,   5)
↓   ↓ +3   ↓ +4   ↓   ↓ +3   ↓ +4   ↓   ↓ +3   ↓ +4
P' (7,   ☐)   Q' (☐,   9)   R' (☐,   ☐)

8 A rectangle, *ABCD*, has vertices at the points *A*(4, 8), *B*(8, 8), *C*(8, 10) and *D*(4, 10).

ABCD is translated 1 square left and 5 squares down. The image of *ABCD* is *A'B'C'D'*.

Copy and complete the workings to find the coordinates of the vertices of *A'B'C'D'*.

A (4,   8)   B (8,   8)   C (8,   10)   D (4,   10)
↓ ↓ -1 ↓ -5   ↓ ↓ -1 ↓ -5   ↓ ↓ -1 ↓ -5   ↓ ↓ -1 ↓ -5
A' (3,   ☐)   B' (☐,   3)   C' (☐,   ☐)   D' (☐,   ☐)

14 Position and transformation

9 The grey cards have different translations written on them. The white cards show what must be added or subtracted to the *x*- and *y*-coordinates of a shape to complete the translation.

Match each grey card (**A** to **D**) to its correct white card (**i** to **iv**). The first one has been done for you: **A** and **iv**.

A	6 squares right and 3 squares down
B	6 squares left and 3 squares up
C	6 squares left and 3 squares down
D	6 squares right and 3 squares up

i	x y
	↓ −6 ↓ −3

ii	x y
	↓ +6 ↓ +3

iii	x y
	↓ −6 ↓ +3

iv	x y
	↓ +6 ↓ −3

10 A rhombus, *PQRS*, has vertices at the points *P*(6, 2), *Q*(7, 4), *R*(6, 6) and *S*(5, 4).

PQRS is translated 3 squares left and 2 squares down. The image of *PQRS* is *P′Q′R′S′*.

Work out the coordinates of the vertices of *P′Q′R′S′*.

 11 This is part of Ivan's homework.

> *Question*
> *A line segment, AB, goes from the point A(4, 7) to the point B(9, 3).*
> *AB is translated 3 squares left and 2 squares down.*
> *The image of AB is A'B'.*
> *Work out the coordinates of A' and B'.*
> *Solution*
> *A' is at (7, 5).   B' is at (12, 1).*

Ivan has worked out the coordinates of *A′* and *B′* incorrectly.

a Explain the mistake that he has made.

b Work out the correct coordinates of *A′* and *B′*.

c Explain how Ivan could check that his answers are correct.

14.3 Translating 2D shapes

 12 Simone translates the triangle XYZ to $X'Y'Z'$.

XYZ has vertices at $X(5, 4)$, $Y(8, 5)$ and $Z(6, 9)$.

$X'Y'Z'$ has vertices at $X'(2, 7)$, $Y'(5, 8)$ and $Z'(3, 12)$.

Which translation, **A**, **B**, **C** or **D**, has she used? Show your working and explain your answer.

A	3 squares right and 3 squares down
B	3 squares right and 3 squares up
C	3 squares left and 3 squares down
D	3 squares left and 3 squares up

Challenge

 13 Alya translates kite $JKLM$ to $J'K'L'M'$. $JKLM$ has vertices at $J(1, 5)$, $K(4, 4)$, $L(1, -1)$ and $M(-2, 4)$.

Alya works out that the vertices of $J'K'L'M'$ are at $J'(-2, 4)$, $K'(1, 3)$, $L'(-2, 2)$ and $M'(-5, 3)$.

Alya has worked out three of the vertices correctly and one incorrectly.

Which vertex, J', K', L' or M', is incorrect? Explain how you worked out your answer.

 14 A rectangle, $CDEF$, has vertices at the points $C(2, -1)$, $D(6, -1)$, $E(6, -3)$ and $F(2, -3)$.

Nadim translates $CDEF$ four times, using four different translations.

He writes down the coordinates of the images of $CDEF$ after each translation. These are the four translations he uses:

A	5 squares right and 3 squares up
B	4 squares right and 2 squares down
C	4 squares left
D	3 squares left and 1 square down

After which translation will the **object** and the image be:
- a touching end to end?
- b touching corner to corner?
- c overlapping?
- d not touching or overlapping?

Explain how you worked out your answers.

Tip

Remember that you must not draw a grid to help you answer this question.

14 Position and transformation

15 a Jon translates shape L 3 squares right and 2 squares up. He labels the shape M.

Jon then translates shape M 4 squares right and 6 squares up. He labels the shape N.

    i What translation could Jon do on shape L to take it to shape N in one step?

    ii Explain the method you used to work out your answer to part **a i**.

    iii What do you notice about your answer to part **a i** and Jon's two translations?

b Jim translates shape L 2 squares left and 4 squares up. He labels the shape P.

Jim then translates shape P 3 squares left and 1 square up. He labels the shape Q.

    i What translation could Jim do on shape L to take it to shape Q in one step?

    ii Explain the method you used to work out your answer to part **b i**.

    iii What do you notice about your answer to part **b i** and Jim's two translations?

> **Tip**
> You could choose your own coordinates for one of the vertices of shape L and test the translations on this point.

16 In a game of chess, in one turn, a knight can move either 1 square left or right followed by 2 squares up or down <u>or</u> 2 squares left or right followed by 1 square up or down. On the chess board shown, K shows the position of the knight.

  a   **i** Describe the translations that the knight must make to get to the square marked X.

      ii What is the fewest number of moves that the knight can make to get from K to X?

  b   **i** Describe the translations that the knight must make to get to the square marked Y.

      ii What is the fewest number of moves that the knight can make to get from K to Y?

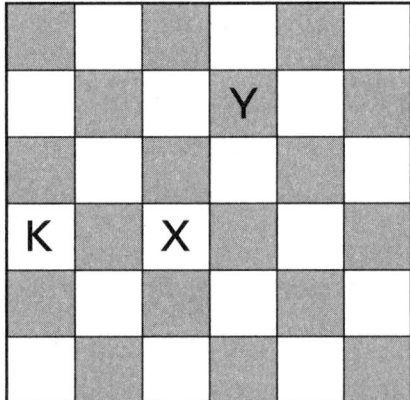

> 14.4 Reflecting shapes

Exercise 14.4

> **Key word**
> reflected

Focus

1 In each of these diagrams, the shape is **reflected** in the *x*-axis. Copy and complete each diagram.

a 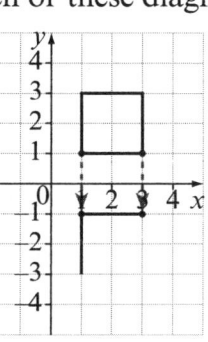   b 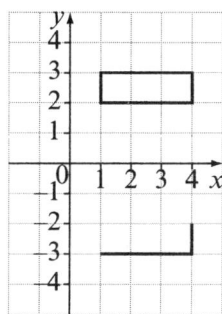   c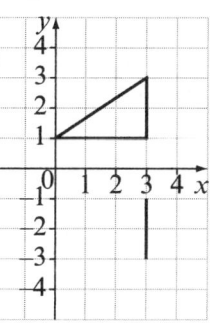

2 In which of these diagrams has shape A been correctly reflected in the *x*-axis?
If the reflection is incorrect, copy the diagram and draw the correct reflection.

a 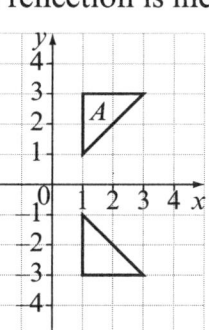   b 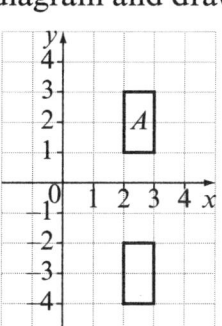   c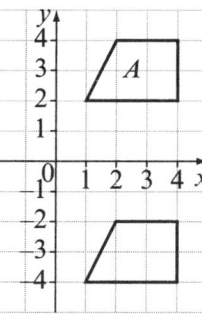

3 In each of these diagrams, the shape is reflected in the *y*-axis. Copy and complete each diagram.

a 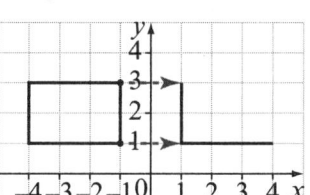   b 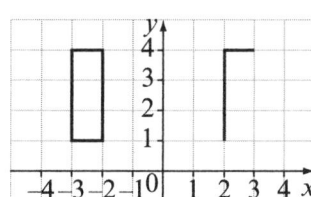   c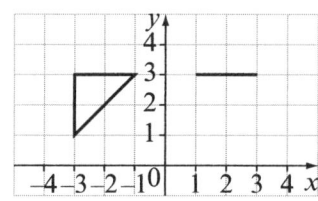

14 Position and transformation

4   In which of these diagrams has shape B been correctly reflected in the *y*-axis?
    If the reflection is incorrect, copy the diagram and draw the correct reflection.

a 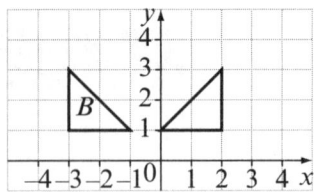   b 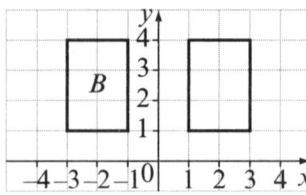   c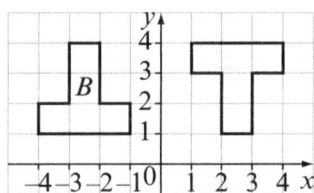

Practice

5   Copy each diagram and reflect the shape in the *x*-axis.

a 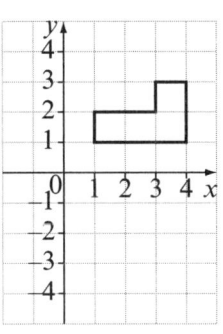   b 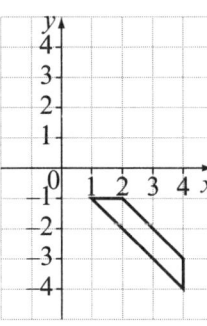   c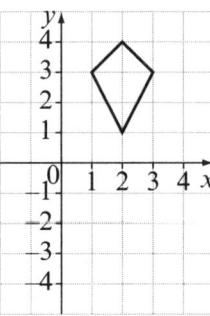

6   Copy each diagram and reflect the shape in the *y*-axis.

a 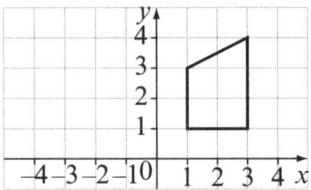   b 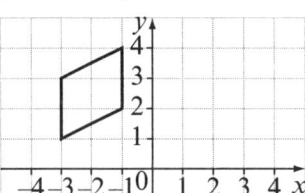   c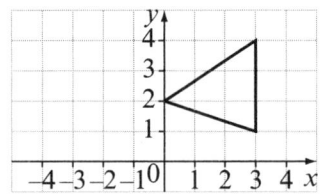

7   Copy each diagram and reflect each letter shape in:
    i   the *x*-axis
    ii the *y*-axis

a 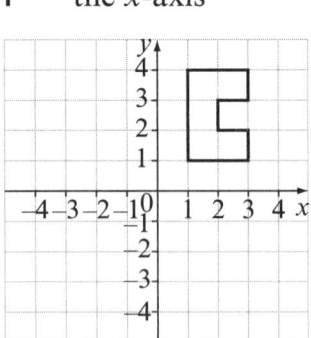   b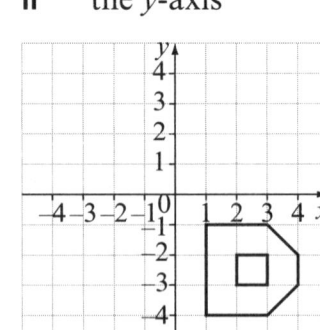

c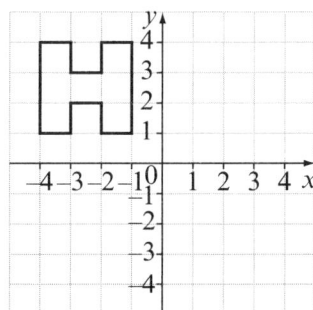

d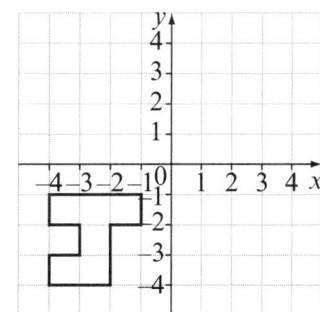

8   The diagram shows ten trapezia, which are labelled A to J.
    Copy and complete these statements. The first one has been done for you.
    a   A is a reflection of G in the x-axis.
    b   D is a reflection of ☐ in the ....
    c   E is a reflection of ☐ in the ....
    d   J is a reflection of ☐ in the ....
    e   H is a reflection of ☐ in the ....
    f   F is a reflection of ☐ in the ....

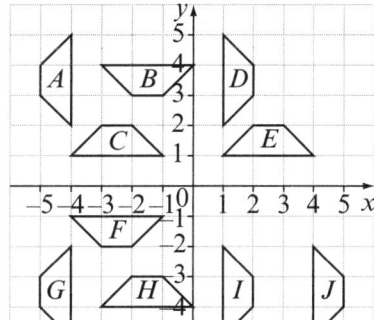

Tip

'Trapezia' is the plural of 'trapezium'.

Challenge

9   a   Helena reflects rectangle JKLM in the x-axis. The vertices of the rectangle have the coordinates J(2, 1), K(5, 1), L(5, 3) and M(2, 3).
        The table shows the coordinates of the vertices of the object and the vertices of its image.
        Copy and complete the table.
        Explain the method you used to work out your answers.

Object	J(2, 1)	K(5, 1)	L(5, 3)	M(2, 3)
Image	J'(☐, ☐)	K'(☐, ☐)	L'(☐, ☐)	M'(☐, ☐)

    b   Helena reflects rectangle JKLM in the y-axis.
        The table shows the coordinates of the vertices of the object and the vertices of its image.
        Copy and complete the table.
        Explain the method you used to work out your answers.

Object	J(2, 1)	K(5, 1)	L(5, 3)	M(2, 3)
Image	J'(☐, ☐)	K'(☐, ☐)	L'(☐, ☐)	M'(☐, ☐)

14 Position and transformation

10 Make a copy of this diagram.
   a Reflect shape A in the *x*-axis. Label the shape B.
   b Reflect shape A in the *y*-axis. Label the shape C.
   c Reflect shape B in the *y*-axis. Label the shape D.
   d Colour in the combined shape of A, B, C and D.
      i   How many lines of symmetry does your combined shape have?
      ii What is the order of rotation of your combined shape?

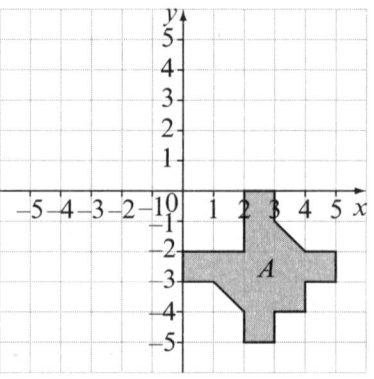

11 Copy each diagram and reflect the shape in the *y*-axis.
   a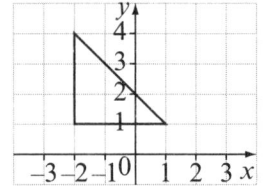
   b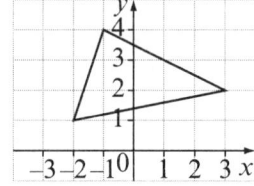
   c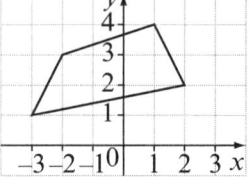

12 The diagram shows kite *PQRS*.
The vertices of the kite have coordinates
$P(1, 3)$, $Q(4, 1)$, $R(1, -5)$ and $S(-2, 1)$.

Arun is going to reflect *PQRS* in the *x*-axis.

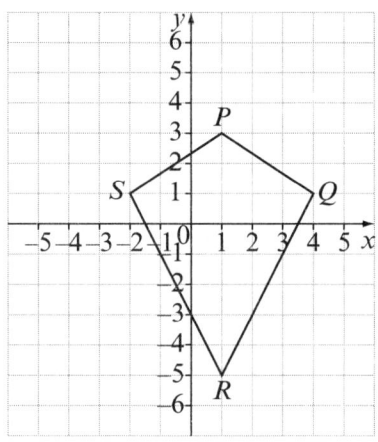

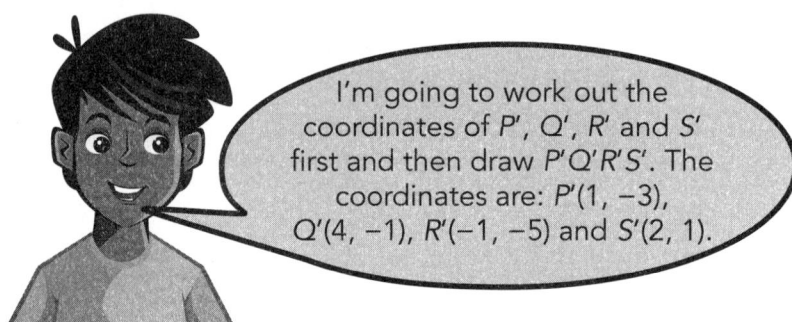

I'm going to work out the coordinates of *P'*, *Q'*, *R'* and *S'* first and then draw *P'Q'R'S'*. The coordinates are: $P'(1, -3)$, $Q'(4, -1)$, $R'(-1, -5)$ and $S'(2, 1)$.

Arun has made some mistakes with his coordinates for *P'Q'R'S'*.
   a Without drawing *P'Q'R'S'*, work out which coordinates are incorrect. Explain the mistakes Arun has made.
   b Copy the diagram. Work out the correct coordinates for *P'Q'R'S'* and draw *P'Q'R'S'* on the diagram.

> 14.5 Rotating shapes

When you rotate a shape, you turn it about a fixed point called the **centre of rotation**.

The centre of rotation is usually shown as a dot • with the letter *C*.

You turn a shape **clockwise** ↷ or **anticlockwise** ↶.

You must give the number of degrees by which you are rotating the object.

The rotations that are most often used are 90° and 180°.

Key words
anticlockwise
centre of rotation
clockwise

Tip
Remember that when a shape (the object) is rotated to a new position (the image), the object and the image are always congruent.

Exercise 14.5

Focus

1   For each of the following, write the number of degrees shape **A** has been turned to get to shape **B**.

    Describe if the turn is clockwise or anticlockwise. The first one has been done for you.

    a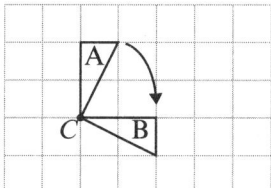
    90° clockwise

    b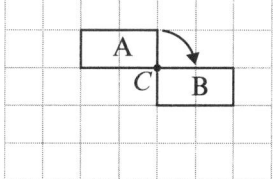

    c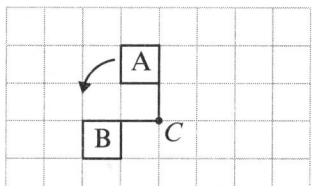

    d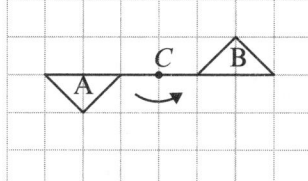

    e

    f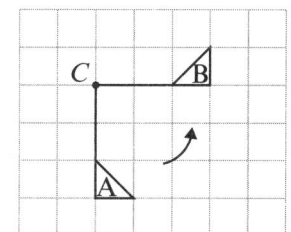

    g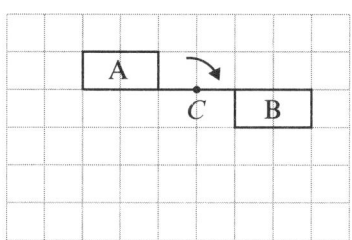

    h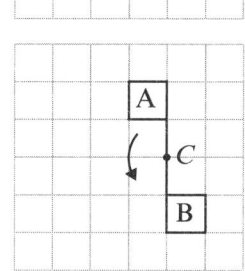

14 Position and transformation

2 Copy each diagram. Rotate each shape 90° clockwise about the centre of rotation, C.

a 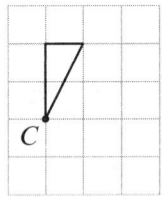 b 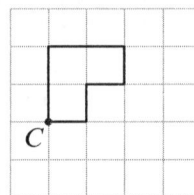 c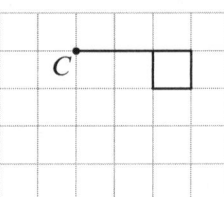

3 Copy each diagram. Rotate each shape 180° about the centre of rotation, C.

a 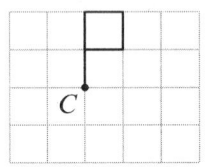 b 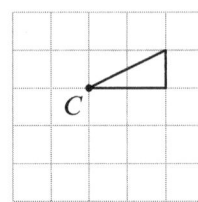 c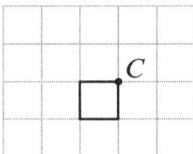

Practice

4 Copy each diagram and rotate the shape about the centre, C, by the given number of degrees.

a 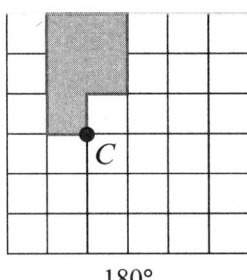 b 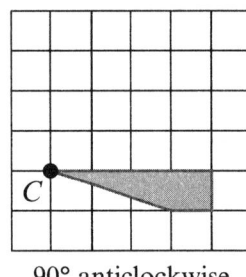 c 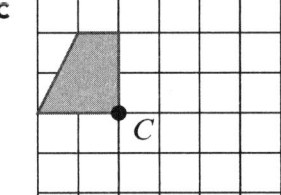 d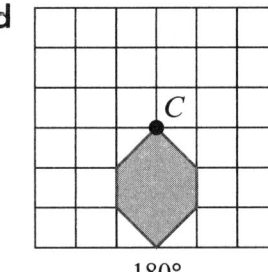

180° 90° anticlockwise 90° clockwise 180°

5 Copy each diagram and rotate the shape about the centre, C, by the given number of degrees.

a 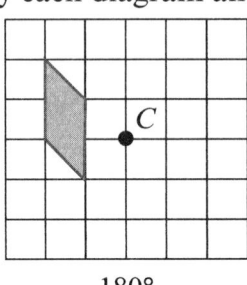 b 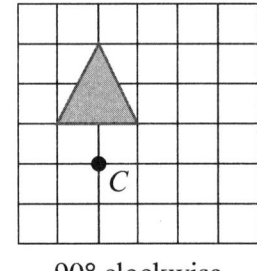 c 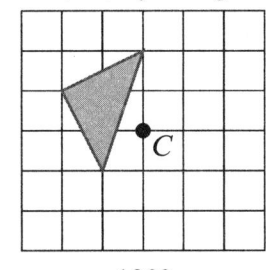 d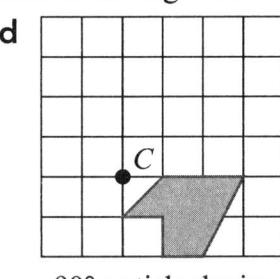

180° 90° clockwise 180° 90° anticlockwise

14.5 Rotating shapes

6 Copy each diagram and rotate the shape, using the information given.

a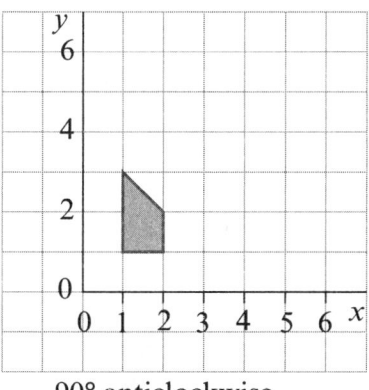
90° anticlockwise
centre (2, 4)

b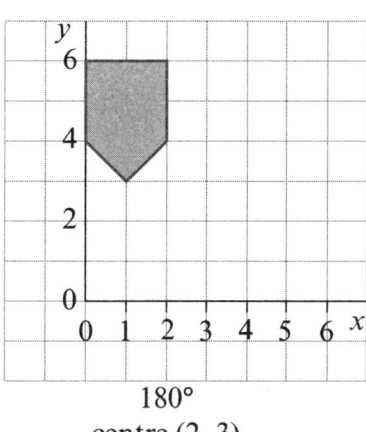
180°
centre (2, 3)

c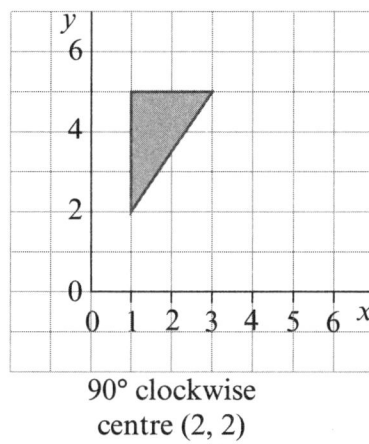
90° clockwise
centre (2, 2)

d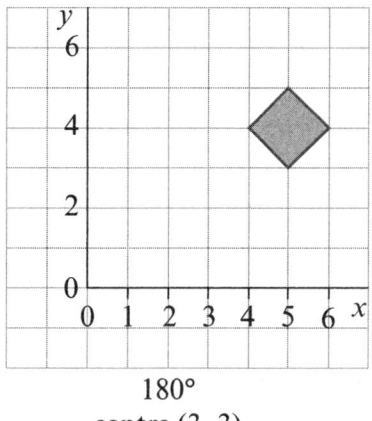
180°
centre (3, 3)

7 a Copy this diagram.
Follow these instructions to make a pattern.
  i   Rotate the pattern 90° anticlockwise about the centre, C.
  ii Draw the image.
  iii Rotate this new image 90° anticlockwise about the centre, C.
  iv Draw the image.
  v   Rotate the third image 90° anticlockwise about the centre, C.
  vi Draw the image.

b What is the order of rotational symmetry of the completed pattern?

c How many lines of symmetry does the completed pattern have?

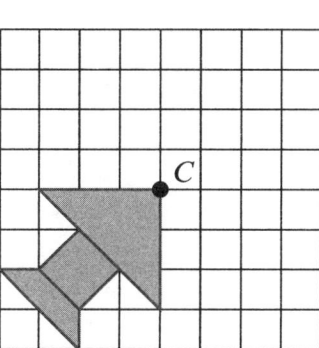

14 Position and transformation

Challenge

 8 Zara draws rectangle A onto this coordinate grid. Each square on the grid has a length of 1 cm.

a What is the perimeter of rectangle A?

Zara rotates rectangle A 180° about the centre (4, 2) to get rectangle B. She joins rectangle A to rectangle B to give a combined shape.

Zara says:

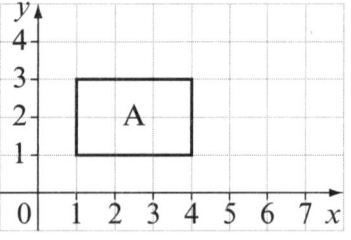

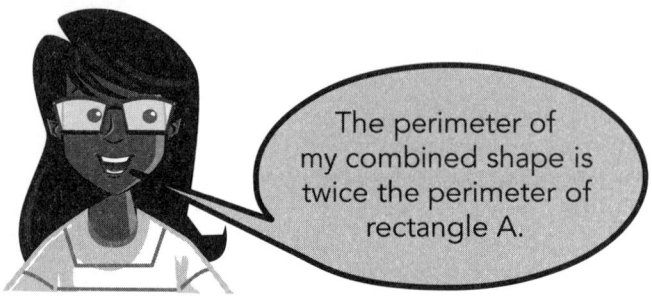

> The perimeter of my combined shape is twice the perimeter of rectangle A.

Tip

You could use a diagram to help you prove or disprove Zara's comment.

b Is Zara correct? Give reasons for your answer.

 9 Make two copies of the diagram shown in Question **8**.

a Using the first copy, rotate the rectangle 90° clockwise about the centre (4, 1). The object and image together make one shape.

i What is the perimeter of this shape?

ii What do you notice about the perimeter of the rectangle and the perimeter of the shape?

b Using the second copy, rotate the rectangle 180° about the centre (4, 3). The object and image together make one shape.

i What is the perimeter of this shape?

ii What do you notice about the perimeter of the rectangle and the perimeter of the shape?

10 a Copy this diagram.

b Rotate rectangle P 180° about the centre (4, 3). Label the image Q.

Shade in the combined shape of rectangles P and Q.

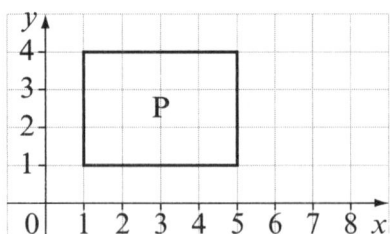

c Sofia says:

> *The two rectangles overlap by four squares, so:*
> 1. *The area of my combined shape is twice the area of rectangle P take away 8 cm².*
> 2. *The perimeter of my combined shape is twice the perimeter of rectangle P take away 8 cm.*

Are Sofia's statements correct? Explain your answers.

11 Make two copies of this diagram.
  a Using the first copy, rotate the shape 90° clockwise about the centre (3, 1).
  b On the second copy, rotate the shape 180° about the centre (4, 2).

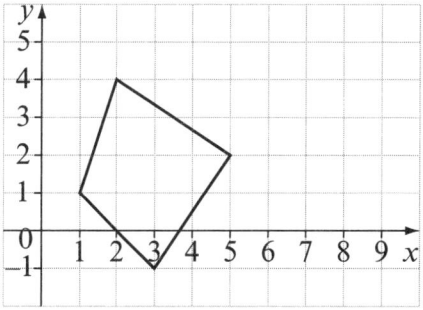

> 14.6 Enlarging shapes

An **enlargement** of a shape is a copy of the shape that is bigger than the original shape.

The original shape and the enlargement are **similar shapes**.

You enlarge a shape using a **scale factor**.

When the scale factor is 2, all the sides of the image must be twice as long as the object.

When the scale factor is 3, all the sides of the image must be three times as long as the object.

Key words
dimensions
enlargement
scale factor
similar shapes

Tips
'twice as long' means two times the length.
'three times as long' means three times the length.

14 Position and transformation

Exercise 14.6

Focus

1 Copy and complete these enlargements. Use a scale factor of 2.

a 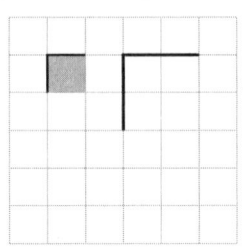   b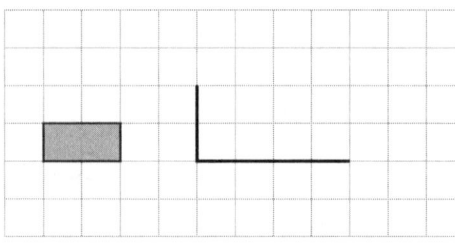

c 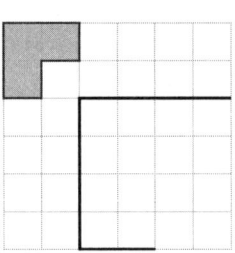   d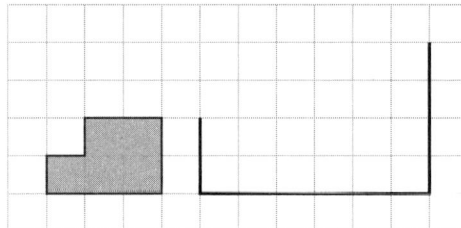

2 Copy and complete these enlargements. Use a scale factor of 3.

a 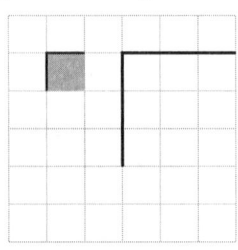   b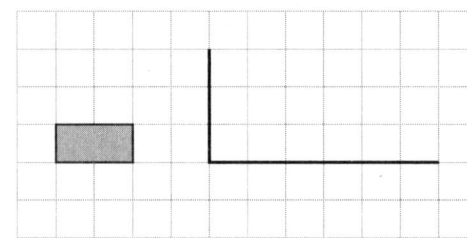

c 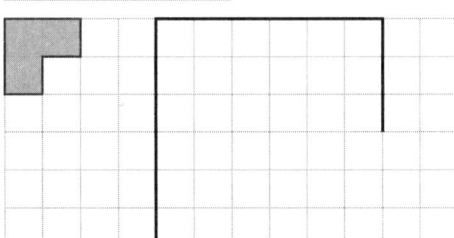   d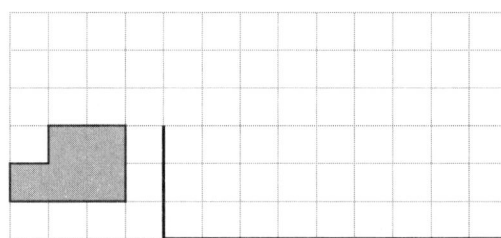

3   Copy each of these shapes onto squared paper. Enlarge each shape using the scale factors given.

   a 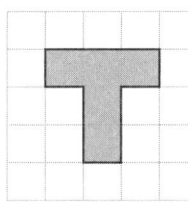   b 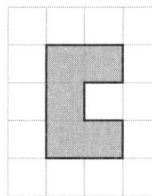   c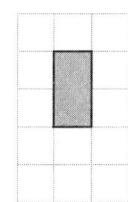

   scale factor 2   scale factor 3   scale factor 4

Practice

4   Copy each of these shapes onto squared paper. Enlarge each shape using the scale factors given.

   a 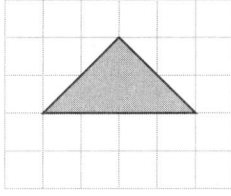   b 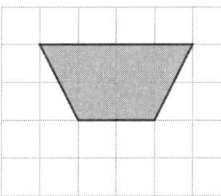   c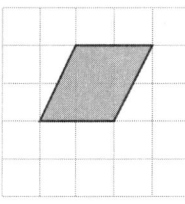

   scale factor 2   scale factor 3   scale factor 4

 5   This is part of Dan's homework.

   Question
   Enlarge this shape using a scale factor of 2.

   Solution

   a   Dan has made some mistakes. Explain the mistakes he has made.
   b   Draw the correct solution.

14 Position and transformation

6 The diagram shows a shape and its enlargement.

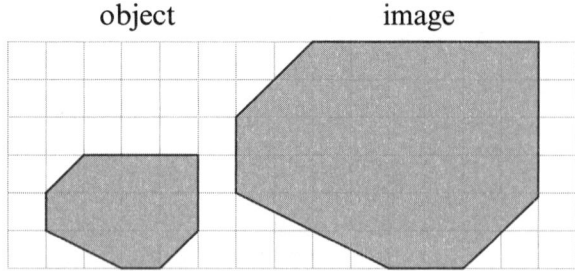

What is the scale factor of the enlargement?

7 Here are some triangles. The triangles are not drawn accurately.

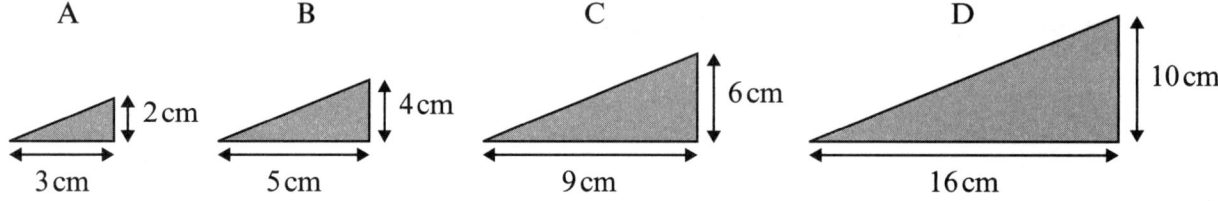

a Explain why triangle B is <u>not</u> an enlargement of triangle A.

b Are triangles C and D an enlargement of triangle A? Explain how you worked out your answers.

Challenge

8 A company makes boxes with square bases. The diagram shows the **dimensions** of the smallest box that it makes.

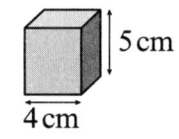

These are the dimensions of the other boxes that the company makes. Some of the boxes are enlargements of the smallest box. Some of the boxes are <u>not</u> enlargements of the smallest box.

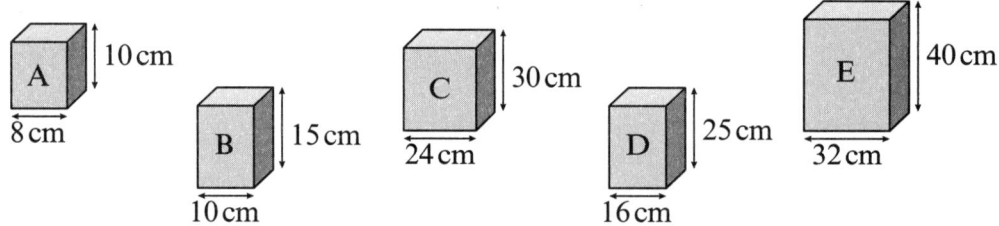

Which of these boxes are enlargements of the smallest box?
Write down the scale factor of each enlargement.

14.6 Enlarging shapes

9 Marcus and Arun look at this diagram.

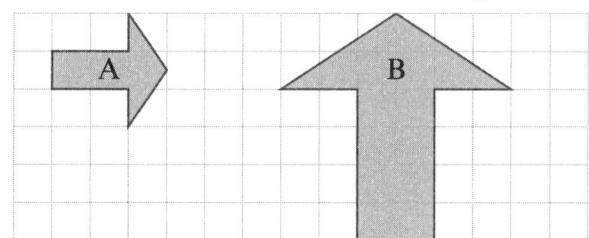

Marcus says: Arun says:

I think that shape B is an enlargement of shape A because all the sides are twice as long.

I don't think that shape A is an enlargement of shape B because the shape has been rotated 90°.

Who do you think is correct, Marcus or Arun? Explain your answer.

10 Naveen enlarges triangle A to get triangle B. He then enlarges triangle B to get triangle C. Finally, he enlarges triangle C to get triangle D.

triangle A   triangle B   triangle C   triangle D

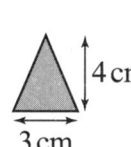 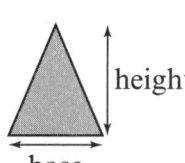 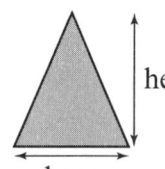 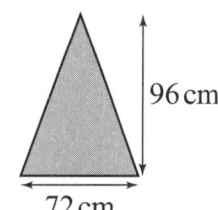

4 cm   height   height   96 cm
3 cm   base   base   72 cm

a i   Work out one possible base length and height for triangles B and C.
   ii Explain how you worked out your answers.
   iii Give the scale factor you used for each enlargement.
b i   Work out a different possible base length and height for triangles B and C.
   ii Explain how you worked out your answers.
   iii Give the scale factor you used for each enlargement.
c i   How many different base lengths and heights could there be for triangles B and C?
   ii Explain how you worked out your answer.

14 Position and transformation

  11 The diagram shows four rectangles, A, B, C and D.

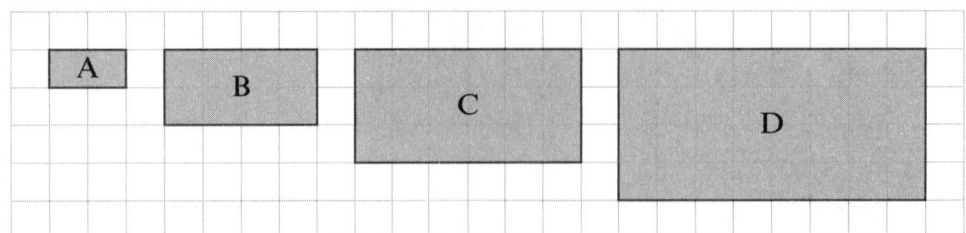

a   Write the scale factor of the enlargement of rectangle:
   i   A to B   ii   A to C   iii   A to D
b   Work out the area of rectangle:
   i   A   ii   B   iii   C   iv   D
c   Copy and complete this table. Write each ratio in its simplest form.

Rectangles	Scale factor of enlargement	Ratio of lengths	Ratio of areas
A : B	2	1 : 2	
A : C			
A : D			

d   Write a rule that connects the ratio of lengths to the ratio of areas.
e   Will this rule work for any scale factor of enlargement?
    Will this rule work, in general, for any shape?
    Explain your answers.

Tip

Remember the square numbers:
$1^2 = 1$, $2^2 = 4$, $3^2 = 9$, $4^2 = 16$, etc.

15 Shapes, area and volume

> 15.1 Converting between units for area

You need to know these **conversion factors**:

$1 \text{ cm}^2 = 100 \text{ mm}^2$ $1 \text{ m}^2 = 10\,000 \text{ cm}^2$

Key words
- area
- conversion factor
- compound shape
- square centimetre (cm²)
- square metre (m²)
- square millimetre (mm²)

Exercise 15.1

Focus

1. Copy and complete these **area** conversions between **cm²** and **mm²**.
   a. $6 \text{ cm}^2 = 6 \times 100 = \boxed{} \text{ mm}^2$
   b. $9 \text{ cm}^2 = 9 \times 100 = \boxed{} \text{ mm}^2$
   c. $2.5 \text{ cm}^2 = 2.5 \times 100 = \boxed{} \text{ mm}^2$
   d. $0.5 \text{ cm}^2 = 0.5 \times 100 = \boxed{} \text{ mm}^2$

   Tip: When you convert from cm² to mm² you <u>multiply</u> by 100.

2. Copy and complete these area conversions between mm² and cm².
   a. $700 \text{ mm}^2 = 700 \div 100 = \boxed{} \text{ cm}^2$
   b. $400 \text{ mm}^2 = 400 \div 100 = \boxed{} \text{ cm}^2$
   c. $1500 \text{ mm}^2 = 1500 \div 100 = \boxed{} \text{ cm}^2$
   d. $650 \text{ mm}^2 = 650 \div 100 = \boxed{} \text{ cm}^2$

   Tip: When you convert from mm² to cm² you <u>divide</u> by 100.

3. Copy and complete these area conversions between **m²** and cm².
   a. $4 \text{ m}^2 = 4 \times 10\,000 = \boxed{} \text{ cm}^2$
   b. $8 \text{ m}^2 = 8 \times 10\,000 = \boxed{} \text{ cm}^2$
   c. $1.5 \text{ m}^2 = 1.5 \times 10\,000 = \boxed{} \text{ cm}^2$
   d. $0.6 \text{ m}^2 = 0.6 \times 10\,000 = \boxed{} \text{ cm}^2$

   Tip: When you convert from m² to cm² you <u>multiply</u> by 10 000.

15 Shapes, area and volume

4 Copy and complete these area conversions between cm² and m².

a $20\,000\,\text{cm}^2 = 20\,000 \div 10\,000 = \boxed{}\,\text{m}^2$

b $50\,000\,\text{cm}^2 = 50\,000 \div 10\,000 = \boxed{}\,\text{m}^2$

c $12\,000\,\text{cm}^2 = 12\,000 \div 10\,000 = \boxed{}\,\text{m}^2$

d $9000\,\text{cm}^2 = 9000 \div 10\,000 = \boxed{}\,\text{m}^2$

Tip

When you convert from cm² to m² you <u>divide</u> by 10 000.

5 Copy and complete these area conversions. All the answers are given in the cloud.

a $8.1\,\text{cm}^2 = \boxed{}\,\text{mm}^2$

b $0.83\,\text{cm}^2 = \boxed{}\,\text{mm}^2$

c $850\,\text{mm}^2 = \boxed{}\,\text{cm}^2$

d $89\,\text{mm}^2 = \boxed{}\,\text{cm}^2$

e $8.4\,\text{m}^2 = \boxed{}\,\text{cm}^2$

f $0.88\,\text{m}^2 = \boxed{}\,\text{cm}^2$

g $88\,000\,\text{cm}^2 = \boxed{}\,\text{m}^2$

h $8200\,\text{cm}^2 = \boxed{}\,\text{m}^2$

Cloud: 0.89   8.8   810   8800   0.82   84 000   83   8.5

Practice

6 Write the units you would use to measure the area of:

a a thumb nail   b a calculator

c an island   d a rugby pitch

7 Copy and complete the following area conversions. Show your working.

a $50\,000\,\text{cm}^2 = \boxed{}\,\text{m}^2$

b $51\,000\,\text{cm}^2 = \boxed{}\,\text{m}^2$

c $251\,000\,\text{cm}^2 = \boxed{}\,\text{m}^2$

d $4\,\text{cm}^2 = \boxed{}\,\text{mm}^2$

e $6.8\,\text{cm}^2 = \boxed{}\,\text{mm}^2$

f $8\,\text{m}^2 = \boxed{}\,\text{cm}^2$

g $3.5\,\text{m}^2 = \boxed{}\,\text{cm}^2$

h $100\,\text{mm}^2 = \boxed{}\,\text{cm}^2$

i $455\,\text{mm}^2 = \boxed{}\,\text{cm}^2$

8 Work out the area of this rectangle. Give your answer in:

a mm²

b cm²

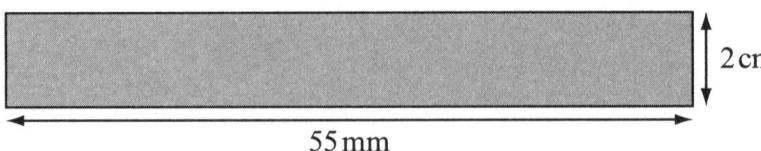

9 Sofia has a rectangular piece of wood. The length is 3.5 m and the width is 50 cm.

   a What is the area of the wood? Give your answer in:
      i   cm²   ii m²
   b The dashed line shows where Sofia cuts a small piece of wood from the end of the rectangle. What is the area of the piece that is left? Give your answer in:
      i   cm²   ii m²

Tip
'Rectangular' means 'in the shape of a rectangle'.

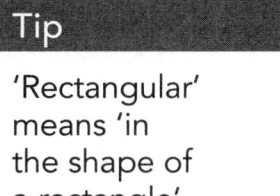
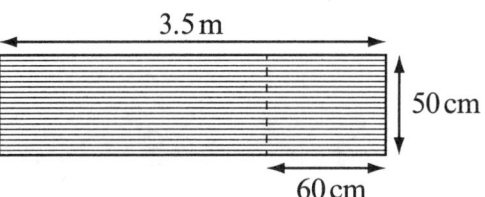

10 Work out the area of this **compound shape**.

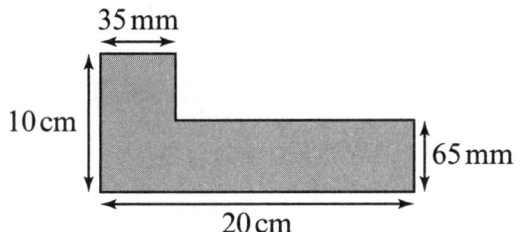
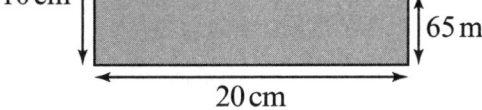

   Give your answer in:
   a mm²   b cm²

11 Sao-Yi says that 8 cm² is the same as 80 mm² because there are 10 mm in 1 cm. Explain why he is incorrect.

Challenge

12 Yuuma says that an area of 75 000 mm² is the same as 750 m².

   Is Yuuma correct? Explain your answer.

13 Freya is going to put tiles on the floor of her kitchen. The diagram shows the dimensions of her floor and the dimensions of one tile.

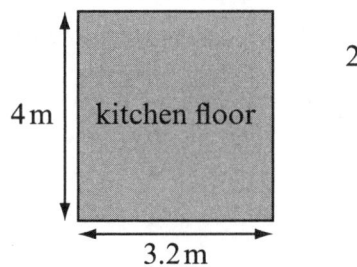
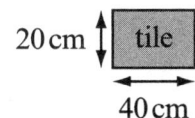

   How many tiles does Freya need to cover her kitchen floor?

14 Work out the answers to the following. Give each answer in:
      i   mm²   ii cm²
   a 8 cm² + 150 mm²   b 12.25 cm² − 950 mm²

15 Shapes, area and volume

15 Work out the answers to the following. Give each answer in:
    i   cm²   ii   m²
    a   0.25 m² + 12 000 cm²   b   595 000 cm² − 12.3 m²

16 Dinesh has a piece of wood with an area of 1.6 m². He cuts the piece of wood into five pieces of equal area. What is the area of each piece in:
    a   m²?   b   cm²?

> 15.2 Using hectares

You need to know this conversion factor:
1 hectare (ha) = 10 000 m²

Key word

hectares (ha)

Exercise 15.2

Focus

1 Copy and complete these area conversions between **hectares** and m².
    a   7 ha = 7 × 10 000 = ☐ m²
    b   13 ha = 13 × 10 000 = ☐ m²
    c   3.5 ha = 3.5 × 10 000 = ☐ m²
    d   0.4 ha = 0.4 × 10 000 = ☐ m²

Tip

When you convert from ha to m² you <u>multiply</u> by 10 000.

2 Copy and complete these area conversions between m² and hectares.
    a   60 000 m² = 60 000 ÷ 10 000 = ☐ ha
    b   120 000 m² = 120 000 ÷ 10 000 = ☐ ha
    c   34 000 m² = 34 000 ÷ 10 000 = ☐ ha
    d   9000 m² = 9000 ÷ 10 000 = ☐ ha

Tip

When you convert from m² to ha you <u>divide</u> by 10 000.

3 Copy and complete the workings to find the area of this rectangle in m² and hectares.
    a   Area = 300 × 50 = ☐ m²
    b   ☐ m² ÷ 10 000 = ☐ ha

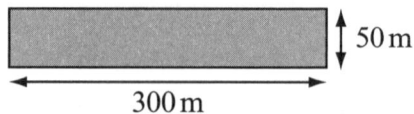

Practice

4   Copy and complete these conversions.
    a   4 ha = ☐ m²
    b   5.2 ha = ☐ m²
    c   0.9 ha = ☐ m²
    d   45.2 ha = ☐ m²
    e   0.82 ha = ☐ m²
    f   0.034 ha = ☐ m²

5   Copy and complete these conversions.
    a   70 000 m² = ☐ ha
    b   32 000 m² = ☐ ha
    c   670 000 m² = ☐ ha
    d   8800 m² = ☐ ha
    e   700 m² = ☐ ha
    f   2 375 000 m² = ☐ ha

6   A rectangular piece of land measures 420 m by 360 m. Work out the area of the land. Give your answer in:
    a   square metres (m²)
    b   hectares (ha)

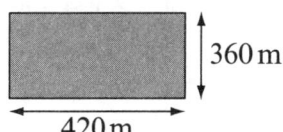

7   A farmer has a T-shaped field. The dimensions of the field are shown in the diagram.
    a   Work out the area of the field, in square metres (m²).
    b   Work out the area of the field, in hectares (ha).
    c   The farmer sells the field for $2200 per hectare. How much money does the farmer receive?

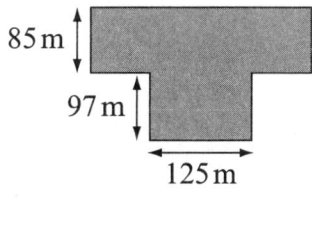

8   a   A rugby pitch has an area of 0.98 ha. Work out the area of the rugby pitch, in m².
    b   The width of the rugby pitch is 70 m. Work out the length of the rugby pitch, in metres.

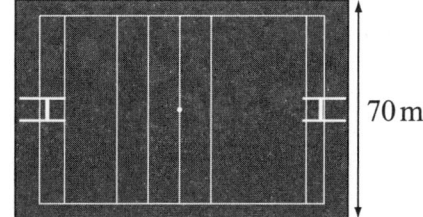

Challenge

9   Asher and Briony share a piece of land in the ratio 2 : 3. The piece of land they share is 3.25 hectares. Work out the area of Asher's piece, in m².

10 A builder wants to buy an area of land. The shape of the land is shown in the diagram.
    The builder wants to spend no more than $40 000 for the land. The area of land is selling for $3900 per hectare.
    Can the builder afford to buy the land? Show all your working.

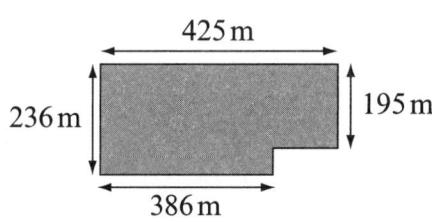

15 Shapes, area and volume

11 In some countries areas of land are measured in hectares (ha) or square kilometres (km²).

In other countries, areas of land are measured in acres (ac) or square miles (mi²).

Here are some conversions.

1 km² = 100 ha   1 mi² = 2.59 km²   1 mi² = 640 ac

The table shows the areas of four islands in the world.

Island	Kilometres²	Hectares	Miles²	Acres
Kyushu	37 437			
Sardinia		2 394 900		
Spitsbergen			15 051	
Timor				7 022 080

a Copy and complete the table. Give each answer to the nearest whole number.

b Write the islands in order of size from the largest to the smallest.

> 15.3 The area of a triangle

This rectangle and triangle are drawn on centimetre squared paper.
Each square has an area of 1 cm².

Area of the rectangle = base × height
$$= 4 \times 2$$
$$= 8 \text{ cm}^2$$

Area of the triangle = $\frac{1}{2}$ × area of the rectangle
$$= \frac{1}{2} \times 8$$
$$= 4 \text{ cm}^2$$

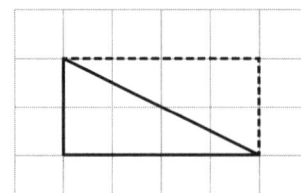

15.3 The area of a triangle

Exercise 15.3

Focus

1   Copy and complete the workings to find the areas of these rectangles and triangles.

   a   Area of rectangle = base × height
   $$= 3 \times \square = \square \text{ cm}^2$$
   Area of triangle = $\frac{1}{2}$ × area of the rectangle
   $$= \frac{1}{2} \times \square = \square \text{ cm}^2$$

   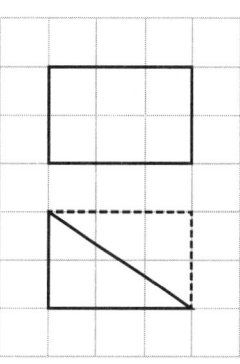

   b   Area of rectangle = base × height
   $$= 4 \times \square = \square \text{ cm}^2$$
   Area of triangle = $\frac{1}{2}$ × area of the rectangle
   $$= \frac{1}{2} \times \square = \square \text{ cm}^2$$

   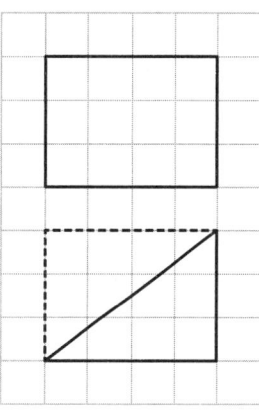

   c   Area of rectangle = base × height
   $$= 5 \times \square = \square \text{ cm}^2$$
   Area of triangle = $\frac{1}{2}$ × area of the rectangle
   $$= \frac{1}{2} \times \square = \square \text{ cm}^2$$

   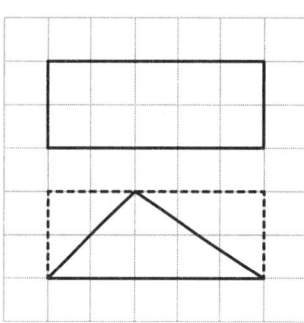

15 Shapes, area and volume

2 Match each triangle (**A** to **E**) to its correct area (**i** to **v**). The first one has been done for you: **A** and **iv**.

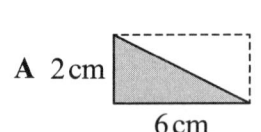 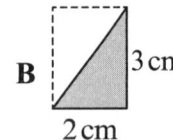 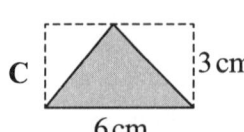 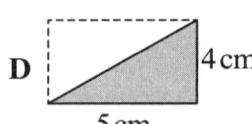 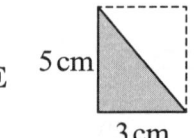

A 2 cm, 6 cm   B 3 cm, 2 cm   C 3 cm, 6 cm   D 4 cm, 5 cm   E 5 cm, 3 cm

i 3 cm²   **ii** 9 cm²   **iii** 7.5 cm²   **iv** 6 cm²   **v** 10 cm²

3 Copy and complete the workings to find the area of each triangle.

Use the formula: Area = $\frac{1}{2}$ × base × height   or $A = \frac{1}{2}bh$

a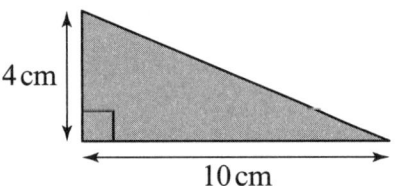

Area = $\frac{1}{2}$ × base × height

= $\frac{1}{2} \times 10 \times \square = \square$ cm²

b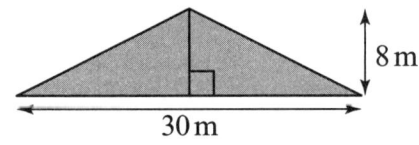

$A = \frac{1}{2}bh$

= $\frac{1}{2} \times \square \times 8 = \square$ m²

c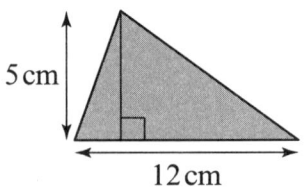

Area = $\frac{1}{2}$ × base × height

= $\frac{1}{2} \times 12 \times \square = \square$ cm²

d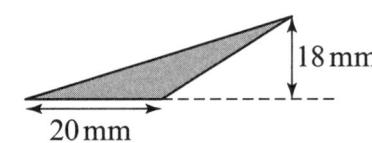

$A = \frac{1}{2}bh$

= $\frac{1}{2} \times \square \times 18 = \square$ mm²

15.3 The area of a triangle

Practice

4   Work out the area of each triangle.

   a 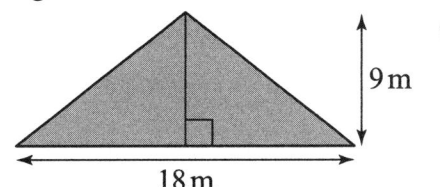   b 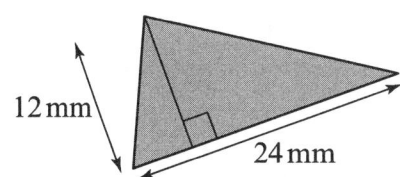   c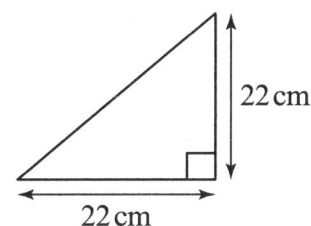

5   A triangle has a base length of 15 cm and a height of 6 cm.
    Work out the area of the triangle.

6   Eira is making a blanket out of fabric. She uses an equal number of red, white, blue and gold triangles. All together she uses 120 triangles.
    Each triangle has a height and base of 22 cm.

    What is the total area of each colour fabric that Eira needs?

 7   This triangle has a height of 8 cm and an area of 32 cm².

   Marcus says:

   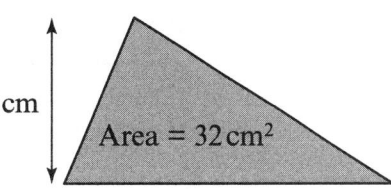

   The base of the triangle is 4 cm because 4 × 8 = 32.

   Is Marcus correct? Explain your answer.

8   Work out the area of each compound shape.

   a 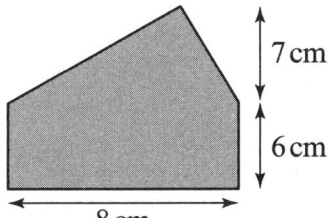   b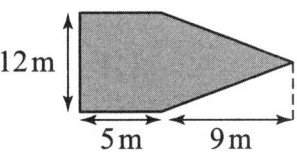

15 Shapes, area and volume

9 Work out the shaded area in this diagram.

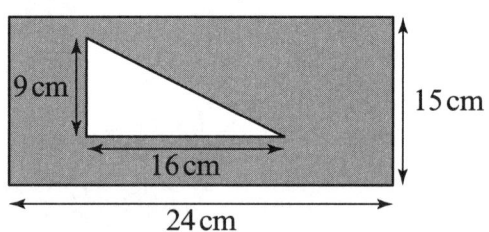

> **Tip**
> To find the shaded area, work out: area of rectangle – area of triangle.

10 The diagram shows a compound shape.
  a Work out the length marked x.
  b Work out the area of the compound shape.

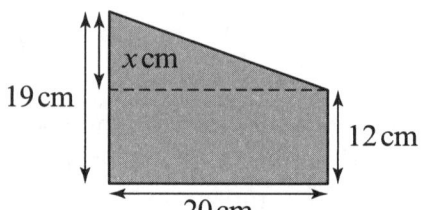

Challenge

11 Work out the missing measurements for each triangle.

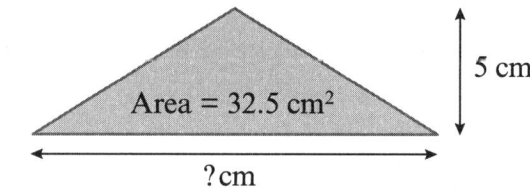

12 Work out the area of each triangle. Remember to give the units with your answers.

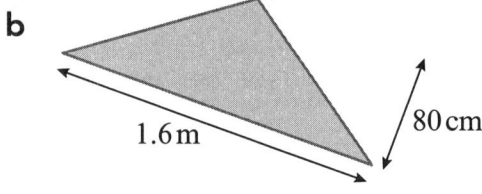

13 Write the base length and height of five triangles that each have an area of $12\,cm^2$.

14 The diagram shows triangles A and B. Triangle A has a base of 15 cm and a height of 9 cm. Triangle B has a height of 6 cm. The area of triangle B is $\frac{4}{5}$ the area of triangle A.

Work out the base of triangle B.

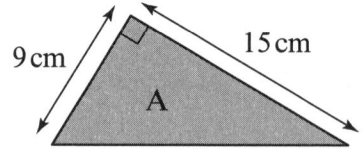 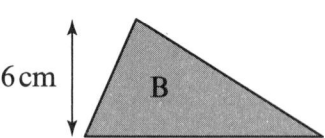

208

15 Rio thinks that the area of this compound shape is 4.42 cm².

Is Rio correct? Explain your answer, showing your working.

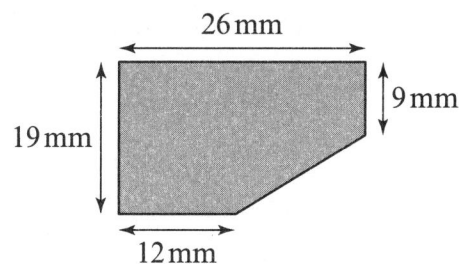

> 15.4 Calculating the volume of cubes and cuboids

This cube has a **volume** of one **cubic centimetre** (1 cm³). You can work out the volume of a cuboid by counting the number of cubes.

This cuboid has a volume of 6 cm³.

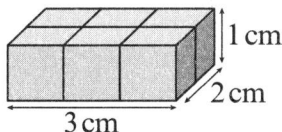

Instead of counting cubes, you can work out the volume of a cuboid using the formula:

Volume = length × width × height or $V = l \times w \times h$

Key words
cubic centimetre (cm³)
cubic metre (m³)
cubic millimetre (mm³)
volume

Tip
You can write the numbers on the cubes as you count them.

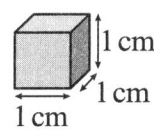

Exercise 15.4

Focus

1 Count the cubes to find the volume of each cuboid. Each cuboid has a height of 1 cm.

a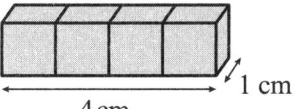

b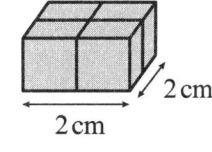

c

d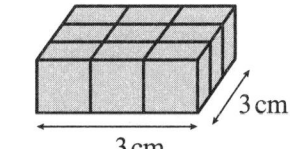

15 Shapes, area and volume

2 Copy and complete the workings to find the volume of each cuboid. The first one has been started for you.

a Number of cubes on top layer = 6
   Number of layers = 2
   Volume of cuboid = 6 + 6 = ☐ cm³

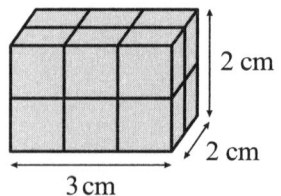

Tip

There are six cubes on each layer, so work out 6 + 6 or 2 × 6 to find the volume.

b Number of cubes on top layer = ☐
   Number of layers = ☐
   Volume of cuboid = ☐ cm³

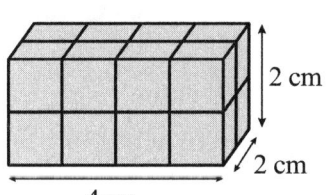

c Number of cubes on top layer = ☐
   Number of layers = ☐
   Volume of cuboid = ☐ cm³

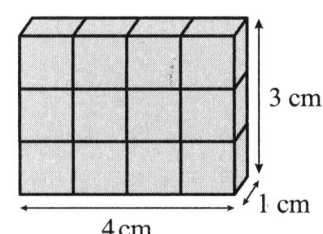

d Number of cubes on top layer = ☐
   Number of layers = ☐
   Volume of cuboid = ☐ cm³

3 Copy and complete the workings to find the volume of each cuboid.

a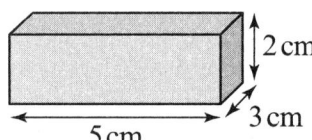

Volume = length × width × height
= 5 × 3 × 2
= ☐ cm³

b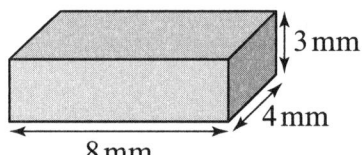

Volume = length × width × height
= 8 × ☐ × ☐
= ☐ mm³

15.4 Calculating the volume of cubes and cuboids

4 Copy and complete the workings to find the volume of these cubes.

a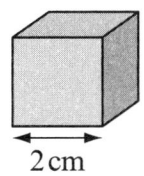

b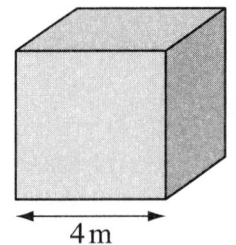

> **Tip**
> Remember that in a cube the length, width and height are all the same.

Volume = length × width × height
= 2 × 2 × 2
= ☐ cm³

Volume = length × width × height
= 4 × ☐ × ☐
= ☐ m³

Practice

5 Work out the volume of each of these cuboids.

a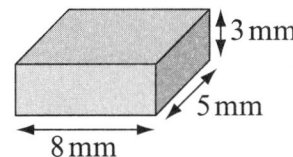

b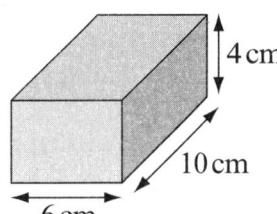

> **Tip**
> Make sure you write the correct units with your answers.

c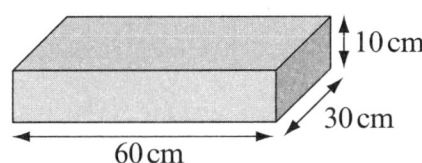

6 Work out the volume of each of these cuboids.

a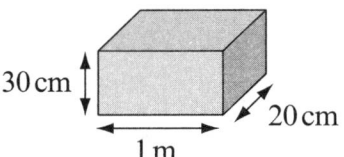

b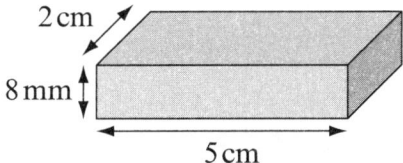

15 Shapes, area and volume

7 Mrs Beecham is marking Arun's homework.

> Question
> A cuboid has a length of 1 m, a width of 10 cm and a height of 2 cm.
> What is the volume of the cuboid?
> Solution
> Volume = 1 × 10 × 2 = 20 m³

Arun's solution is incorrect. Explain the mistake that Arun has made and work out the correct answer.

8 The table shows the lengths, widths and heights of four cuboids. Copy and complete the table.

	Length	Width	Height	Volume
a	5 cm	50 mm	5 mm	☐ mm³
b	8 cm	4 cm	5 mm	☐ cm³
c	50 cm	60 cm	4 m	☐ m³
d	2.2 m	15 cm	30 cm	☐ cm³

9 Look at this compound shape.

  a Write the value of y.
  b Copy and complete these workings to find the volume of the shape.

  Top cuboid: $V = l \times w \times h = 4 \times \Box \times 2$
  $ = \Box$ cm³
  Bottom cuboid: $V = l \times w \times h = 12 \times 5 \times 8$
  $ = \Box$ cm³
  Volume of shape: $\Box + \Box = \Box$ cm³

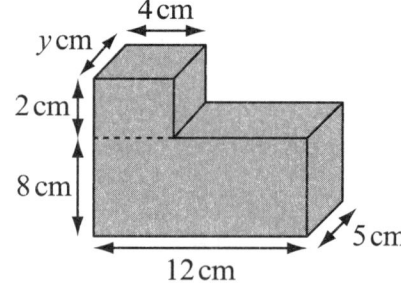

10 Work out the volume of each of these compound shapes.

a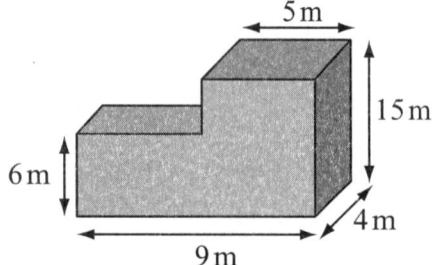

b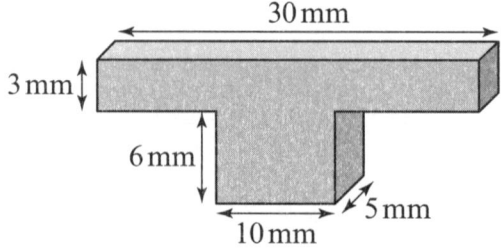

15.4 Calculating the volume of cubes and cuboids

Challenge

11 A wooden cuboid has a length of 35 mm, a height of 5 mm and a volume of 1225 mm³.
What is the width of the cuboid?

12 A cube has a volume of 216 cm³. What is the side length of the cube?

13 A cuboid has a length of 8 cm, a width of 6 cm and a height of 10 cm.
   a What is the volume of the cuboid?
   b Write the dimensions of another three cuboids that each have the same volume as the cuboid in part **a**.

14 The diagram shows a shape made from silver. The shape is melted and made into silver cubes. The side length of each cube is 9 mm.
How many whole cubes can be made from this shape?

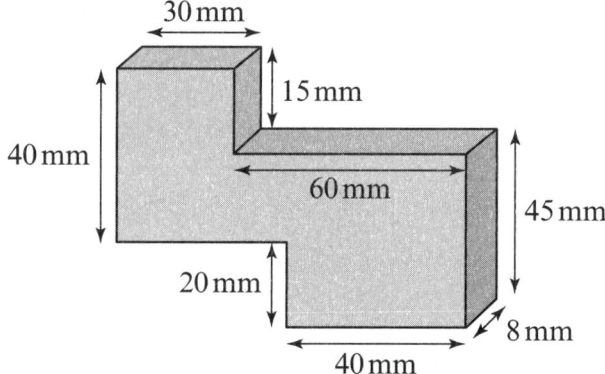

15 Nadia buys a fish tank. The dimensions of the fish tank are shown in the diagram.
Nadia fills the tank with water to $\frac{3}{4}$ of the height of the tank.
She knows that 1 cm³ of water has a mass of 1 gram.
What is the mass of the water in the fish tank?
Give your answer in kilograms.

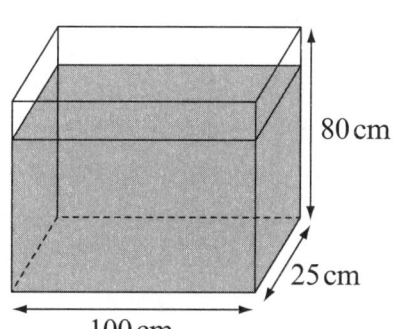

16 The diagram shows two shapes, A and B.
A is a compound shape. B is a cuboid.

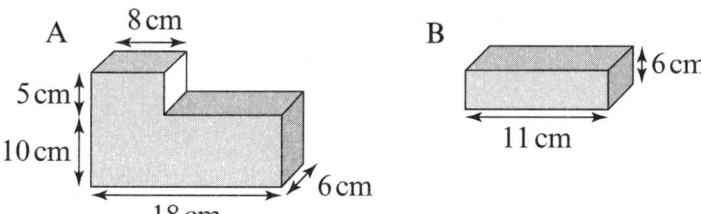

The volume of shape B is 40% of the volume of shape A.
Work out the width of shape B.

15 Shapes, area and volume

> 15.5 Calculating the surface area of cubes and cuboids

The **surface area** of a cube or cuboid is the total area of all its faces.
The side lengths of this cube are all 2 cm.
You can work out the surface area of the cube like this:
Area of one face = $2 \times 2 = 4 \, cm^2$
Total surface area = $6 \times 4 \, cm^2 = 24 \, cm^2$
Follow these steps to work out the surface area of a cuboid.

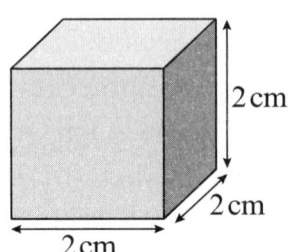

Step 1 Make a sketch of every face of the cuboid and write its length and width.
Step 2 Work out the area of every face and write it in the centre of the face.
Step 3 Add together all the areas.

Tip

The area of one face = length × width

The six faces of a cube are all the same size.

Make sure you have worked out the area of all six faces.

Exercise 15.5

Focus

1   Copy and complete the working to find the surface area of each cube.

   a   Area of one face = ☐ cm²
       Total surface area = 6 × ☐ = ☐ cm²

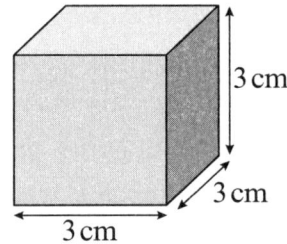

   b   Area of one face = ☐ cm²
       Total surface area = 6 × ☐ = ☐ cm²

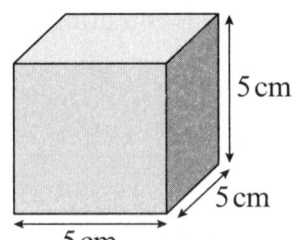

214

c   Area of one face = ☐ cm²
    Total surface area = 6 × ☐ = ☐ cm²

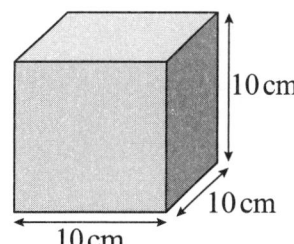

2 Copy and complete the working to find the surface area of each cuboid.

a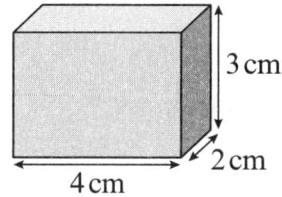

Front face 12 cm² 3 cm   Back face   12 cm² 3 cm
            4 cm   4 cm

Top face   8 cm²   2 cm   Bottom face ☐ cm²   ☐ cm
            4 cm   4 cm

Left end face 6 cm² 3 cm   Right end face ☐ cm² ☐ cm
               2 cm   ☐ cm

Total surface area = 12 + 12 + 8 + ☐ + 6 + ☐ = ☐ cm²

b   Front face = 30 cm²
    Back face = ☐ cm²
    Top face = 18 cm²
    Bottom face = ☐ cm²
    Left end face = ☐ cm²
    Right end face = ☐ cm²
    Total surface area = 30 + ☐ + 18 + ☐ + ☐ + ☐ = ☐ cm²

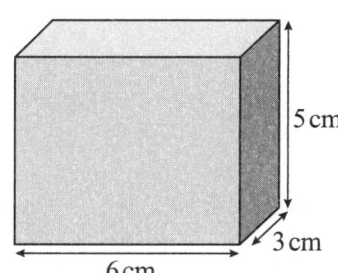

15 Shapes, area and volume

3 Copy and complete the workings to find the surface area of each cube.

a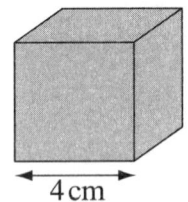

Area of one face
= ☐ × ☐ = ☐ cm²
Surface area of cube
= 6 × ☐ = ☐ cm²

b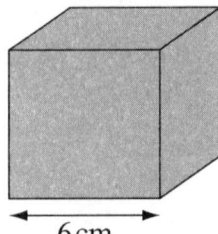

Area of one face
= ☐ × ☐ = ☐ cm²
Surface area of cube
= 6 × ☐ = ☐ cm²

4 Copy and complete the workings to find the surface area of each cuboid.

a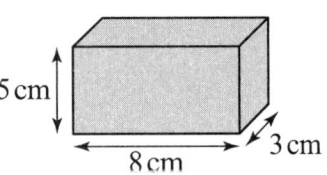

Area of top face
= 8 × 3 = ☐ cm²
Area of front face
= 8 × 5 = ☐ cm²
Area of side face
= 5 × 3 = ☐ cm²
Surface area = 2 × ☐ + 2 × ☐ + 2 × ☐
= ☐ + ☐ + ☐
= ☐ cm²

b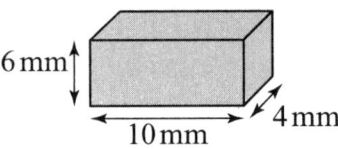

Area of top face
= 10 × ☐ = ☐ mm²
Area of front face
= 10 × ☐ = ☐ mm²
Area of side face
= 6 × ☐ = ☐ mm²
Surface area = 2 × ☐ + 2 × ☐ + 2 × ☐
= ☐ + ☐ + ☐
= ☐ mm²

Practice

5 Work out the surface area of each cuboid.

a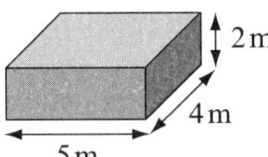

b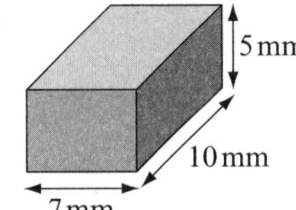

c

6 Which of these shapes has the smaller surface area: cube A or cuboid B? Show your working.

A 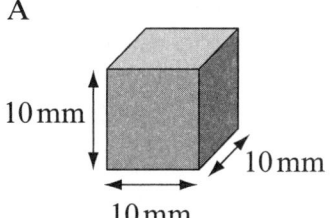 B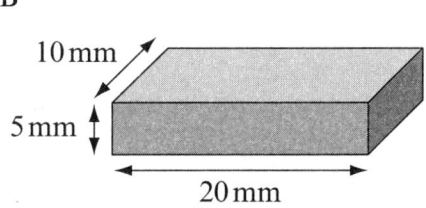

7 Which of these shapes has the smaller surface area: cube A or cuboid B? Show your working.

A 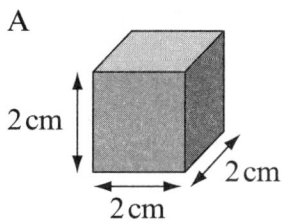 B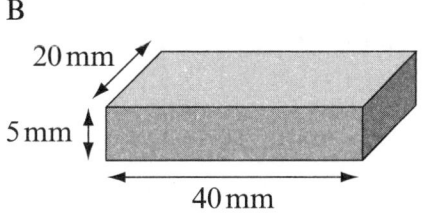

8 Work out the surface area of this cuboid. Give your answer in:
  a cm²
  b m²

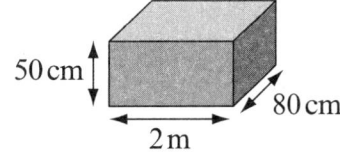

9 Emma has a wooden sculpture in the shape of a cuboid. The sculpture has a height of 2 m, a length of 1.5 m and a width of 1 m. Emma plans to paint all the faces of the sculpture with three coats of wood varnish.

varnish $12.99

(Size of tin: 500 mL)
1 litre covers 12 m²

  a Use the information given in the diagram to work out how many tins of wood varnish Emma will need to buy.
  b What will be the total cost of the wood varnish?

10 Work out the surface area of a cube with side length 0.8 m. Give your answer in cm².

> **Tip**
> First, change 0.8 m to cm.

11 The surface area of a cube is 384 m².
  a What is the area of one face of the cube?
  b What is the side length of the cube?

> **Tip**
> The area of six faces is 384 m².

15 Shapes, area and volume

12. A cuboid has a length of 15 cm, a width of 0.2 m and a height of 12 mm. Work out the surface area of the cuboid, in cm².

Tip
Make sure all the dimensions are in cm before you work out the surface area.

Challenge

13. The length of a cuboid is 25 cm. The width of the cuboid is $\frac{2}{5}$ of the length of the cuboid.
    The height of the cuboid is 80% of the length of the cuboid.
    What is the surface area of the cuboid?

14. Liwei wants to paint the inside and outside of this open box.
    He has enough paint to cover 30 000 cm².
    Does Liwei have enough paint to paint the box? Show all your working.

    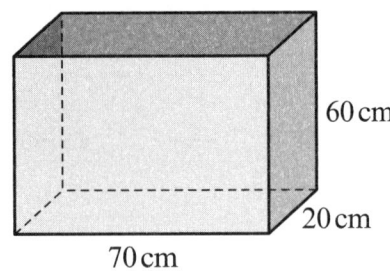

    Tip
    An open box is a box with no lid.

15. The surface area of this cuboid is 2 cm² more than four times the surface area of this cube.

    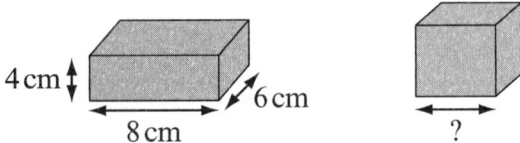

    What is the side length of the cube?

16. This cuboid has a volume of 864 cm³.

    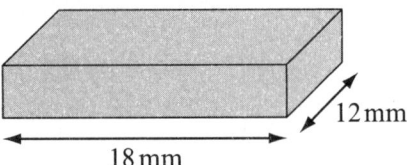

    Show that the surface area of the cuboid is 672 cm².

17 These three boxes have the same volume.

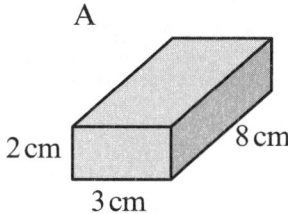 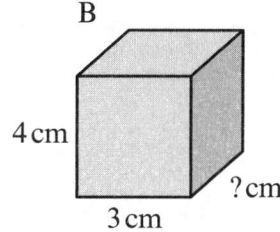 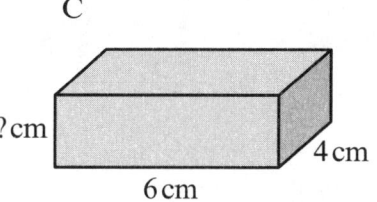

- **a** Work out the missing lengths.
- **b** Work out the surface area of each cuboid.
- **c** If you managed a business that needed to make a box with this volume, would you make box A, B or C? Explain your answer.
- **d** These are the dimensions of three boxes that each have a volume of 64 cm³.
    - **D** 4 cm by 4 cm by 4 cm
    - **E** 2 cm by 8 cm by 4 cm
    - **F** 1 cm by 4 cm by 16 cm

    Which box do you think will have the:
    - **i** largest surface area?
    - **ii** smallest surface area?

    Explain your answers. Work out the surface area of each cuboid, then check to see if your answers to parts **i** and **ii** are correct.

16 Interpreting and discussing results

> ## 16.1 Two-way tables

Exercise 16.1

Key word

two-way table

Focus

1 Some students are asked if they have any brothers or sisters.
   They answer either 'yes' or 'no'.
   The **two-way table** shows some of the results.
   Copy and complete the table.

	Yes	No	Total
Girls	25	3	
Boys	20	2	
Total			

In here is the total number of girls.

In here is the total number of boys.

In here is the total number who answered 'yes'.

In here is the total number who answered 'no'.

In here is the total number of students asked.

16.1 Two-way tables

2 Some students are asked if they like pineapple. They answer either 'yes' or 'no'.
The two-way table shows the results.

	Yes	No	Total
Boys	20	6	26
Girls	13	11	24
Total	33	17	50

  a How many boys answer 'yes'?
  b How many girls answer 'no'?
  c How many boys are asked the question?
  d How many students in total answer 'no'?
  e How many students in total are asked the question?

3 The two-way table shows the eye colour of the adult men and women in a fitness class.

	Brown eyes	Blue eyes	Total
Men	6	2	8
Women	5	7	12
Total	11	9	20

  a How many of the men have brown eyes?
  b How many of the women have blue eyes?
  c How many of the adults do <u>not</u> have brown eyes?
  d How many adults are there in total in the fitness class?

4 The two-way table shows the type of clothes a group of surfers on a beach are wearing.

	Swimwear	Wet suit	Other clothing	Total
Male	6	12	3	21
Female	2	7	0	9
Total	8	19	3	30

  a How many of the female surfers are wearing wet suits?
  b How many of the surfers are wearing swimwear?
  c How many surfers are on the beach?
  d How many of the surfers are <u>not</u> wearing wet suits?

16 Interpreting and discussing results

5 This two-way table shows the favourite racket sport of the students in class 7H. Copy and complete the table.

Use the 'Total' column and the 'Total' row to help you to work out the missing numbers in the table. All the missing numbers are shown in the cloud.

	Tennis	Squash	Badminton	Total
Girls	6		8	15
Boys		7	6	
Total	10			32

Cloud: 1, 4, 17, 8, 14

Practice

6 This two-way table shows the favourite coffee type of 40 adults. Copy and complete the table.

Use the 'Total' column and the 'Total' row to help you to work out the missing values in the table.

	Latte	Cappuccino	Americano	Total
Men	8		10	
Women	5	3		
Total		3		40

7 The two-way table shows some information about the breeds of horses competing at a horseshow.

	Arabian	Morgan	Thoroughbred	Other	Total
Female owner	42	18		4	119
Male owner	26		25		
Total		62			222

  a Copy and complete the table.
  b How many of the Morgan horses have a male owner?
  c How many of the horses are <u>not</u> thoroughbred horses?

8   The two-way table shows the favourite topics of a group of 50 maths students.

	Algebra	Geometry	Number	Statistics	Total
Girls	12	6		2	
Boys	8		6	1	
Total		11			50

a   Copy and complete the table.
b   How many of the boys choose geometry as their favourite topic?
c   How many girls are in the group?
d   How many of the students did <u>not</u> choose algebra or geometry as their favourite topic?

9   Sofia and Zara keep a record of the number of essays, poems and stories they write for English homework in one year. The two-way table shows their results.

	Essays	Poems	Stories	Total
Zara	16		10	
Sofia		11		38
Total		20	28	

a   Copy and complete the table.
b   Sofia says:

I wrote twice as many stories as I did essays.

Show that Sofia is correct.
c   What fraction of Zara's total number of homework tasks were stories? Write your answer in its simplest form.
d   Zara says:

I wrote 45% of our total number of poems.

Show that Zara is correct.

16 Interpreting and discussing results

e What percentage of the total number of essays did Sofia write?

f What is the ratio of essays to stories for Zara? Write your answer in its simplest form.

10 Erin records the food she sells in her café during one weekend. The two-way table shows her results.

	Saturday	Sunday	Total
Salads	20		30
Sandwiches		8	33
Cakes		25	
Fruit	18	12	
Total	75		130

a Copy and complete the table.

b On which day does Erin sell the most items of food?

c Which item of food is the most popular?

d Erin makes a profit of:
- $2.80 on each salad
- $2.50 on each sandwich
- $1 on each cake
- 80 cents on each piece of fruit.

Erin thinks she makes the most profit from cakes during the weekend because the food item she has sold the most is cakes. Do you think Erin is correct? Explain your answer.

e What is the total amount of profit that Erin makes this weekend?

Challenge

11 A factory manufactures 30 500 batteries an hour. 6500 of these batteries are rechargeable.

The factory makes 3000 ordinary AAA batteries an hour.

Of the 10 000 AA batteries the factory makes an hour, 4000 are rechargeable.

The factory makes 15 000 ordinary and 1500 rechargeable C cell batteries an hour.

Copy and complete the two-way table to show the numbers of batteries made per hour.

	AAA	AA	C cell	Total
Ordinary				
Rechargeable				
Total				

12 Thirty friends go to the cinema. They each buy one snack.
They buy a chocolate bar, an ice cream or some popcorn.

Thirteen of the group buy a chocolate bar; only three of them are boys.

Four of the 16 girls buy popcorn. Eight of the boys buy popcorn.

Copy and complete the two-way table to show the snacks the group of friends buy.

	Chocolate bar	Ice cream	Popcorn	Total
Boys				
Girls				
Total				

13 Eighty students are asked which is their favourite English football team.

Of the 48 boys asked, $\frac{1}{4}$ choose Arsenal and $\frac{1}{3}$ choose Liverpool, but none choose Chelsea.

Of the girls asked, 25% choose Manchester City. This number is the same as the total number of girls who choose Chelsea.

None of the girls choose Liverpool and only one girl chooses Manchester United.

The total number who choose Manchester United is three more than the total number who choose Manchester City.

Copy and complete the two-way table showing the information given above.

	Arsenal	Chelsea	Liverpool	Manchester City	Manchester United	Total
Boys						
Girls						
Total						

16 Interpreting and discussing results

14 While on safari, Greg takes 1500 photos of animals either eating, walking, running or playing.

$\frac{3}{10}$ of all the photos are of monkeys, and half of those are of monkeys playing, but none of them are of monkeys eating.

The rest of the monkey photos are walking : running in the ratio 4 : 1.

There are the same number of photos of warthogs running as there are of monkeys running.

Of the 120 warthog photos, 30 show warthogs walking.

The remainder of the warthog photos show them eating.

$\frac{1}{2}$ of all the photos are of elephants.

$\frac{2}{3}$ of the elephant photos are of them eating and 20% of them are of them walking.

The rest of the elephant photos are of them playing.

The total number of photos of animals playing is 350.

There are 15 photos of impala walking.

The ratio of the photos of impala eating : running is 5 : 2.

Copy and complete the two-way table to show the information given above.

	Eating	Walking	Running	Playing	Total
Elephant					
Monkey					
Impala					
Warthog					
Total					

> 16.2 Dual and compound bar charts

Exercise 16.2

Focus

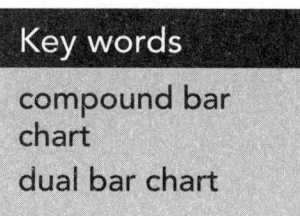

1   This **dual bar chart** shows the favourite type of film of the students in class 7B.

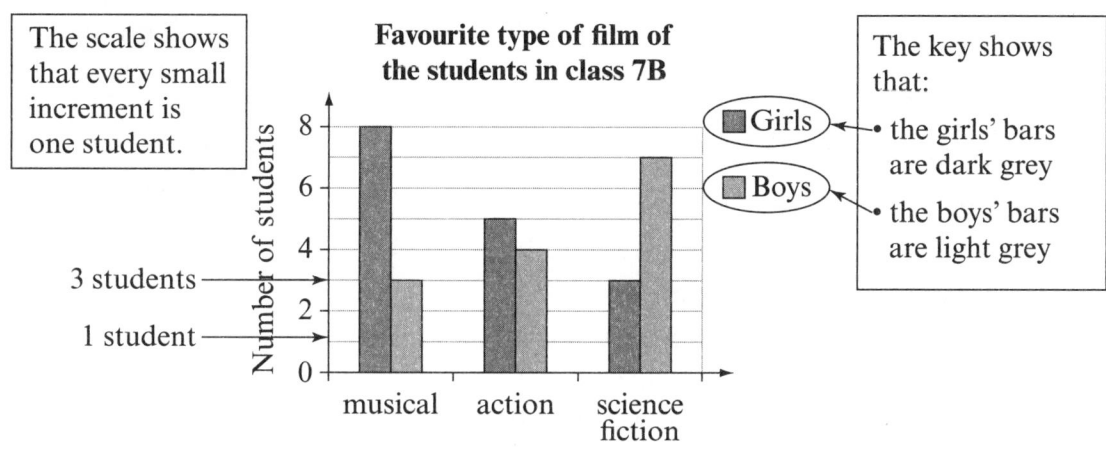

a   How many of the girls choose 'musical' as their favourite film?
b   How many of the boys choose 'action' as their favourite film?
c   How many more boys than girls choose 'science fiction' as their favourite film?
d   How many students are there in class 7B?
e   Which type of film is chosen most by the:
    i   girls?   ii   boys?   iii   whole class?

16 Interpreting and discussing results

2 This dual bar chart shows the types of emails received one day by two teachers.

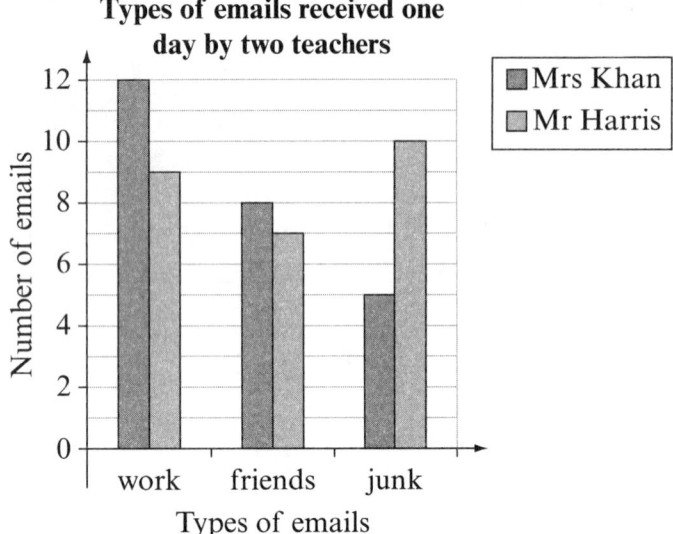

Tip

Junk emails are unwanted emails. They are usually sent out by companies trying to sell you something.

  a Which teacher received the most work emails?
  b Which teacher received the most junk emails?
  c How many more emails from friends did Mrs Khan receive than Mr Harris?
  d Work out the total number of emails received by:
   i Mrs Khan
   ii Mr Harris

3 This **compound bar chart** shows the types of emails received one day by Miss Davies.

Copy and complete these statements. All the numbers you need are in the cloud.

  a Miss Davies received …… work emails.
  b Miss Davies received a total of …… emails from work and from friends.
  c Miss Davies received a total of …… junk emails and emails from work and from friends.
  d Miss Davies received 18 − 6 = …… emails from friends.
  e Miss Davies received 20 − 18 = …… junk emails.

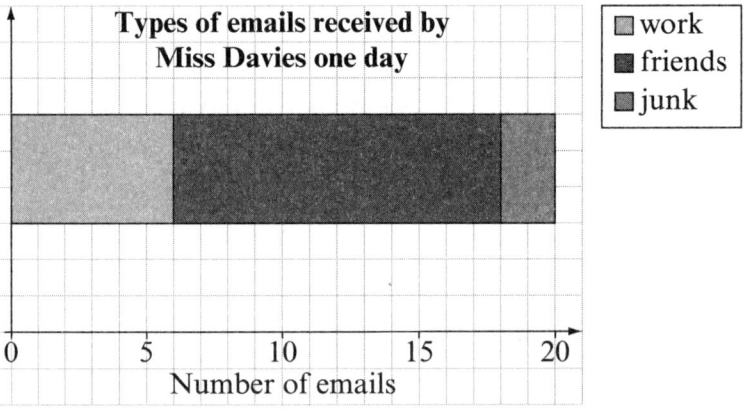

20 6 18
2 12

4 This compound bar chart shows the favourite types of magazines of the students in class 7D.

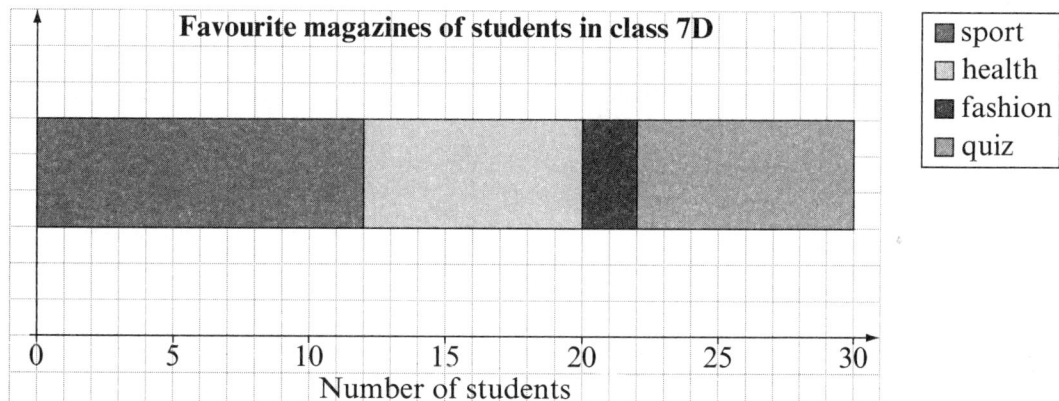

a What is the total number of students in class 7D?
b Which type of magazine is the:
   i most popular?   ii least popular?
c How many students chose these types of magazines as their favourite?
   i sport   ii health   iii fashion   iv quiz

5 This compound bar chart shows the science exam results for class 11C.

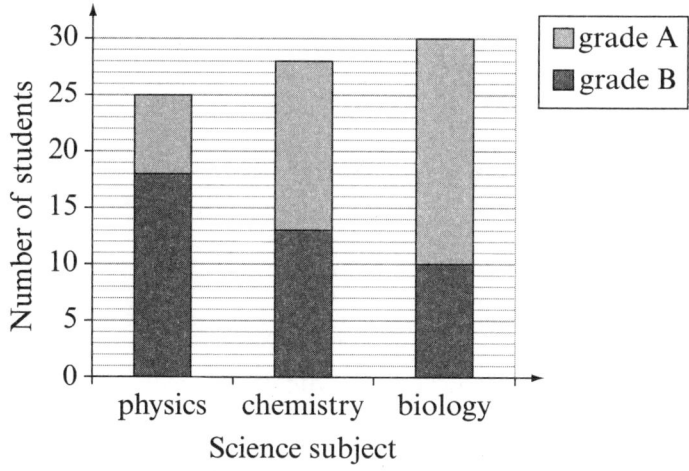

a In which science subject did the students get the most:
   i grade As?   ii grade Bs?
b How many students achieved a:
   i grade B for biology?   ii grade A for biology?
c How many students achieved a:
   i grade B for chemistry? ii grade A for chemistry?

16 Interpreting and discussing results

Practice

6 This dual bar chart shows the number of gold and silver medals won by four countries competing in the 2016 Olympic Games.

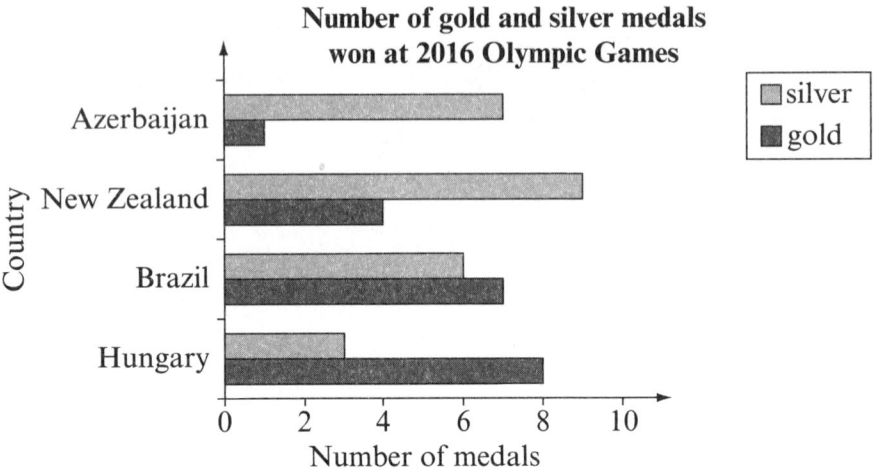

a Which country won the most:
   i gold medals?   ii silver medals?
b Which country won the least number of medals in total?

Marcus says:

"Hungary won twice as many gold medals as New Zealand."

c Show that Marcus is correct.
d Make two other comments that compare the number of medals won by the different countries.

7 The two-way table shows the number of items Nahla and Ayana recycle in one week.

	Plastic bottles	Glass bottles	Tin cans
Nahla	6	4	8
Ayana	3	8	5

a   Copy and complete the dual bar chart to show this information.

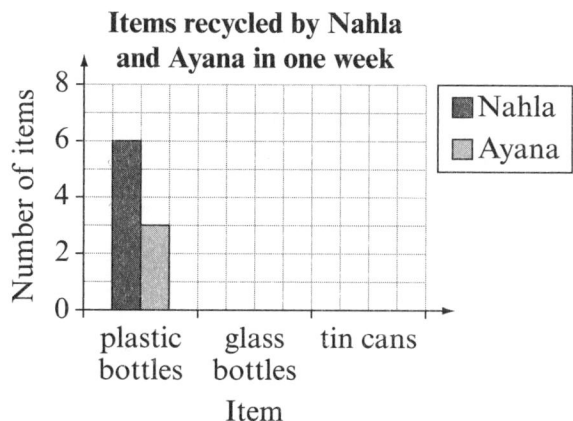

b   Make two comments about what the bar chart shows.

8 This two-way table shows the favourite activities of the students in class 7P.

	Gym	Dance	Swimming	Cricket
Girls	4	6	2	5
Boys	5	2	3	8

a   Draw a dual bar chart to show this information.
b   Make two comments about what your bar chart shows.

9 The compound bar chart shows the number of minutes that Carlos and Rio spend sending text messages, making calls and browsing the internet on their smartphones.

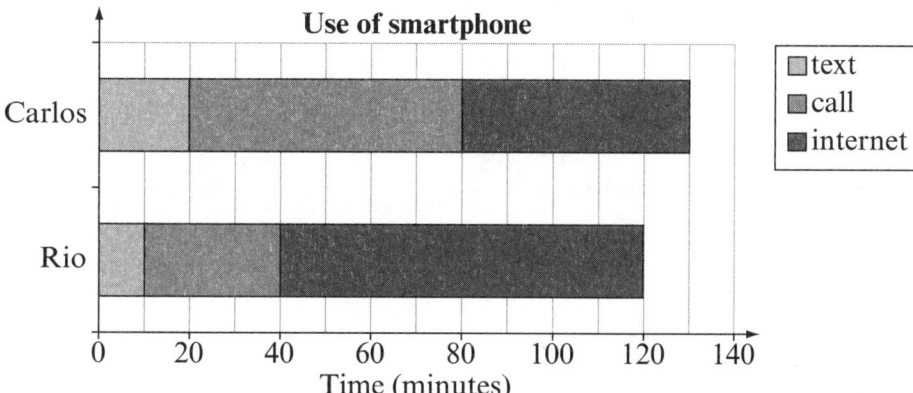

a   For how many minutes does Carlos send text messages?
b   For how many minutes does Rio browse the internet?
c   How many minutes more does Carlos spend on calls than Rio?
d   Carlos says that he spends the same amount of time sending text messages and calls as Rio spends on the internet. Is Carlos correct? Explain your answer.

16 Interpreting and discussing results

10 This two-way table shows the number of kitchen appliances sold by a store in two weeks.

	Type of kitchen appliance			
	Fridge	Freezer	Washing machine	Dishwasher
Week 1	8	3	12	2
Week 2	10	1	6	4

a   Copy and complete this compound bar chart.

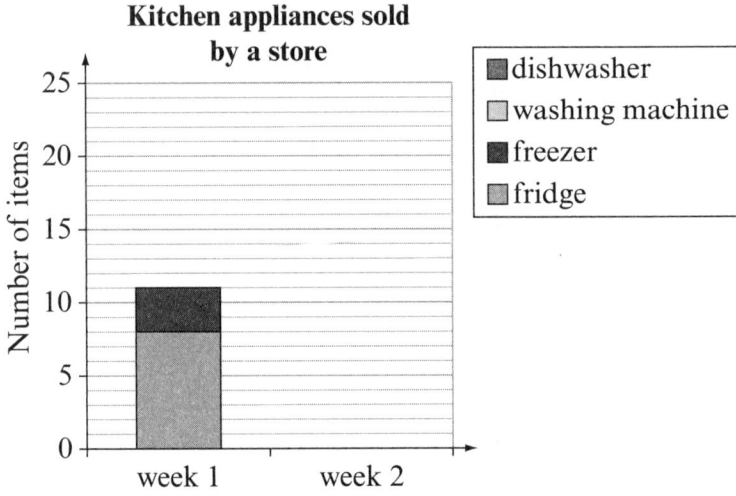

b   Make two comments about what the bar chart shows.

Challenge

11 Brad and Kurt compare their scores from four spelling tests. The compound bar chart shows their test scores.

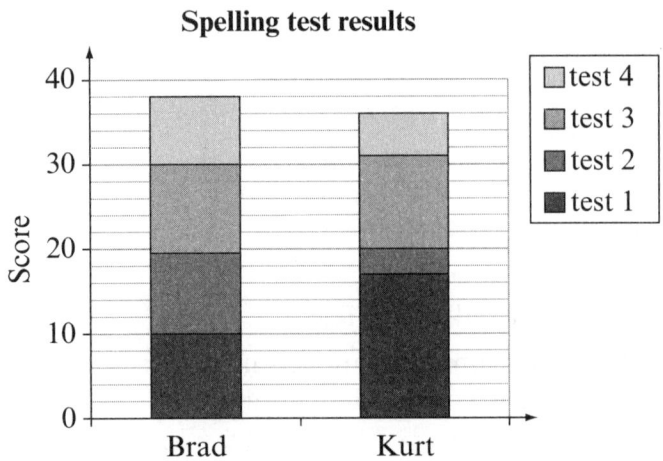

a In which test did Brad and Kurt get the same score?
b In which tests did Brad get a higher score than Kurt?
c Arun says:

Brad scored 3 more than Kurt in test 2.

Is Arun correct? Explain your answer.
d Write down two comments that compare the test results of Brad and Kurt.
e Do you think Brad or Kurt is better at spelling? Explain your answer.
f Each test was out of a mark of 15. Write Kurt's total score for the four tests as a:
  i fraction   ii percentage

12 The compound bar chart shows the number of flights that arrived early, on time or late on one day at three airports in the United Kingdom.

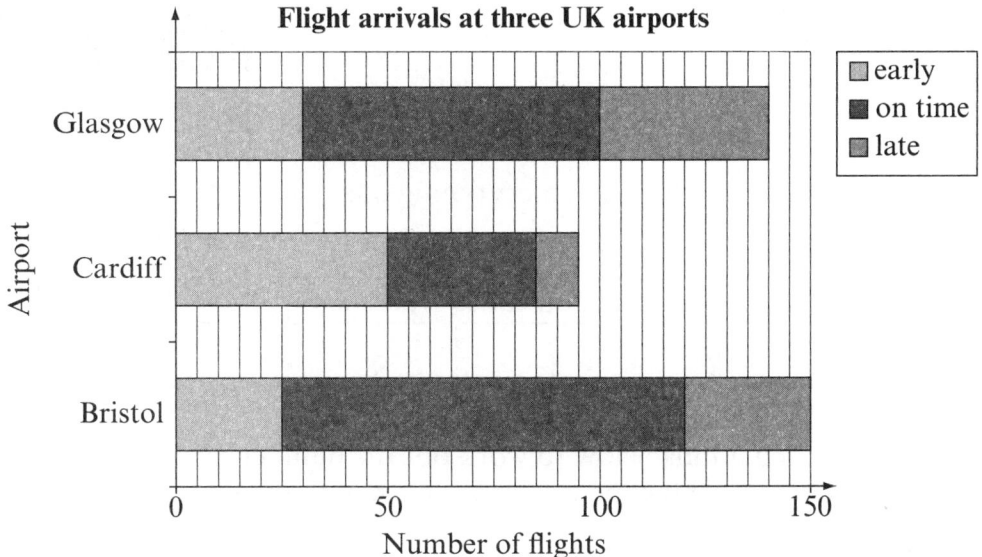

a Use the information in the chart to copy and complete this two-way table.
b What fraction of the Bristol flights were late? Give your answer in its simplest form.
c What percentage of the 'on time' flights were at Glasgow?
d What is the ratio of Bristol early flights to Cardiff early flights? Give your answer in its simplest form.

	Early	On time	Late	Total
Glasgow				
Cardiff				
Bristol				
Total				

16 Interpreting and discussing results

 13 This two-way table shows the favourite type of chocolate of 100 adults.

	Type of chocolate	
	Milk	Dark
Men	39	32
Women	13	16

a i   Draw a dual bar chart to show this information.
  ii Make one comment on what your chart shows.
b i   Draw a compound bar chart to show this information.
  ii Make one comment on what your chart shows.
c Which do you think is the best chart to use to display this information? Give reasons for your answer.

> 16.3 Pie charts and waffle diagrams

Exercise 16.3

Focus

Key words
label
pie chart
proportions
sector
waffle diagram

1 The table shows the desserts chosen by the customers dining in a restaurant one evening.

Dessert chosen	ice cream	cheesecake	lemon cake	fruit salad
Number of customers	9	12	11	8

a Copy and complete the calculations below to work out the number of degrees for each **sector** of a **pie chart**, to show the information given in the table.

> Total number of customers = 9 + 12 + 11 + 8 = ☐ customers
> Number of degrees per customer = 360 ÷ ☐ = ☐°
> Number of degrees for each sector:
> Ice cream = 9 × ☐ = ☐°   Cheesecake = 12 × ☐ = ☐°
> Lemon cake = 11 × ☐ = ☐°   Fruit salad = 8 × ☐ = ☐°

Tip
Remember **to label** each sector and to give the pie chart a title.

b Draw a pie chart to represent the data given in the table.

2 The table shows the results of a survey about students' favourite weekdays.

Favourite weekday	Monday	Tuesday	Wednesday	Thursday	Friday
Number of students	5	8	14	6	27

a Copy and complete the calculations below to work out the number of degrees for each sector of a pie chart, to show the information given in the table.

> Total number of students = 5 + 8 + 14 + 6 + 27 = ☐ students
> Number of degrees per students = 360 ÷ ☐ = ☐°
> Number of degrees for each sector:
> Monday = 5 × ☐ = ☐°   Tuesday = 8 × ☐ = ☐°
> Wednesday = 14 × ☐ = ☐°   Thursday = 6 × ☐ = ☐°
> Friday = 27 × ☐ = ☐°

Tip
Remember to label each sector and to give the pie chart a title.

b Draw a pie chart to represent the data given in the table.

3 The bar chart shows the number of times 24 people ate potatoes in one week.

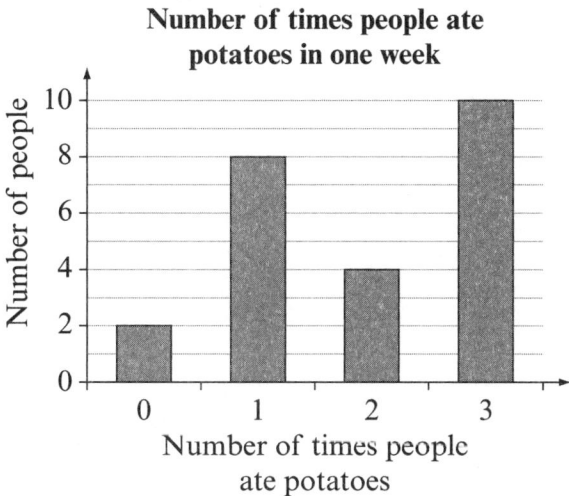

a Use the bar chart to copy and complete this table.

Number of times people ate potatoes	0	1	2	3	Total
Number of people	2				24

16 Interpreting and discussing results

b Copy and complete the calculations below to work out the number of degrees for each sector of a pie chart, to show the information given in the table.

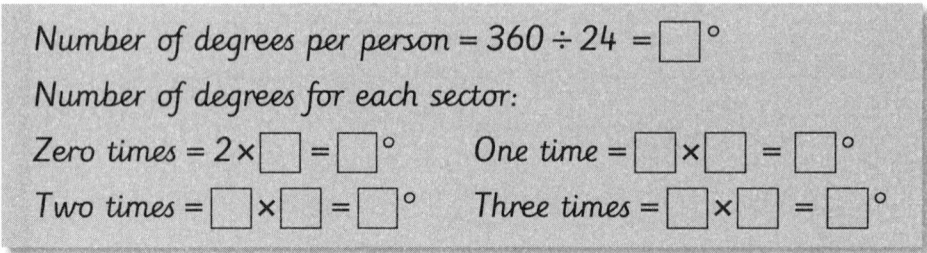

Number of degrees per person = 360 ÷ 24 = ☐°

Number of degrees for each sector:

Zero times = 2 × ☐ = ☐°   One time = ☐ × ☐ = ☐°

Two times = ☐ × ☐ = ☐°   Three times = ☐ × ☐ = ☐°

c Draw a pie chart to represent the data given in the table.

4 The **waffle diagram** shows the favourite fruit of the students in class 7P.

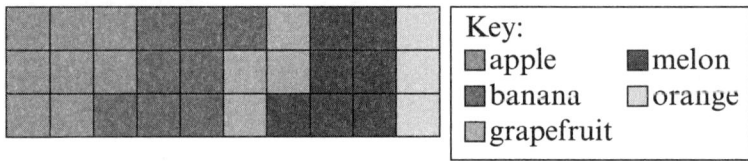

Key:
- apple
- banana
- grapefruit
- melon
- orange

a Copy the table and use the waffle diagram to complete it, showing the number of students that chose each fruit.

Fruit	Number of students
apple	8
banana	
grapefruit	
melon	
orange	

b Draw a pie chart to show the information given in the table.

Practice

5 Frank owns a bicycle shop. The pie chart shows Frank's sales in October of four different BMX bike models. Altogether Frank sold 200 BMX bikes in October.

  a Which model of BMX bike was the most popular?

  b What fraction of the bikes sold were Mudds?

  c What percentage of the bikes sold were Tungstens?

  d How many of the bikes sold were Xtremes?

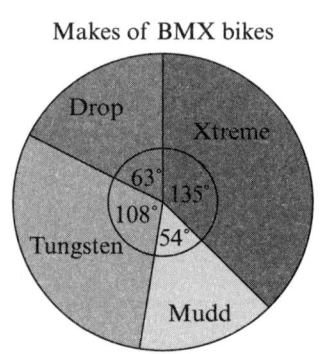

Makes of BMX bikes

6 A supermarket sells five types of rice. The pie chart shows the **proportion** of the different types of rice it sold one day.

    a Which rice was the most popular?
    b What fraction of the rice sold was brown rice?
    c What percentage of the rice sold was black rice?
    d Altogether the supermarket sold 400 kilograms of rice on this day. How many kilograms of red rice was sold on this day?

Type of rice sold by a supermarket

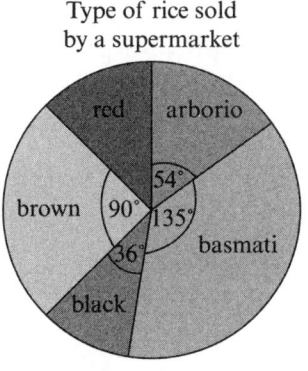

7 The pie chart shows the favourite type of cookie of the members of a netball club.

    a Which type of cookie is the least popular?
    b What fraction of the members chose coconut?

Altogether there are 24 members of the netball club.

    c How many members chose ginger?
    d How many more members chose choc-chip than raisin?

Favourite type of cookie

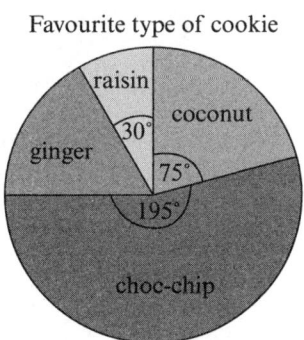

Challenge

8 The waffle diagram shows the number of sandwiches sold in a café one day.

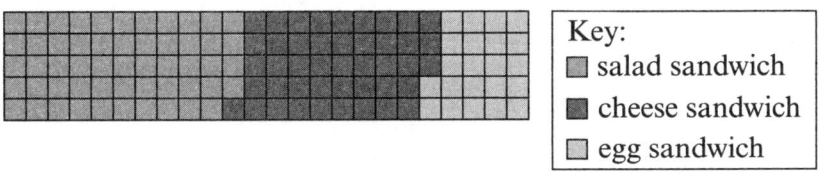

Key:
- salad sandwich
- cheese sandwich
- egg sandwich

Draw a pie chart to show the information given in the waffle diagram.

9 The pie chart shows the results of a survey on the favourite type of fruit preferred by a group of men. Nine men chose bananas as their favourite.

Men's favourite fruit

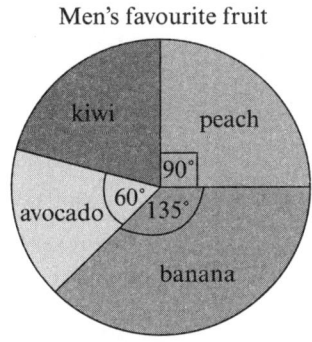

Bo thinks that six men chose kiwis. Is Bo correct? Explain your answer.

16 Interpreting and discussing results

10 The pie chart shows the results of a survey on the favourite type of fruit of a group of women. Eight <u>more</u> women chose bananas than those who chose peaches.

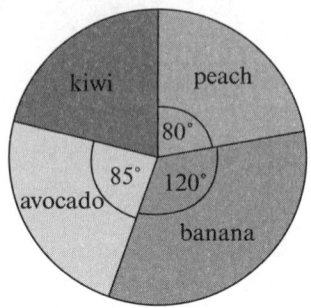

Women's favourite fruit

How many women chose kiwis? Show all your working.

11 Shani asks 60 people what their favourite type of book is.
She works out the percentage and the number of degrees for each sector of a pie chart.

The table shows some of her results.

Favourite type of book	Frequency	Percentage	Number of degrees
thriller	9		
romantic		30	108
history			
nature	12	20	

Draw a pie chart to show the information given in the table.

> 16.4 Infographics

Exercise 16.4

> Key word
> infographic

Focus

1 This **infographic** shows the number of cell phones used in five countries in Africa.

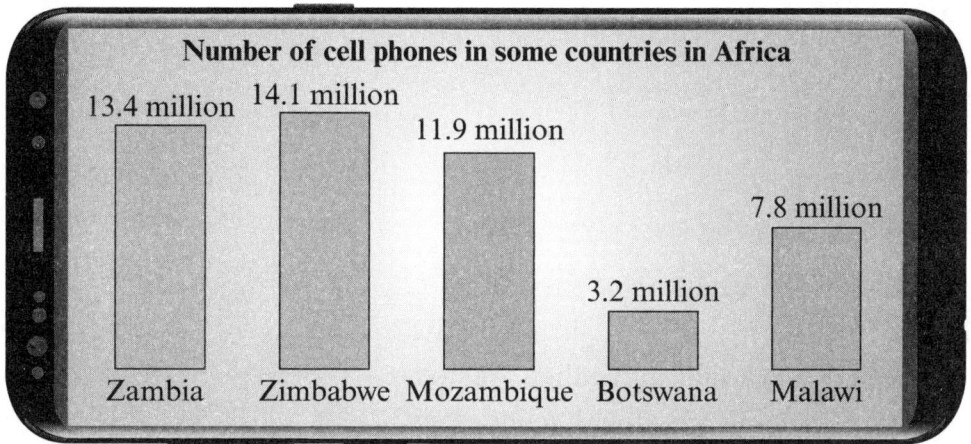

   a In which country are the most cell phones used?
   b How many cell phones are used in Malawi?
   c What is the missing number from this sentence?

   In Mozambique ___ million more cell phones are used than in Botswana.

2 Zara sees this infographic in a magazine.
   Zara says:

"More than half the people in the world have never received a phone call in their life."

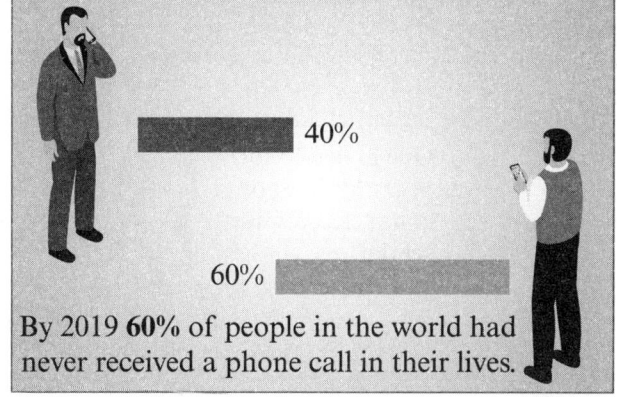

By 2019 **60%** of people in the world had never received a phone call in their lives.

   a Is Zara correct? Explain your answer.
   b What fraction of the people in the world have never received a phone call in their lives? Write your answer in its simplest form.
   c What percentage of the people in the world <u>have</u> received a phone call in their lives?

> **Tip**
> The percentages for 'have' and 'have never' must add up to 100%.

16 Interpreting and discussing results

3   A group of adults were asked five questions about themselves. The infographic shows the percentage of adults that agree with the statements.

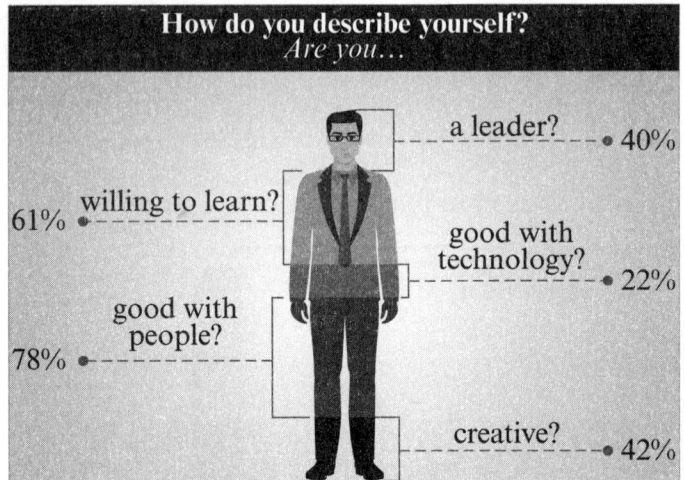

a   What percentage of the adults agree they are:
   i   willing to learn?   ii   creative?
b   What percentage of the adults agree they are <u>not</u>:
   i   a leader?   ii   good with technology?

Tip

The percentages for 'agree' and 'disagree' for each question must add up to 100%.

Practice

4   This infographic shows some facts about education around the world.

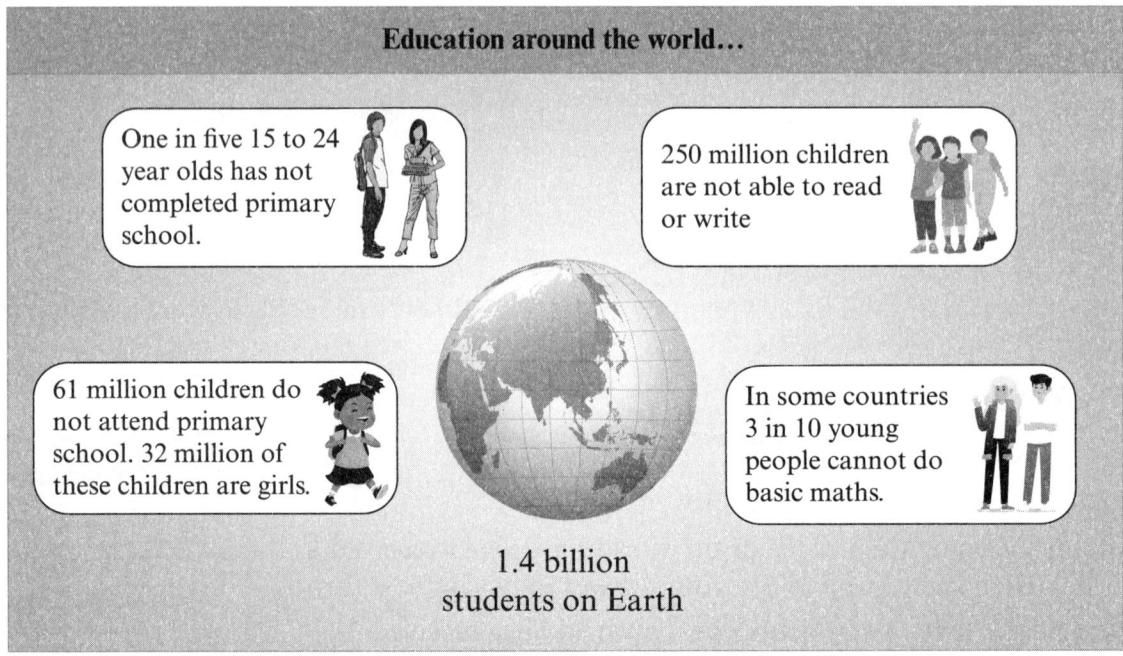

Choose the correct answer, **A**, **B** or **C**, for each of these questions.

a The number of students on Earth is:
  A 32 million   B 250 million   C 1.4 billion

b The number of children not able to read or write is:
  A 25 000 000   B 250 000 000   C 2 500 000 000

c In some countries the percentage of young people that cannot do basic arithmetic is:
  A 30%   B 3%   C 0.3%

d The fraction of 15 to 24 year olds that <u>have</u> completed primary school is:
  A $\frac{1}{5}$ B $\frac{4}{5}$ C $\frac{5}{6}$

e The percentage of children who do not attend primary school that are girls is:
  A exactly 50%   B less than 50%   C more than 50%

5 Sofia asks 400 students in her school to choose their favourite subject out of geography, computing, maths, english, physics and chemistry. She draws this infographic to show her results.

  a Which subject is chosen the most?
  b Which subject is chosen the least?
  c What percentage of students chose English?

  d Sofia says:

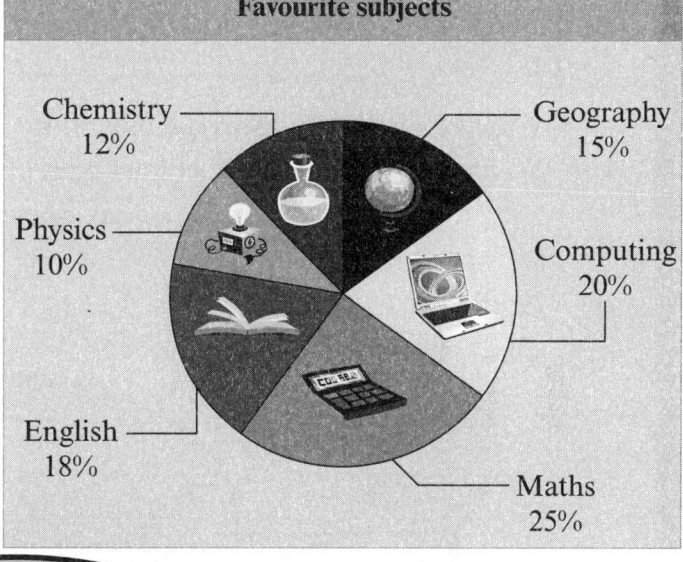

  > 25% of the students chose maths. I asked 400 students. 25% of 400 = 100, so 100 students chose maths.

  Work out how many students chose:
  i   physics
  ii computing

16 Interpreting and discussing results

6 This infographic shows information about the top five oil-producing countries.

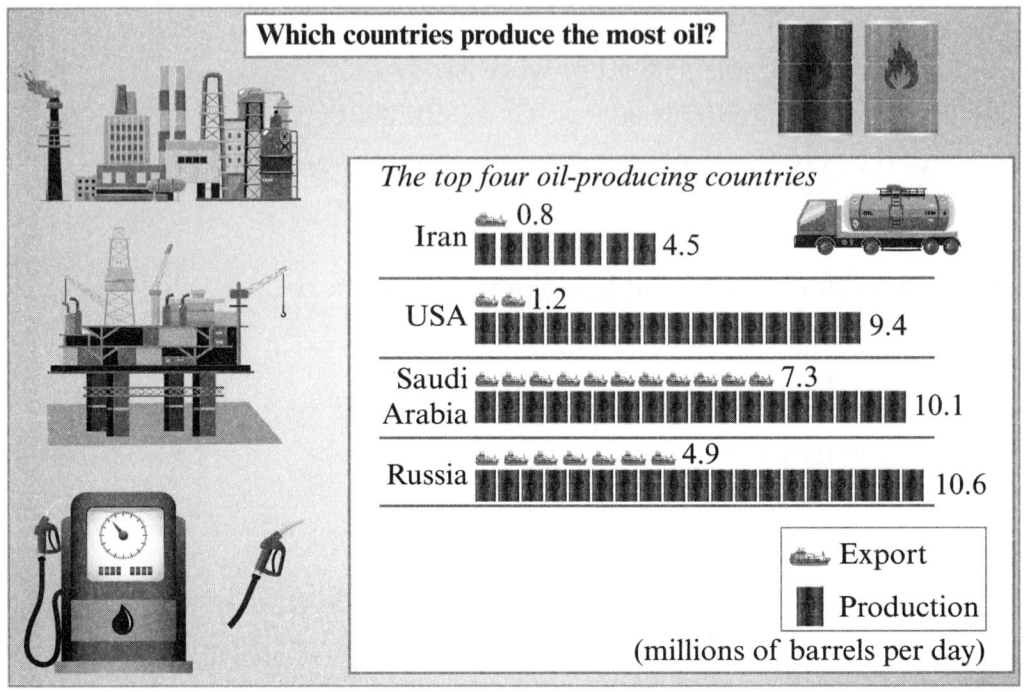

a Which country produces the most oil?
b Which country exports the most oil?
c How many million barrels per day does the USA:
  i produce?   ii export?
d Arun says:

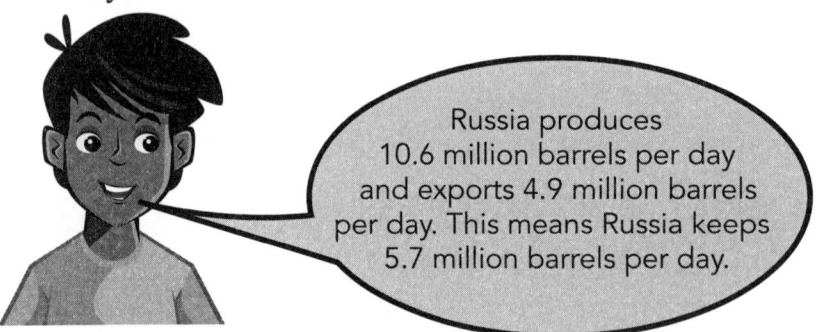

Russia produces 10.6 million barrels per day and exports 4.9 million barrels per day. This means Russia keeps 5.7 million barrels per day.

Show that Arun is correct.

e i Which country keeps the most oil? Explain how you can tell from the graph which country this is.
  ii How many million barrels per day does this country keep?

Tip

'Production' is the amount of oil a country produces. 'Export' is the amount of oil a country sells to other countries.

f   Arun says:

Russia exports about half of the oil it produces.

    Is Arun correct? Explain your answer.
g   Make two more comments about what the infographic tells you.

Challenge

7   This infographic shows what land is used for in four countries in South America.

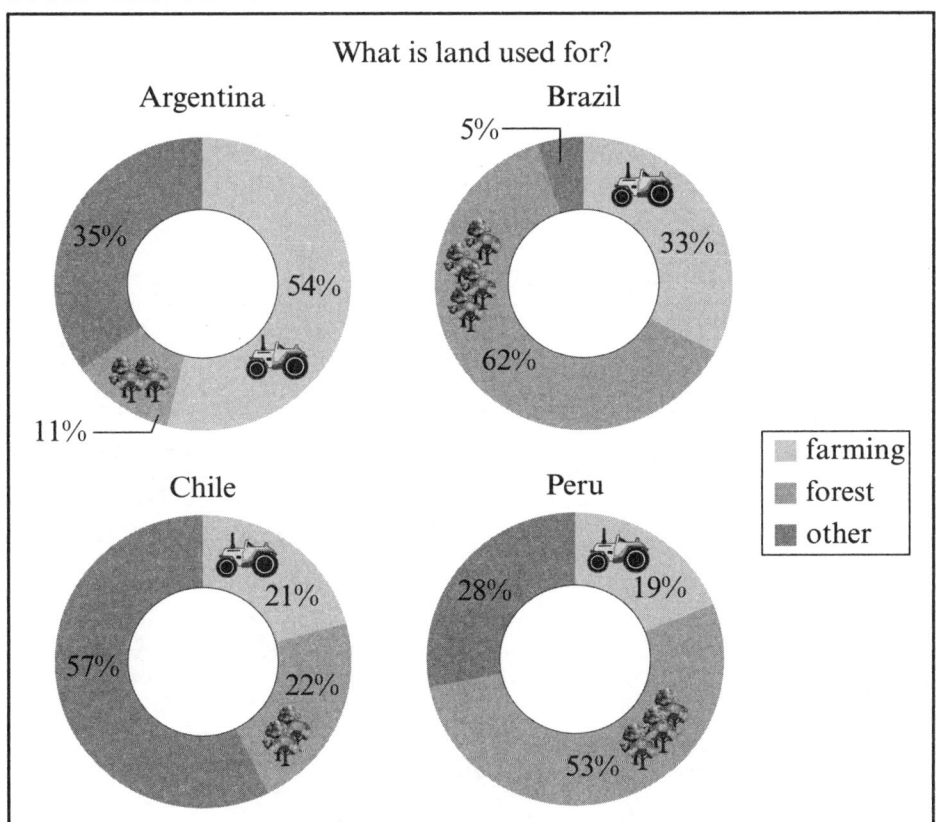

a   Which country has the greatest percentage of land used for farming?
b   Which country has the greatest percentage of land that is forest?
c   What do you think the 'other' use of land might be?
d   Compare the charts in the infographic and write a short paragraph describing what they tell you.

8 Sue manages a snack bar. She finds this infographic in a magazine.

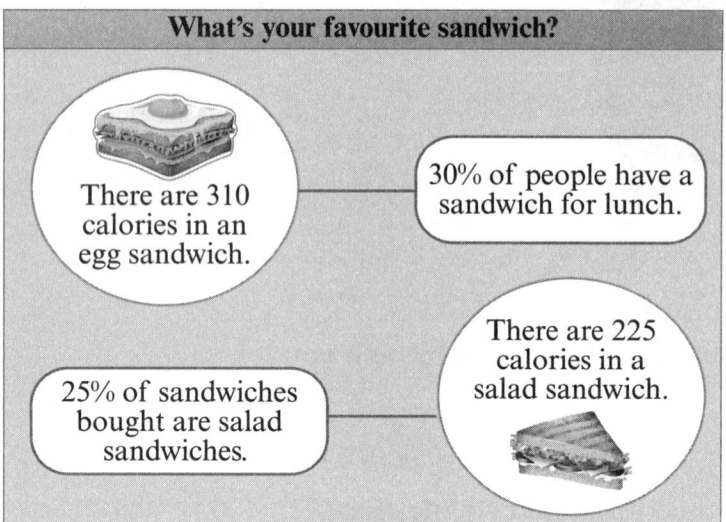

- **a** Sue usually has 150 customers in her snack bar on a Monday. How many of these customers are likely to buy a sandwich?
- **b** On a Tuesday Sue usually sells 68 sandwiches. How many of these sandwiches are likely to be salad sandwiches?
- **c** One week Pepe buys two egg sandwiches and three salad sandwiches. What is the total number of calories in these sandwiches?

9 Jim wants to make an infographic to display the information given in this table.

Name of planet	Mercury	Venus	Earth	Mars	Jupiter
Time it takes for the planet to orbit the Sun	88 days	225 days	365 days	687 days	12 years

This is the infographic he makes:

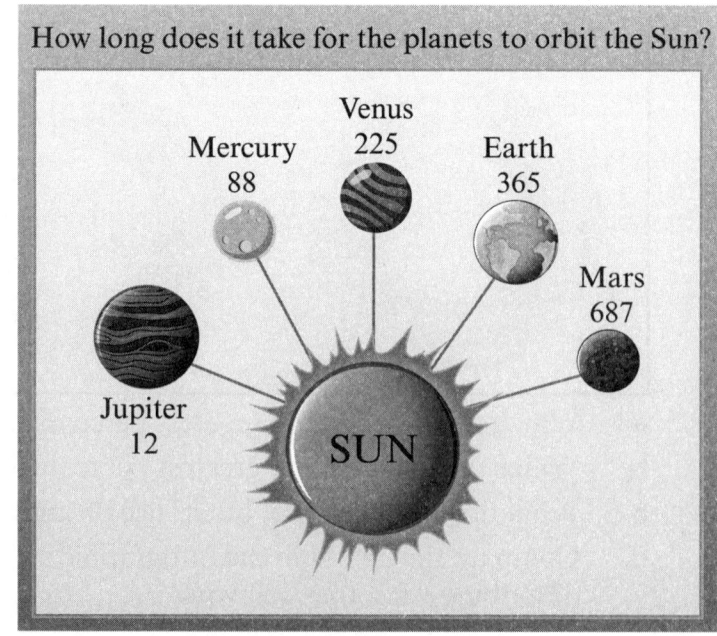

- **a** Critique Jim's infographic by answering the following. Explain your answers.
  - **i** Do you think Jim's infographic shows the information in the table correctly?
  - **ii** Do you think the way it shows the information is misleading?
- **b** How do you think you could improve this infographic?

> 16.5 Representing data

Exercise 16.5

Key words

frequency table
justify

Focus

1   Look at the following sets of data. Which type of diagram, graph or chart do you think is best to use to display the data? Choose from the words in the box. **Justify** your choice.

   line graph   bar chart   scatter graph   dual bar chart

   a   The number of adult and child tickets sold at a theme park on two different days.
   b   The amount of electricity that is produced by wind power in five countries.
   c   The change in sales of cellular phones over time.
   d   The exam scores for 12 students in music and maths.

2   Allana collects glass bottles, plastic bottles, cans, cartons and newspapers for recycling. The table shows the number of each item that she collects in one week.

Item	glass bottles	plastic bottles	cans	cartons	newspapers
Number collected	8	28	25	9	12

   a   Draw a diagram, graph or chart to represent the data.
   b   Justify your choice of diagram, graph or chart.
   c   Make one comment about what your diagram, graph or chart shows.

3   Ana, Bea, Carla, Dion, Elin, Fi, Gail and Holly are members of a tennis club.
   There are tournaments in which they can enter in May, June and August.
   The girls who enter the tournament in May are: Ana, Bea, Fi and Gail.
   The girls who enter the tournament in June are: Bea, Carla, Elin, Fi and Gail.
   The girls who enter the tournament in August are: Ana, Bea, Dion and Elin.
   a   Draw a diagram, graph or chart to represent the data.
   b   Justify your choice of diagram, graph or chart.
   c   Make one comment about what your diagram, graph or chart shows.

245

16 Interpreting and discussing results

Practice

4 The table shows the age and height of ten trees.

Height (metres)	4	5.5	1.5	2	6.5	8	7	5	6	7.5
Age (years)	6	8	1	3	12	20	17	7	9	18

a Draw a diagram, graph or chart to represent the data.
b Justify your choice of diagram, graph or chart.
c Make one comment about what your diagram, graph or chart shows.

5 Sadie counts the number of butterflies and bees that land on flowers of different colours in her garden. The table shows her results.

	Yellow	Red	Blue
Butterfly	8	4	1
Bee	12	6	5

Sadie wants a graph that compares the number of flowers of different colours, and also shows the total number of flowers landed on by the butterflies and bees.

a Draw a diagram, graph or chart to represent the data.
b Justify your choice of diagram, graph or chart.
c Make one comment about what your diagram, graph or chart shows.

6 The table shows the mean monthly temperatures in Cape Town over one year.

Month	Jan	Feb	Mar	Apr	May	Jun	Jul	Aug	Sep	Oct	Nov	Dec
Temperature (°C)	22	23	21	18	16	13	12	13	14	16	18	20

a Draw a diagram, graph or chart to represent the data.
b Justify your choice of diagram, graph or chart.
c Make one comment about what your diagram, graph or chart shows.

Challenge

7 Prakash measures the heights of the students in his class. The **frequency table** shows his results.

a Draw a diagram, graph or chart to represent the data.
b Justify your choice of diagram, graph or chart.
c Make one comment about what your diagram, graph or chart shows.

Height, h (cm)	Frequency
120–129	6
130–139	12
140–149	8
150–160	4

d Prakash estimates that 18 students are more than 135 cm tall.

    i Explain how Prakash worked out this number.

    ii Do you think this is a good method to use to work out this estimate? Explain your answer.

8 The two-way table shows the hair colour and gender of the students in Mr Singh's class.

	Brown hair	Black hair	Other hair colour	Total
Girls	6	5	3	14
Boys	10	4	2	16
Total	16	9	5	30

a Draw four different diagrams, graphs or charts to represent the data.

b Explain when you think it is best to use each of the diagrams, graphs or charts that you have drawn.

> **Tip**
>
> For example: if you draw a pie chart, you could say it is best to use this chart if you want to see the proportion of the students in the class with different colour hair.

> 16.6 Using statistics

Exercise 16.6

You need to remember how to work out the mode, median, mean and range.

> The **mode** is the most common value or number.
> The **median** is the middle value when they are listed in order of increasing size.
> The **mean** is the sum of all the values divided by the number of values.
> The **range** is the largest value <u>minus</u> the smallest value.

Key words

bimodal
mean
median
mode
range

Tips

Remember that when a set of data has two modes, it is called **bimodal**.

16 Interpreting and discussing results

Focus

1. A group of students are timed as they completed a task. Their times, in seconds, are shown below.

10	12	14	14	15	18	20	20	20	29	37

   a Work out the:
      i mode   ii median   iii mean time

   b Marcus, Arun and Zara discuss which average; that is, the mode, the median or the mean, best represents the data.

   Marcus says: Arun says:

   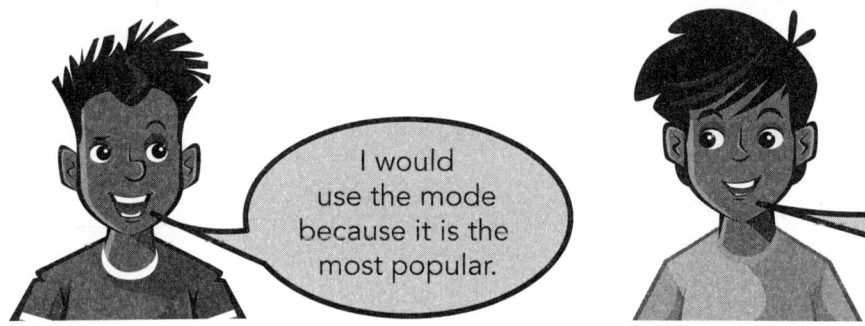

   Marcus: "I would use the mode because it is the most popular."

   Arun: "I would use the mean because the calculation uses all the values."

   Zara says:

   Zara: "I wouldn't use the mode because only two of the times are greater than the mode. I wouldn't use the mean because there is one really large value that will make the mean too large to represent the data. I would use the median because it is nicely in the middle of the data."

   Who do you think is correct?

2. Students in a science class take a test. Here are their marks.

32	32	33	34	39	41	42	43	44	44

   a Work out the:
      i mode   ii median   iii mean

   b Which average best represents the data? Give a reason for your choice of average.

3 These are the numbers of goals scored
in 20 football matches played in January.

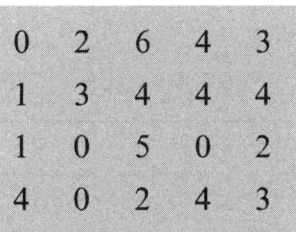

a Write the number of goals scored in
order of size, starting with the smallest.
b Find the:
i mode
ii median
iii mean number of goals scored
c Which average best represents the data? Give a reason for your choice of average.
d Work out the range in the number of goals scored.
e In February the range in the number of goals scored is four. Is there more variation in the number of goals scored in January or in February?

Tips

Range = largest value − smallest value

The month with the larger range has more variation in the number of goals scored.

4 This table shows the numbers of cars owned by 20 different families living in the same street.

Number of cars	0	1	2	3	4
Number of families	5	8	4	2	1

a Write down the modal number of cars.
b Write down the median number of cars.

Tip

There are 20 families, so the median will be the number of cars owned by the 10th/11th family. The first five families have no cars, families 6 to 13 have one car, so the median is ….

c Copy and complete the working to find the mean number of cars per family.

Total number of cars = $0 \times 5 + 1 \times 8 + 2 \times 4 + 3 \times 2 + 4 \times 1$
= $0 + 8 + \square + \square + \square$
= $\square$

Mean number of cars = $\square \div 20 = \square$

d Which average best represents the data? Give a reason for your choice of average.
e Work out the range in the number of cars owned.
f A different group of families has a range of two cars. Which group of families, the first or the second, has more variation in the number of cars owned?

Tip

The greatest number of families in the table is eight. This means that the modal number of cars is …

Tip

Range = largest number of cars owned (4) − smallest number of cars owned (0)

16 Interpreting and discussing results

Practice

5 These are the ages of 50 children at a small school.

Age (years)	6	7	8	9	10	11
Frequency	12	9	8	10	8	3

a Work out the:
  i mode   ii median   iii mean age
b Which average best represents the data? Give a reason for your choice of average.
c Work out the range in the age of the children.
d A different school has a range of seven years. Which school, the first or the second, has more variation in the age of the children?

6 Some children in a swimming club recorded how many lengths they could swim without stopping. Here are the results.

Lengths	0	1	2	3	4
Number of children	8	2	2	6	10

a Work out the:
  i mode   ii median   iii mean number of lengths
b Which average best represents the data? Give a reason for your choice of average.
c Work out the range in the number of lengths the children could swim.
d A different club has a range of eight lengths. Which club, the first or the second, has less variation in the number of lengths the children could swim?

7 a Here are the scores of the hockey matches played in League One on 20th September.

```
4-2   3-4   2-2   6-0   4-1   2-3   2-4   3-2   3-3
2-1   1-3   2-2   4-1   5-0   0-3   1-3   1-5   4-2
```

Copy and complete this frequency table. It shows the total number of goals per match.

Total number of goals in the match	Tally mark	Frequency
3		
4		
5		
6			
7			

The first score is 4-2, so the total for this match is 6 goals. Put a tally mark in the 6 row.

The second score is 3-4, so the total for this match is 7 goals. Put a tally mark in the 7 row.

b Work out the:
  i mode ii median iii mean number of goals
c Which average best represents the data? Give a reason for your choice of average.
d Work out the range in the total number of goals.
e On 27th September the range in the total number of goals was 6. Which day, the 20th or the 27th of September, has more variation in the total number of goals?

8 The table shows how many days 30 people worked, over a period of two weeks.

Number of days	4	5	6	7	8	9	10
Number of people	2	0	4	2	1		18

a Work out the missing frequency.
b Arun says:

I think the median number of days people worked is 7 because it is the value in the middle of the table.

Explain the mistake that Arun has made.
c By looking at the table, how can you tell that the mode is 10 days?
d Arun works out that the mean number of days worked is 8.7. Show that Arun is correct.
e Which average best represents the data? Give a reason for your choice of average.

16 Interpreting and discussing results

Challenge

9   This table shows the number of goals scored by a football club in each match in one season.

Goals	0	1	2	3	4	5	6	7	8
Frequency	6	11	5	11	4	0	2	0	1

a   Find the:
   i   number of games played   ii   mode
   iii median   iv   mean number of goals

b   Zara asks, 'What is the average number of goals?'
    Which would be the best average to use to answer this question? Give a reason for your answer.

10 This table shows the numbers of matches in 60 matchboxes.

Number of matches	47	48	49	50	51	52	53	54
Number of matchboxes	4	5	7	11	14	9	7	3

a   Find the:
   i   mode   ii median
   iii mean   iv range of the numbers

b   The writing on the matchbox says: 'Average contents 50 matches'.
    Is this correct? Give a reason for your answer.

11 The table shows the lengths of lessons per day, in some schools.

Length of lesson (minutes)	35	40	45	50	55	60
Number of schools	6	5	1	2	1	5

a   Find the:
   i   range   ii mode
   iii median   iv mean length of each lesson

b   One school is thinking of changing the length of its lessons. Which would be the most useful average for it to know? Why?

c   Two of the schools increase the length of their lessons from 35 minutes to 45 minutes. Find the new value of the:
   i   range   ii mode
   iii median   iv mean lesson length

12 The table shows the ages of 50 members of a club.

Age (years)	11	12	13	14	15	16
Frequency	10	21	8	5	3	3

a Find the:
 i   mean age
 ii median age
 iii modal age
 iv age range

b Arun says:

I think the mode is the best average to represent the data.

What do you think? Explain your answer.

c Marcus says:

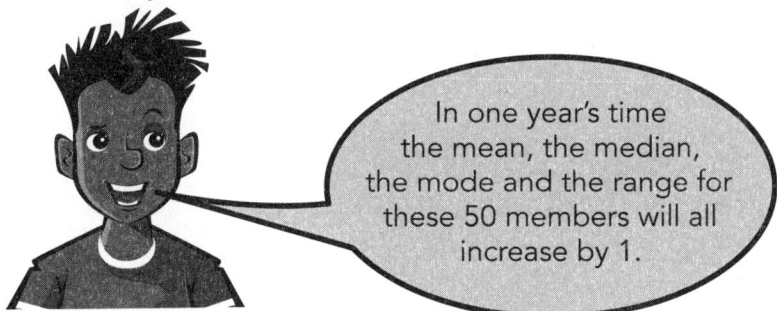

In one year's time the mean, the median, the mode and the range for these 50 members will all increase by 1.

Is he correct? Explain your answer.